THE STRATEGY OF PEACE

Books by John F. Kennedy

THE STRATEGY OF PEACE (EDITED BY ALLAN NEVINS)
PROFILES IN COURAGE
WHY ENGLAND SLEPT

THE
STRATEGY
OF PEACE

EDITED BY ALLAN NEVINS

SENATOR
JOHN F.
KENNEDY

HARPER & BROTHERS · NEW YORK

Contents

The dogmas of the quiet past are inadequate to the stormy present. The occasion is piled high with difficulty, and we must rise with the occasion. As our case is new, so we must think anew and act anew. We must disenthrall ourselves.

—ABRAHAM LINCOLN

Introduction: A Believer in the American Mission

"What is the use," Grover Cleveland once growled, "of being elected or re-elected unless you stand for something?" Whether an office-holder is a mayor, governor, or President he should be held to the spirit of that question; he can be a mayor like Tom L. Johnson of Cleveland, a governor like Altgeld of Illinois, or a President like Franklin D. Roosevelt, who stood not only for *something*, but for something well in advance of accepted goals. In American political life the stand is all-important. One of our national faults is our tendency to pay too much attention to personalities and too little to policy and argument; we are lazy, we like to drift, and we are willing to accept gestures for courage, and catchwords for ideas. This tendency helped to nurture the long vogue in our history of the stump speech tradition; the tradition that it did not much matter that a political leader had nothing to say if he just said it with the magnetism of James G. Blaine, the grace of Chauncey M. Depew, or the spellbinder rhetoric of Theodore Bilbo. The strength of that tradition explains why few volumes of American political speeches have been published, and fewer still read. Most speeches were not worth publishing or reading.

Happily, the tradition has changed. Speaking for good old Buncombe County in Congress, and standing by the flag and the country on the stump, are not enough. Joseph Chamberlain once remarked to his followers: "The trouble with you young men is that you don't take enough pains with your speeches"—by which he meant pains to assume a strong stand and defend it by logic and fact; and as if in answer to that challenge, young Winston Churchill said that he wrote a speech six times over with his own hand. In the heyday of stump speech demagogy, Lincoln grappled squarely with questions that most politicians were trying frantically to evade, and put honest reason behind the solutions he offered. The people responded to his determined effort to think his way through the difficulties facing the country. They will always respond to decision, candor, and earnestness backed by ability, and since our difficulties thickened, they have increasingly made this clear. The speeches of Theodore Roosevelt, Elihu Root, Woodrow Wilson, and Franklin D. Roosevelt, torches in the murk of their times, are worth reading still; they set standards which cannot be forgotten. We demand new torchbearers, and we are getting them. One of the ablest, with the enthusiasm of comparative youth and the idealism of dedicated purpose, lifts his lamp in the pages of this volume.

This book has special value in coming at a time when a mood of national complacency and inertia has again gained disturbing strength. The mood is keyed, as always, to notes of ease and slackness in high places; it is based on prosperity—an uneven prosperity, an inflation-bred prosperity, but prosperity enough to make tranquilizer pills for millions. The actual situation of the republic, surrounded by problems of desperate character, is quite different from what lazy minds think it is. It is so grim that the tone of urgency in Senator Kennedy's book ought to sound like a tocsin.

As a century ago the United States stood on the verge of a catastrophe to which political drift, cowardice, and fanaticism had brought it, today nobody can be sure it does not stand on the verge again.

The Cold War damps down the flames of latent hot war as uneasily as ever; armaments in the two great hostile camps of the world are piling higher and higher; the danger of a sudden explosion remains almost as terrifying as before, and that explosion could precipitate the most cataclysmic disaster of history. While we talk of hemispheric solidarity as an element in our strength, demonstrations against the United States break out in Cuba, Panama, Bolivia, and Venezuela. Our national debt creeps higher and higher. Inflation clamps an ever-crueler fetter on people of low and fixed incomes. The budget is unbalanced, and the international trade balance becomes so heavily adverse that the Secretary of the Treasury makes alarmed speeches, and the Under Secretary of State goes abroad to demand that other nations take immediate steps to improve our position. The national outlay for agriculture is estimated at more than six billions, yet the farm problem remains unsolved, with the stored crop surpluses approaching a ten-billion-dollar total. A forum of economists brought together by the National Industrial Conference Board concludes that the rate of industrial growth in the United States has dropped to almost the slowest pace among the great Western nations.

A time for complacency!—it is a time for anxiety, for tough thinking, for resolute action. This is what Senator Kennedy tries to drive home.

We need leaders who will accomplish two great objects. First, they will awaken responsible citizens out of their mood of acquiescence and drift, showing them that only timely, determined action can create a better future; and second, they will discuss our problems in constructive terms, or at least terms that clarify the possible solutions.

The diffusion of a new national mood, the outlining of a fresh political philosophy, was the central aim of Franklin D. Roosevelt's "Forgotten Man" speech and Commonwealth Club speech in 1932. The careful analysis of specific issues and presentation of programs for dealing with them was the primary object of Adlai E. Stevenson's admirable speeches in 1956, published later under the title *The New America*. In this volume Senator Kennedy endeavors, with thoughtful force, both to convert men to a more strenuous and idealistic mood, and to discuss in concrete terms some pressing situations we face, and the best paths through them.

Any attempt to bring Americans to a new national mood must reach deeper than most people suppose; it must reach down to fundamentals. In this attempt he has the advantage of representing a party which Woodrow Wilson, Franklin D. Roosevelt, Harry S. Truman, and Adlai E. Stevenson infused with their own spirit. We are often told that our two great parties are essentially alike, and foreigners profess difficulty in finding what separates Democrats and Republicans. The statement has some truth. Our parties are heterogeneous, composite organizations which bring into adjustment many different groups; each is a party of rich, well-to-do, and poor, of farmers, factory workers, and professional people, of Protestants, Catholics, and Jews, of radicals, moderates, and conservatives. They unify the nation rather than divide it. Nevertheless, vital differences of philosophy are evident. President Eisenhower once said that he and his party stand for "dynamic conservatism"; all the Democratic leaders just named, including Senator Kennedy, would say that their party stands for "dynamic liberalism." It is noteworthy that these speeches are never marred by loose abuse of Republicanism or its leaders. But the distinction between the parties would seem to have a threefold implication.

First, although both parties believe in a steady expansion of the American economy, the Democrats wish to effect it primarily by an increase in consumer buying power—by higher wages and ampler employment. The Republicans wish to achieve it rather by encouraging capital investment—by tax policies and other measures promoting larger profits and larger savings. In the second place, although both parties are in favor of retaining and enlarging the main socio-economic reforms of the New Deal, the Democrats would do it with only a reasonable emphasis on budget-balancing, debt reduction, and other cautionary measures. The Republicans, on the other hand, as Mr. Eisenhower has shown in his end-of-term utterances, would emphasize a balanced budget, a reduced debt, and a conservative fiscal management generally. In meeting the demands of labor and the farmers, the Democrats would thus move with more quickness and energy than the Republicans, who would act with caution if not reluctance.

And in the third place, the Democrats are now in some respects much more a Federal-action party than the Republicans, and the Republicans much more inclined to shelter conservatism behind States' Rights ramparts than the Democrats—a reversal of their historic roles. It would be fair to say that since Franklin D. Roosevelt the Democrats have cherished Jeffersonian ideals but acted on Hamiltonian ideas. That is, the Democrats in their aids to education, housing, and roadbuilding, their expansion of social security, their reduction of maximum hours and increase in minimum wages, would rely primarily on Federal action. The Republicans, however, would prefer to reserve a large area to state effort. In dealing with waterpower and conservation, too, the Democrats would give the national Government a larger sphere of responsibility than the Republicans, who, as Mr. Eisenhower has repeatedly said, would strive for a balance in the activities of private enterprise, the states, and the Federal authority.

These are large differences in political philosophy. While any statement of them has to be attended by many reservations and exceptions, they certainly exist. Unfortunately, neither differences in principle nor the main specific measures before the country have lately received the thorough discussion they merit. The complacency and apathy which a plodding Republican leadership, a Presidential reliance on general staff methods, have fostered, have been against tough-minded analysis. Mr. Stevenson has said that one of his keenest disappointments in 1956 was his failure to bring on a hard fight over issues. "In the climate of opinion which then prevailed, it was easy—and politically astute—for my opponents to brush them aside." Mr. Kennedy's main general object is to put an end to this Laodicean drift. He wants to shake people out of their dangerous torpidity. Why worry? The bombs are not yet falling. Venezuela is not yet Communist. The wretched schoolhouses, the inadequate roads, the insufficient health and medical programs can be shored up a while yet. Mr. Kennedy shows here why people *should* worry. If they awaken to quarrel with him, well and good—but let them awaken.

This volume is focused on problems of peace: on the place of America in the world, relations with post-Stalinist Russia, the hope that armaments may be reduced, the importance of assisting underdeveloped nations, and the means of making our influence felt in North Africa, the Near East, and the satellite nations. A volume of even greater size, equally forthright in its challenge to wisdom and generosity, could be compiled from Mr. Kennedy's utterances on home affairs. Primacy is given the international scene because of its urgency, and because his views on domestic questions are well known.

Everyone knows his friendship for labor, expressed in many ways, but most dramatically in his stubborn battle, against overwhelming odds, for the moderate Kennedy-Ervin bill which unfortunately failed late in 1959. Everyone knows of his interest in a liberalization of our immigration legislation, which has aligned him with Senator Lehman in urging abolition of the national quota system and the lifting of visas to 250,000 a year. All are familiar with his interest in the rights of the Negro, most recently expressed in his speech at the Alfred E. Smith dinner of 1959, urging bolder measures to earn world respect in the treatment of minorities.

His devotion to civil liberties, and detestation of McCarthyism and all similar invasions of decency and justice, is thorough and well documented here. He has spoken against the requirement of a loyalty oath from beneficiaries of the National Defense Education Act and joined with Senator Clark in introducing a bill for its repeal. No one feels a stronger concern for the strengthening of the public school system. He showed his desire to assist both agriculture and the under-privileged in proposing unlimited distribution of the farm surplus through the Department of Health, Education and Welfare. He has stood with Senators Fulbright, Lehman, and Paul Douglas in a special concern for the promotion of culture on both a national and an international basis.

But it was important to concentrate in this book his opinions on peace, defense, and foreign policy. This is not because it is now necessary to combat isolationism; observers on Mr. Kennedy's Western tours have been impressed by the absence of even the faintest echo of old isolationist cries. It is because the Administration has shown a signal lack of imagination and thrust in world affairs. It has awaited disclosure of the point where Communist aggression would next be felt—in Berlin, in Iraq, in the Taiwan Straits, on the Nepal border—and then taken belated steps to meet them. Almost never has it offered bold initiative of its own. Professing democratic principles, it has given as much support in Latin America to reactionary governments and dictators as to popular movements and free regimes; with the result that students jeer at Uncle Sam and liberals denounce us as fawners on power, no matter how the power is obtained. It has taken fumbling, ill-planned steps in the Near East to buttress Arab governments which fail to join hands against the Communist threat. In Egypt its cancellation of proffers of help on the Aswan Dam mortally wounded the pride of a sensitive people and government; and it then used abusive language and humiliating measures to interpose between the provoked Egyptians and three of our most important friends, Great Britain, France and Israel. We proclaim our desire for arms reduction; but whereas Khrushchev found means of making a dramatic gesture on the subject that impressed half the world, we seem timid and reluctant.

Senator Kennedy's volume exhorts us to turn a new page; to show courage, resourcefulness, originality, and flexibility. He wishes the nation kept strong militarily and economically, but it must use its strength with a vision which in recent years has been lacking. It is to be noted that in these speeches he never once appeals to motives of selfishness, of nationalist prejudice, or of fear. Instead, he calls for effort, sacrifice, and magnanimity. We must not hesitate to help Poland and Hungary by expanding travel and trade, exchanging students and teachers, investing capital, and lending technological aid. We must discard old prejudices in broadening the area of common purpose and action with Russia; for both nations want peace, both want to lighten the burden of arms, both want to stop air-pollution by unlimited atomic explosions, and both want to make scientific advances which pooled effort and information can best promote. We must give more money in foreign aid. He is a patriot, but his book echoes Nurse Cavell: "Patriotism is not enough."

In stating these aims, with faith that the people will support them, he reawakens memories of some of the finest moments of our history. We may instance but one. In fifteen weeks of historic achievement in 1947 three leaders, President Truman, Secretary Marshall, and Under Secretary Acheson, with encouragement from Senator Vandenberg, brought the United States to the assistance of Turkey and Greece against Russian encroachments, proclaimed the Truman Doctrine, and offered to the world the Marshall Plan.

These three steps constituted an epochal advance. They not only bulwarked the weakest flank of the West against Communist subversion, and took the United States far outside its old spheres of action in pledging armed aid to nations weak and threatened, but provided a basis on which the war-shattered nations of Europe and Asia could find sure recovery, health, and strength. Marshall's proposals at the Harvard Commencement changed the climate of the globe; they brought sunshine where gloom had brooded. His plan for co-ordinated effort by all the leading nations to restore social and economic vigor on a global scale was an unforgettable example of imaginative leadership; and it rested on Truman's courage in committing America to a bold new stand—or rather as Truman has said, the doctrine and the plan were "two halves of the same walnut." This is the imagination and the courage for which Mr. Kennedy calls.

Readers will find here instruction and sagacity on our knottier problems. They will find also a true philosophy of government, for the Senator has his own vision and his own system of ideas. The speeches will accomplish their best aim if they raise others to the level of the vision. They are rooted in a faith that the greatness of the nation lies in its plain people, who have always profoundly believed that America has a mission, and in that belief are ready to respond to calls to their higher motives. This was the faith of Woodrow Wilson, who said once that "up from the common soil, up from the great heart of the people, rise joyously streams of hope and determination that are bound to renew the face of the earth in glory"; that "this great American people is at bottom just, virtuous, and hopeful; the roots of its being are in the soil of what is lovely, pure, and of good report; and the need of the hour is just that radicalism that will clear a way for the realization of the aspirations of a sturdy race."

ALLAN NEVINS

I
THE
POSSIBILITIES
OF PEACE

1. The Global Challenge

WASHINGTON, D.C.
JANUARY 1, 1960

This volume is born of the reminder that "in the beginning is the word"—and particularly so, in the case of a democratic government. For in such a government it is the freely spoken and freely challenged word that is meant to lay open a vision of the realities lying beyond the sweep of naked eyesight. Surely, then, the first duty of an officer in a democratic government is to uphold the integrity of words used in public debate; and to do this by himself using them in ways where they will stand as one with the things they are meant to represent.

In the last several years, I have been serving as a member of the United States Senate, as a member of the Foreign Relations Committee, and as the Chairman of the Senate Foreign Relations Subcommittees on the U.N. and on African Affairs. Here, in these posts, the mechanical act of casting a yea or a nay vote is the least part of the work to be done. The greater part is the act of educating oneself about the play of forces which call for a yea or a nay decision; of sifting, defining, and choosing between alternative policies; and of explaining why this instead of that policy commends itself to one's reason. The statements contained in this volume represent my own attempt to make plain to myself and to others my thoughts on the leading questions of foreign policy that have borne down so hard on all of us. I do not claim to have all the answers. But Professor Allan Nevins and Harper & Brothers have very kindly asked to bring together some of my main addresses to the Senate and other public forums on foreign policy and related areas over the last several years. To these I have added my own current comments.

Except for the elimination of repetition, the statements that follow are a fair transcript of the texts as they were originally given amid the oceanic heavings of fast-breaking world events. No man can see to the end of time. But while the immediate crises and occasions for these statements have changed or passed, the remarkable and disturbing thing is that the issues, the basic themes, the central criticism remain essentially unchanged.

The central theme which runs throughout these statements is that we move from crisis to crisis for two reasons: first, because we have not yet developed a strategy for peace that is relevant to the new world

3

in which we live; and secondly, because we have not been paying the price which that strategy demands—a price measured not merely in money and military preparedness, but in social inventiveness, in moral stamina, in physical courage. Because that strategy has not been developed nor that price paid, it has not been too difficult to forecast with a reasonable degree of precision where our national fortunes would trend. They would trend in the direction of a slide downhill into dust, dullness, languor, and decay.

It is only fair to say that in the years immediately after the end of the Second World War, when the Russian thrust was embodied in the person of Joseph Stalin, we did have a strategy for peace. Its aim was clear-cut, and its distinguished successes were measurable.

Its aim was to preserve the political and physical integrity of Western Europe from the danger of a Communist takeover; and to preserve it, moreover, without a resort to war. Not that other areas of the world were written off or even discounted in value. Rather, Western Europe with its human and material resources was seen as the key to everything else. If they fell under Russian control and were combined with Russian resources, the United States would be dwarfed in comparative strength. On the other hand, if Europe's resources were combined with those of the United States in a mutual security system, they would far exceed the components of Russian power, and make possible the assistance needed by other peoples elsewhere anxious to preserve their own independence and the right to develop in their own way.

Known as the "policy of containment," this strategy of peace was based on two monopolies we then enjoyed. One was a monopoly in the power to export capital and technical assistance to Europe and to underdeveloped countries. By means such as the Marshall Plan and the Point Four Program, we had no competition from the Russians as we restored or strengthened the economic foundations, and hence the social and political foundations, of nations menaced from within by Communist subversion, or which lay in the path of a direct Communist attack from without.

The second monopoly we enjoyed subdivided into two parts. We enjoyed a monopoly in nuclear weapons and in the capacity to deliver them to a target. The original strategy of NATO was cast in the mold of this twin fact. It assumed that an alliance of land forces in Western Europe could be formed with sufficient strength to contain any probing operations the Communists might launch to test the West's will to resist. On the other hand, any prospective full-scale attack by Communist arms would be deterred or broken up by the United States Strategic Air Command, carrying nuclear bombs. Though the land components of the NATO forces never reached their originally scheduled levels, and though the political composition of the forces in being became unbalanced, the strategic conception had enough material vitality to it to preserve the independence of Western Europe.

But beginning in 1949, the Russians began to challenge the double monopoly the United States enjoyed. They did much more than merely make themselves the equal of the United States in the actual possession of nuclear bombs. Their startling advances in the techniques of rockets and missiles made them the superior of the United States in the power to deliver nuclear warheads onto a target. Thus they invalidated the original strategic conception of NATO, by outflanking its key element—the deterrent power of the U.S. Strategic Air Command. In this way, they also enlarged the military importance of Russia's vast conventionally equipped land army.

While the American public is no longer in doubt that the Soviet Union has broken the American monopoly in nuclear weapons and the means of delivering them, neither the Administration nor the public mind has been brought abreast of the full implications in Russia's challenge to the second monopoly we once enjoyed—namely, the power to export capital and technical assistance. Russia's day-to-day successes in this area do not lend themselves to melodramatic headlines, suitably illustrated with photographs and art sketches. Nevertheless her successes have been startling, and in the long run may be even more significant than her triumph in military technology.

Russia's bid to win Europe to itself by the indirect route of winning the vast outlying raw materials region is further served by the many simultaneous revolutions now under way in those very regions. In Asia, the Middle East, and Africa, peoples long dormant under colonial rule are now for the first time in a ferment of a newly won national identity and independence. Joined also by Latin America, they are swept up by the revolution of industrialization; the revolution of an explosive population growth; the revolution of consumer demands; the revolution of colored peoples to shake off the badge of inferiority white peoples imposed on them. All this makes for a paramount revolution in the outlook on life itself.

Now, as never before, hundreds of millions of men and women—who had formerly believed that stoic resignation in the face of hunger and disease and darkness was the best one could do—have come alive with a new sense that the means are at hand with which to make for themselves a better life.

If the title deeds of history applied, it is we, the American people, who should be marching at the head of this world-wide revolution, counseling it, helping it to come to a healthy fruition. For whenever a local patriot emerges in Asia, the Middle East, Africa, or Latin America to give form and focus to the forces of ferment, he most often quotes the great watchwords we once proclaimed to the world: the watchwords of personal and national liberty, of the natural equality of all souls, of the dignity of labor, of economic development broadly shared. Yet we have allowed the Communists to evict us from our rightful estate at the head of this world-wide revolution. We have been made to appear as the defenders of the *status quo*, while the Communists have portrayed themselves as the vanguard force, pointing the way to a better, brighter, and braver order of life.

Some say we are losing out for lack of a national purpose. We need to find, it is said, a new sense of great purpose.

In my view the American purpose remains what it has been since the nation's founding: to demonstrate that the organization of men and societies on the basis of human freedom is not an absurdity, but an enriching, ennobling, practical achievement. Our purpose is to demonstrate at home that this great continental democracy can solve its problems by the method of consent—by a system of freedom under law. With respect to the world outside, our purpose is not only to defend the integrity of this democratic society but also to help advance the cause of human freedom and world law—the universal cause of a just and lasting peace.

Every generation of Americans has faced a different set of problems in carrying forward these abiding purposes of our society. The problems have changed; the purposes have remained constant.

And so it is with us. At home, we must demonstrate that we can educate our children adequately in a world where ideas and technology are increasing in importance, and where excellence must be nurtured and cherished. Our democracy must demonstrate that it can restructure its urban organization, in the light of the revolutionary enlargement of our population, now increasingly concentrated in metropolitan areas. Our democracy must demonstrate that it can use constructively—at home and on the world scene—the enormous surge of abundance in our agricultural sector.

In relation to the world outside, our democracy must demonstrate that it has the capacity to defend itself in a world of intercontinental ballistic missiles; and that it has the energy and the sense of adventure —as well as the technical skill—to play a role of leadership in the exploration of space. Our democracy must demonstrate that it is still prepared to contend patiently, as well as with insight and passion, for the cause of human freedom in Asia, the Middle East, Africa, and Latin America, as well as in the areas now held in satellite status by the Soviet Union. Our democratic society must demonstrate that it can convert the North Atlantic ties, forged in the precarious war and postwar years, into a stable, creative partnership among equals. Finally, our democratic society must demonstrate that it has the wisdom and maturity to engage in constructive exchanges and in negotiation with the Soviet Union. For over two years I have been urging that we should negotiate with the Russians at the summit or anywhere else. For all the risk involved in bilateral discussions with Mr. Khrushchev, I favored his coming and Mr. Eisenhower's visit to the Soviet Union. We should be ready to take risks to bring about a thaw in the Cold War. While blocking the routes to Communist expansion, we must—at American initiative—exploit every opportunity that the dynamics of change in Soviet life may offer, to move toward peace.

This generation does not have to find new purposes. The old American purposes are still wholly relevant. What this generation must do is to face its problems—at home and abroad. They cannot be divided.

Instead, with the present Administration setting the example, we have lapsed back into a frame of mind where we assume that we are at liberty to deal with domestic and foreign affairs separately, and each in its own good time. We assume that the Good Life we have been enjoying here at home is somehow the same as building the Good Society here at home and abroad. We have posed the abstraction of a budgetary balance against the lunging physical reality of Communist power. Attitudes, platitudes, and beatitudes have taken the place of a critical and vigilant intelligence marching in advance of events, and by the measures taken, producing the events we want. We have allowed a soft sentimentalism to form the atmosphere we breathe. And in that kind of atmosphere, a diffuse desire to do good has become a substitute for tough-minded plans and operations—a substitute for a strategy.

The American, by nature, is optimistic. He is experimental, an inventor and a builder who builds best when called upon to build greatly. Arouse his will to believe in himself, give him a great goal to believe in, and he will create the means to reach it. This trait of the American character is our greatest single national asset. It is time once more that we rescue it from the sea of fat in which it has been drowning. It is time once more to get on with the business of being true to the work of a Choosing People—a people who voluntarily assume the burden and the glory of advancing mankind's best hopes.

2. *The Khrushchev-Eisenhower Visits*

UNIVERSITY OF ROCHESTER
ROCHESTER, NEW YORK
OCTOBER 1, 1959

There is only one supreme, overriding issue confronting the American public today—one critical issue that affects, and is affected by, everything else we do as a nation and as individuals. Whether we call that issue by the name of national security, or foreign policy, or the quest for peace, the fact remains that in this the nuclear age no other public matter touches all of our lives so directly and so decisively.

Now the American people have taken a new look at this issue— they have given it new attention—and it is largely because they have seen it in personal, human terms, in terms of the extraordinary tour of one extraordinary man: Nikita Khrushchev.[1] If there were no other benefit at all from this visit—if all the traveling and all the

[1] The results of Nikita S. Khrushchev's visit to the United States in September of 1959 were hard to appraise. Everybody agreed with Churchill, however, that "jaw-jaw is better than war-war." Without making any observable concessions, Khrushchev did something to improve the atmosphere of Soviet-American relations. One of his statements was particularly felicitous: "I have seen how the slaves of capitalism live, and they live pretty well. The slaves of Communism live pretty well too, and let's live the way we want to live."
Senator Kennedy had special opportunities to hear and observe Mr. Khrushchev, and the speech he made at Rochester a week after the Prime Minister returned home is a tolerant but realistic analysis of the visit, and of the possibilities of using it to improve the prospects of peace.—A.N.

talking produced no other result besides this new and renewed interest of the American people in the image of our adversary—that result alone has certainly been worth while.

But what are the results of Mr. Khrushchev's visit? What has been its contribution, if any? The visit is over—Mr. Khrushchev is no longer in every American headline—but he should still be in every American mind. It seems to me imperative that all of us—public servants and private citizens alike—now reflect on the meaning of this visit and try to put it into some kind of long-range perspective. I do not mean that we should continue to wrangle over whether Mr. Khrushchev should have been invited in the first place. Whether that decision was wise, or necessary, or unavoidable is no longer at issue, except for narrow political purposes. And I do not believe the American people respect that kind of partisanship on sensitive international issues.

But now that the dust of the departing Soviet jet has settled, there are questions we must ask—not of the President, who has probably revealed all he can, but of ourselves. What lessons did we learn? What manner of man was this Khrushchev? What did we learn about our future relations?

A few years ago, at a diplomatic party in Moscow, Premier Khrushchev told the assembled guests about the Russian who suddenly began to run through the corridors of the Kremlin shouting: "Khrushchev is a fool! Khrushchev is a fool!" He was sentenced, the Premier said, to twenty-three years in prison—"three for insulting the Party Secretary—and twenty for revealing a state secret."

But Mr. Khrushchev is no fool—and the American people now know that beyond a doubt. He is shrewd, he is tough, he is vigorous, well informed, and confident. Americans traditionally like to picture hostile dictators as unstable and irrational men, the almost comic captives of their moods and manias. There was some feeling in recent years that even Mr. Khrushchev could be pictured largely as a short-tempered, vodka-drinking politician-buffoon, alternately scheming and screaming inside the Kremlin's walls.

But the Khrushchev with whom I met, in his session with the Senate Foreign Relations Committee, was a tough-minded, articulate, hard-reasoning spokesman for a system in which he was thoroughly versed and in which he thoroughly believed. He was not the prisoner of any ancient dogma or limited vision. And he was not putting on any act—he was not engaging in any idle boasts— when he talked of the inevitable triumph of the Communist system, of their eventual superiority in production, education, scientific achievement, and world influence.

I think it is well that the American people saw and heard this kind of man and this kind of talk. I think it is important that we realize what we are up against. And I think it is important also that Mr. Khrushchev recognize what he is up against—so that he does not miscalculate our determination or underestimate our resources. A confrontation of adversaries gives each a picture of the other. After Samuel Adams, following the Boston Massacre, had confronted the British Colonial Governor in his office with a warning of revolution, he wrote in his diary: "It was then I fancied that I saw his knees tremble." Mr. Khrushchev was shown our nation—our might, our strength, our determination. But he did not tremble.

Some have hailed his visit as a prelude to a new, great era of peace—the end of the Cold War—the relaxation of tensions. This is the way Mr. Khrushchev most often talked—this is what the American people most want—and the wish, we know, is so often father to the thought.

But a more careful reflection on Mr. Khrushchev's visit, it seems to me, is cause for redoubled efforts, not relaxation. It justifies more, not less, sacrifice to protect and extend the world's frontiers of freedom. For after seeing Mr. Khrushchev's hard, tough manner and confidence on a supposed good-will mission, we should recall Winston Churchill's memorable question: "If this is what they do in the green wood, what will they do in the dry?"

There is no evidence, judging from his remarks in Peking, that Mr. Khrushchev has been deterred in the slightest from his objective of overcoming in every way short of world war what he called "the senile capitalist system . . . this exhausted, limping and stumbling . . . horse."

I do not mean to minimize the values of the talks at Camp David. Communication is important. Understanding is important. Making clear our peaceful but determined intentions is important. And there is real hope now for further talks on Berlin, disarmament, cultural exchanges, trade, the old lend-lease debts, nuclear tests, and the peaceful uses of atomic energy. All of these are important.

It is far better that we meet at the summit than at the brink.[2]

[2] When 1959 ended, the American, British, French, and Soviet Governments stood committed to a meeting of the heads of the states. The question of its time gave rise to difficulties. Prime Minister Macmillan wanted it as soon as possible in order to "keep up the momentum" of progress

But let us remember that assurances of future talks are not assurances of future success or agreement. We in this country did not invent the Cold War. The real test of Mr. Khrushchev's desire to end it will be in his deeds, not his words—his deeds in Germany and Eastern Europe where he has been rattling his missiles—or in advising the Red Chinese on Laos—or in charging his emissaries at the United Nations and the Geneva nuclear test conferences.

We look for deeds, not words. And we, too, must offer deeds, not words. We need to think through more carefully our own positions on such questions as disarmament and troop withdrawals, instead of offering only proposals which we know in advance must be rejected.

But the hard facts of the matter are that the real roots of the Soviet-American conflict cannot be easily settled by negotiations. Our basic national interests and their basic national interests clash—in Europe, in the Middle East, and around the world. Our aspirations as the most powerful leader of the Free World conflict with their aspirations as the most powerful leader of the Communist world. No negotiations can end those differences. No exchange of personal visits, no amount of summit conferences, can cause either side to compromise away its fundamental position in Germany, Europe, or the world community.

But that does not mean that all is hopeless. An excess of pessimism is no more called for than an excess of optimism. The fact is that we can find certain basic interests or objectives which the United States and the U.S.S.R. have in common—and we should concentrate our efforts on those potential areas of agreement. We need a new

---

toward assured peace. President Eisenhower was also ready for an early meeting, but only on condition that preliminary talks showed a likelihood of success. President de Gaulle for his part favored delay. He thought that the Western leaders should hold two preliminary conferences among themselves; he wanted time allowed for a visit by Khrushchev to France in the second half of March; and altogether he thought that May or June would be the best time for the summit gathering. A question of policy was involved in all this. The British leaders wished to confirm and strengthen the "Camp David spirit" at once, trusting that settlements of specific issues could then follow. De Gaulle, on the other hand, believed that careful negotiations should precede the summit conclave, which could then itself make decisions on important questions. The Big Four— Eisenhower, Macmillan, de Gaulle, and Adenauer—meeting in Paris on December 18, agreed to join Khrushchev at the summit in the spring, the exact date to be fixed later.

Mr. Kennedy's Rochester speech outlined some real areas of possible agreement between East and West at a summit meeting.—A.N.

approach to the Russians—one that is just as hard-headed and just as realistic as Mr. Khrushchev's, but one that might well end the current phase—the frozen, belligerent, brink-of-war phase—of the long Cold War.

For we can discern in Mr. Khrushchev's speeches the germs of these potential common interests. Let me mention a few:

First, both the U.S. and the U.S.S.R. would like to be free of the crushing burden of the arms race. We would much prefer to use these resources in developing our own and other nations, in raising our standard of living, in improving education and health and housing.

Secondly, neither the U.S. nor the U.S.S.R. wants a nuclear war. Neither wants to set the fire that may extinguish civilization as we know it before its own flames are finally extinguished—the war that would leave not one Rome intact but two Carthages destroyed—and would at the very least set back by a generation or more the efforts in both nations to make economic, social, and cultural progress.

Third, neither the U.S. nor the U.S.S.R. wants nuclear weapons—and the power to initiate nuclear war—to pass into the hands of too many other nations—Red China, France, Sweden, and a host of others now preparing to join the atomic club.

Fourth, neither Americans nor Russians want to breathe radio-active air. On both sides of the Iron Curtain, in every continent, we all breathe the same atmosphere—and we do not want it polluted by an excess of nuclear tests.

Fifth, both nations seek to advance their own economies and scientific achievements—and would benefit by a much greater exchange and pooling of goods, ideas, and personnel between our two nations.

These are the real areas of potential agreement with the Russians—because these are the real interests we could share in common. If we could succeed in reaching practical, enforceable agreements in these areas, there would still be fierce competition. But it would be competition in trade and aid, in production and propaganda, in seeking friends and building fences. Our security would still be at stake in this competition—let us never forget that. We could still not relax our effort. Mr. Khrushchev would still be out to "bury" us. But the world's very survival would be less endangered—the Cold War would be less likely to become hot—and the competition would be one that we should accept with pleasure.

Let Mr. Khrushchev try to surpass the United States in the production of corn and butter, homes and TV sets. Let him turn his nation's energies to this pursuit. And let him educate a new generation of Russians—scientists and engineers and language specialists, but also inevitably restive with questions about the world. For once the Pandora's box of learning is opened, truth will be loose in the land of the Soviets—and the truth may make them free.

But I do not hold out any magic hopes for a sudden thaw or a certain timetable. The Chinese Communists, in particular, may upset it all as they go through a Stalinist phase. But we must always be pressing for a gradual thaw, and make that alternative seem more feasible, more desirable to Mr. Khrushchev than the alternative of armed conflict.

If Mr. Khrushchev chooses otherwise, then we must be ready: politically, economically, and militarily. But we can make it difficult for him to choose otherwise. And we must make it difficult for him to repudiate the words of his American tour—his expressions of hope for peace, his stated belief in self-determination of peoples, his insistence that the Kremlin neither controlled nor spoke for other Iron Curtain nations.

All this we can do, with imagination, patience, determination and, above all, effort. For Mr. Khrushchev may have known his Marx— but his Marx did not know the United States of America. This is no atrophied capitalist society, declining, splitting, failing. We do not live under a dying system, fading from the scene as feudalism faded some centuries ago.

On the contrary, modern American capitalism, with its unique combination of public effort and private competitive enterprise, is dynamic, progressive, and still evolving. It may, from time to time, pause or show weakness. But it is still capable of greater heights than any Mr. Khrushchev has ever seen or imagined. It is still capable of building all the defenses we need *and* all the schools and homes and industries, too—and at the same time helping to build situations of strength and stability throughout the non-Communist world.

This is the real lesson for the future we should take from the Khrushchev visit. As Winston Churchill said in June of '39: "We shall not escape our dangers by recoiling from them." Unfortunately for the British, Churchill had inherited the fate of Cassandra—the mythical daughter of Priam to whom the god Apollo had first given the gift of accurate prophecy but, later angered, then ordained that her prophecies would never be believed. Like Cassandra, Winston Churchill was neither believed nor beloved for his warnings of danger and his calls for sacrifice at a time when the hopes for relaxation were high.

Here, too, our hopes for relaxation are high. But the hard facts of the matter are that we here in the United States, in the year 1959, cannot escape our dangers by recoiling from them—or by being lulled to sleep.

Mr. Khrushchev had reason to be confident on his visit here. His country was the first into outer space and the first to the moon. Its growth in productivity, resource development, and education has been phenomenal. Its successes in penetrating non-Communist areas politically and economically has been unprecedented.

But now that we know what we are up against—now that we see where we should concentrate our efforts for agreement—now that we accept his challenge to compete in nonmilitary affairs—we, too, can be confident. We, too, can be just as tough, just as realistic, just as hard bargainers as Mr. Khrushchev. And we can win. For this is still the greatest country on earth. And though Mr. Khrushchev may claim that his nation, like ours, is also a home of the brave, this nation—not Russia—is still the land of the free. And that, in the last analysis, is going to make the difference.

3. The Captive Nations

No problem of American foreign policy was more sharply brought to mind by Mr. Khrushchev's visit than the problem of the captive nations. Newspaper ads were taken to remind the Soviet Premier—and us all—of the fate of Budapest. Picket lines were formed by refugees from Eastern Europe. The chief criticisms of the visit, the chief cause of security problems, the chief mass protest meetings all stemmed from the feelings aroused by Soviet oppression in the so-called satellite states. The following talk was an attempt to consider the implications of a thaw in Soviet-American relations in terms of our abiding interest in the freedom of the Eastern European peoples suffering under Communism.

The proposition that peace is the necessary precondition for the advance of freedom applies generally, as does the proposition that we must be prepared to deal realistically and imaginatively with nations under many different—and often detestable—economic systems and forms of government. But they apply especially to Eastern Europe, where it is now clear that we cannot expect freedom to come by means of dramatic or violent revolution.

Having made it clear in 1956 that we would not help these people revolt or send them arms if they did, we must not in any way incite them to what might be national suicide. Our best hope, and theirs, is rather in having more nations follow the example of Poland, Yugoslavia, and Finland in moving gradually, if cautiously, away from total Soviet political domination and in seeking greater economic independence as well. This process is hindered by woodenly lumping all Eastern European nations together under one label regardless of the differences in their aspirations or operation. We can, however, help by offering the best possible concrete alternatives, by being prepared to take advantage of every opening to establish better relations with the West, by having ready various forms of economic aid to lessen their dependence upon the U.S.S.R. or China. Unfortunately, we cannot do more—certainly we dare not do less.

Under the original Battle Act, we are able to grant assistance only on a finding that a given country is not Soviet "controlled" or "dominated"—a finding which is difficult to make in a twilight situation such as existed in Poland in 1956. The talk below discusses the amendment I proposed in 1957 to permit the more flexible policy required for the changing situation in the post-Stalin Communist world—an amendment that I hope will become law in 1960.[3]

PULASKI DAY DINNER
MILWAUKEE, WISCONSIN
OCTOBER 17, 1959

In August, 1955, more than a year before the peaceful Polish revolution of 1956, I walked through the historic Cathedral of Częstochowa. There I saw a small cross noted by every visitor to that museum—the cross of Casimir Pulaski.

One hundred and eighty years ago this very month the body of Casimir Pulaski was lowered into the Atlantic Ocean somewhere off

[3] The Battle Act, introduced by Representative Laurie C. Battle of Alabama, became law in October, 1951. It authorized the government to cut off military, economic, and financial aid from countries dominated by the Soviet Union, or countries which exported arms, or other war materials, to Russia or her satellites; but it gave the government considerable authority to permit exceptions in the interests of a broader national security. This authority Senator Kennedy now wished to enlarge.—A.N.

the coast of Georgia. He was only thirty-two. He had been on these shores little more than two years. And yet his death was mourned by Americans high and low. For Pulaski the Polish count was a hero of the American Revolution who had crossed an ocean to dedicate himself to the cause of liberty and independence.

We think of Casimir Pulaski tonight because his beloved Poland has once again fallen victim to a foreign power. Were he alive tonight, the hero of Savannah and Charleston would weep for his homeland —and we, inwardly or outwardly according to our custom, weep with him.

But weeping is not enough. We know it is not enough. And yet, while we give vent to our feelings of resentment and outrage, we are also caught up in a feeling of frustration. What can we do about the situation in the satellites? How can we help those liberty-loving peoples regain their liberty, without subjecting them to even more cruel repression—or subjecting the world to an even more disastrous war? How can we let them know their fate is not forgotten—that we have not abandoned them to be—as the Irish of 1647 considered themselves when Owen Roe O'Neill was poisoned—"sheep without a shepherd when the snow shuts out the sky?"

This is the dilemma we face, as the President and Premier Khrushchev are pictured together in the press on both sides of the Iron Curtain. And this is the dilemma with which this Administration has been confronted, in trying to make good on its tarnished promises of a new "liberation" policy. For this is no longer an age when minutemen with muskets can make a revolution. Hungary, we know, is not Cuba—and neither is Poland. Mr. Khrushchev is not to be overthrown like Mr. Batista. Brave bands of young men and women may be able to stop a few tanks—but street barricades and homemade hand grenades cannot long stand against a modern army and an atomic air force.

The facts of the matter are that—no matter how bitter some feelings may be, or how confident some are of a victorious war for liberation—freedom behind the Iron Curtain and world peace are actually inextricably linked. For if war should ever break out, the control and occupation of Eastern Europe would certainly be even more rigid and repressive than it is today. That is why, in the days of upheaval in 1956, when Poland could have turned to violent rebellion as Hungary did, Cardinal Wyszynski kept advising his people that the condition of Polish freedom was peace. Many scoffed—many thought him fainthearted. But by following his advice, Poland has now attained at least a measure of national independence and at least a relaxation of Communist rule. Forced collectivization of the farmers has ceased and most of the collectives were dissolved—religious freedom has been restored in considerable degree—and a limited freedom of speech exists albeit precariously.

No one says that land of ancient freedom is once more free again. But if Poland had not accepted this halfway house to freedom, it could have been, as Prime Minister Gomulka warned, wiped off the map of Europe. If the present emphasis on a thaw in the Cold War should end and tensions rise again, the present good relations between Poland and the United States would undoubtedly cease, the growing contacts between the Polish people and the West would be cut off, and the present degree of freedom of speech and religion in Poland would prove to be short-lived. On the other hand, if a real thaw develops and Soviet-American relations improve, the prospects for the continuation and perhaps the expansion of this limited degree of Polish freedom are good. So, in a real sense, the condition for Polish freedom—the condition for the freedom of the still captive peoples—*is* peace.

But if freedom in Eastern Europe is to come only by peaceful change, what can we do to encourage this gradual evolution—this ferment that recalls the warning of Jefferson that "the disease of liberty is catching"?

Unfortunately, in recent years, our hands have been tied by a rigid statutory perspective of the Communist world. We have, in our laws, seen it in wholly black and white terms. Nations were either for us or against us—either completely under Russian domination or completely free. We did not recognize that the Communist world is no longer a solid monolith—that the Iron Curtain is no longer an impenetrable wall. We admitted that we were not willing to help violent revolution—but neither were we prepared to help peaceful evolution.

Fortunately, in its final week of the 1959 session, the Senate passed an amendment to the Battle Act—cosponsored by Senator Aiken of Vermont and myself—which was designed to provide our Government with a more flexible set of economic tools to promote peaceful change behind the Iron Curtain. It would permit the use of such tools whenever it appeared to the President that such encouragement would help wean the so-called captive nations away from their Kremlin masters. We urgently need such legislation, which was originally defeated in the Senate by a one-vote margin when I offered it a year ago. We need that legislation if our policy toward Polish liberation is to be one of action instead of slogans—if it is to move with flexibility and imagination instead of being limp with caution and conservatism. We need that legislation if we in this country are finally going to take the initiative in Eastern Europe, instead of merely reacting to every move by the Kremlin.

If this amendment can pass the House of Representatives in 1960 —if our policy can finally begin to recognize that there are varying shades and degrees within the Communist world—then, and only then, can we take the initiative away from the Soviets in Eastern Europe. In Poland—and in any other crack that appears in the Iron Curtain—we can then begin to work gradually, carefully, and peacefully to promote closer relationships and nourish the seeds of liberty. Expanded trade between Poland and the United States, increased travel and tourism by Americans in Poland, the use of our capital and technology for Polish industry and housing projects, expanded student and teacher exchanges, and more people-to-people contacts —all of these could play important parts in such a policy—in addition to the usual diplomatic and information projects.

But such a policy, we can be sure, would not encounter a smooth course. Mr. Khrushchev knows the dangers of relaxing tensions too far. The leaders of Communist states, including Poland's Mr. Gomulka, will take pains to make clear their agreement with Soviet objectives that are despicable to us—and ironically enough they will do so in order to remain in a position whereby they can still accept our aid and friendship.

So let us remember that all of this will require patience, imagination, and strength on the part of our own Government. It will require that we do everything we can to make it easier for the Soviets to take the risks of relaxation—and make it harder for them to revert to the tactics, the tensions, and the terrors of Stalin's Cold War. To reach these ends, there are no magic policies of liberation—there is only hard work—but that hard work can and must be done.

4. Nuclear Tests

STUDENT CONVOCATION AT U.C.L.A.
LOS ANGELES, CALIFORNIA
NOVEMBER 2, 1959

No change in a fast-changing world presents a greater challenge—no problem in a world full of problems calls for greater leadership and vision—than the control of nuclear weapons, the utter destruction which would result from their use in war, and the radioactive pollution of our atmosphere by their continued testing in peacetime.

It is not a simple problem with simple answers. The experts disagree—the evidence is in conflict—the obstacles to an international solution are large and many. But the issue of nuclear tests and their effects is one which should be discussed in the coming months—not as a purely partisan matter, but as one of the great issues on the American scene.

It was well, therefore, that this issue was raised in a constructive way by the Governor of New York. His statement contributed to the dialogue on this basic issue—it represented the position of a leading figure in the Republican party—and he did not attempt to evade the question. So I commend Governor Rockefeller for stating his views, and I hope they will be considered and debated by interested citizens everywhere.

But I must also express my own emphatic disagreement with his statement, which called for this country to resume nuclear test explosions. Such a proposal, it seems to me, is unwise when it is suggested just prior to the reopening of negotiations with the British and Russians at Geneva on this very question. It is damaging to the American image abroad at a time when the Russians have unilaterally suspended their testing and the peoples of the world are fearful of continued fall-out. And, while Mr. Rockefeller did suggest that the testing take place underground to prevent fall-out, he also —according to press reports—"discounted" the harmful effects of fall-out—which I am unwilling to do.

While many competent scientists agree that there has been no great harm done to mankind as a whole from the amount of radiation created by bomb tests so far, it is also true that there is no amount of radiation so small that it has no ill effects at all on anybody. There is actually no such thing as a minimum permissible dose. Perhaps we are talking about only a very small number of individual tragedies—the number of atomic age children with cancer, the new victims of leukemia, the damage to skin tissues here and reproductive systems there—perhaps these are too small to measure with statistics. But they nevertheless loom very large indeed in human and moral terms. Moreover, there is still much that we do not know— and too often in the past we have minimized these perils and shrugged aside these dangers, only to find that our estimates were faulty and the real dangers were worse than we knew.

Let us remember also that our resumption of tests would bring Russian resumption of tests—it would make negotiations even more strained—it would spur other nations seeking entry into the "atomic club," with their own tests polluting the atmosphere—and, in short, it could precede the kind of long, feverish testing period which all scientists agree would threaten the very existence of man himself. And, perhaps even more importantly, the ability of other nations to test, develop and stockpile atomic weapons will alter drastically the whole balance of power, and put us all at the mercy of inadvertent, irresponsible, or deliberate atomic attacks from many corners of the globe. This problem—called the "Nth country" problem, because we do not know how many nations may soon possess these weapons— is at the real heart of the Geneva negotiations. For once China, or France, or Sweden, or half a dozen other nations successfully test an atomic bomb, then the security of both Russians and Americans is dangerously weakened.

The arguments advanced in favor of a test resumption are not unreasonable. The emphasis is on weapons development—the necessity to move ahead "in the advanced techniques of the use of nuclear material." This reason is not to be dismissed lightly. Our basic posture in world affairs relies on technical military superiority. We need to develop small tactical nuclear weapons and so-called "clean" nuclear weapons, in order to deter their use or other forms of limited aggression by the enemy. We need to increase the flexibility and range of weapons in our arsenal in order to increase our flexibility and range of diplomatic possibilities. This is not, I might add, justification for cutting back our ground forces and our ability to wage conventional warfare—but it is nevertheless important. Certainly the destruction rained upon us all by a small nuclear battle—and this our weapons development program is intended to deter—would be many times the damage caused by all the test fall-out in the future. Moreover, such a weapons development program cannot be suspended indefinitely in a free country without our scientists and technicians scattering to other positions in other laboratories. In addition, France and other nations on the verge of becoming nuclear powers will resent a ban—and their good will is also important.

But it is even more important that we find a way out of the present menacing military situation. And let us remember that our present test suspension is implicitly conditional on a continued Russian test suspension. If we are not developing new weapons in the absence of tests, neither are they. If we will make progress militarily through the resumption of tests, so, in all probability, will they. And the facts of the matter are that, generally speaking, we are ahead of the Russians in the development of atomic warheads of all sizes but behind in the development of delivery systems. Until this lag can be overcome, there is a lesser value for us in testing and developing further "techniques in the use of nuclear material." In short, for both sides to resume atomic tests today might well turn out to be more of a disadvantage to the West militarily than a help. The Soviet Union—which apparently made great progress in its 1958 tests—is quite as likely as we in any new tests to score a break-through with some new means of destruction which will make all the more delicate the present balance of terror.

I would suggest, therefore, the following alternative position:

1. *First*, that the United States announce that it will continue its unilateral suspension of all nuclear tests as long as serious negotiations for a permanent ban with enforceable inspection are proceeding with tangibly demonstrated good faith, *provided* that the Russians do not meanwhile resume their own tests. The latest extension of our test suspension announcement expires on December 31—and we cannot take the chance of continuing it indefinitely without an inspection system—or afford the cost of extending a temporary suspension so long that our scientists disperse and our laboratories break down. But neither can we afford to undercut negotiations close to success—to resume polluting the atmosphere while the Russians pose as moral leaders. As long as serious, good-faith negotiations continue into the early months of 1960—and are not prolonged indefinitely beyond that—we must continue our suspension beyond December 31.

2. *Second*, the United States must redouble its efforts to achieve a comprehensive and effective agreement to ban all nuclear tests under international control and inspection—and this means develop-

ing a single, clear-cut, well-defined, realistic inspection proposal of our own. We do not have this today. We have not made as concentrated an effort on techniques for preserving mankind as we have on techniques of destruction. Nor do we have a clear, concrete policy for the general arms control or disarmament program which must necessarily follow an agreement on testing if it is to be meaningful. But the whole international climate could benefit from this demonstration that East and West can reach significant, enforceable agreements. At least a part of the burdensome arms race would come to a halt. The danger of new nuclear powers emerging would be lessened. For the first time the Russians would have accepted effective international controls operating within their own territory. The hazards to health would be over. Such an agreement, in short, even if not perfect—even, for example, if it looks to further modification regarding inspection systems for underground or outer-space tests—would nevertheless be well worth far more effort than we are presently exerting. And it would be far more valuable than the military benefits to be gained from test resumption.

3. *Third,* if our best efforts do not succeed, the negotiations collapse, the Russians resume testing, and it becomes necessary for our tests to resume, even then they should be confined to underground and outer-space explosions, and to the testing of only certain small weapons in the upper atmosphere, in order to prevent a further increase in the fall-out menace—and in the hope, moreover, that the Russians and others will be forced by world opinion to follow our example.

4. *Fourth and finally,* we must step up our studies of the impact of radioactive fall-out and how to control it, through the Public Health Service here at home and a special United Nations monitoring commission abroad. Let us not discover the precise point of danger after we have passed it. Let us not again reject these warnings of peril as "catastrophic nonsense" (to quote Mr. Nixon), as they were rejected in 1956 when put forward by a great Democratic standard-bearer, Adlai E. Stevenson. There is every indication that had a test ban been accomplished *then,* it would have been far more useful, far more easily accomplished, and far more beneficial to our national security than it would today, now that the missile gap has widened so far.

These four policy positions that I have stated are no magic solution—nor can they be achieved overnight without effort. The course which I am suggesting is full of risks. It will require more effort, more leadership, more moral courage than merely "running scared." But the new and terrible dangers which man has created can only be controlled by man. And if we can master this danger and meet this challenge, we will have earned the deep and lasting gratitude, not only of all men, but of all yet to be born—even to the farthest generation.

PORTLAND, OREGON
AUGUST 1, 1959

There is a tendency today to dismiss the efforts for international agreement on nuclear tests as visionary and unrealistic. But the harsh facts of the matter are that the time is not far off when many nations in many parts of the world of many political shades and commitments will possess nuclear or even thermonuclear weapons.

Think for a moment what that means.

Many nations now possess, or have access to, the scientific personnel and know-how, the power and fuel supplies, the mineral and chemical resources, the industrial base and the transportation facilities which combined to make the United States the first great nuclear power. These other nations have not obtained the necessary technical information through espionage or accidental leaks. On the contrary, there have been such enormous developments in pure and applied science since Hiroshima that today there are, for all practical purposes, no longer any real atomic secrets—except for methods of detonation and isotope separation. The basic knowledge required is possessed by practically every country—the only question is how many will commit themselves politically and economically to joining the nuclear club.

Canada, Communist China, Sweden, Switzerland, and particularly France have all given various indications this past year that they are on the way to the development of such weapons. French tests in the Sahara are about to begin. Sweden has doubled its budget in this field during the current fiscal year. Canada already possesses a variety of reactors, as well as adequate uranium supplies and trained personnel. On the other side of the Iron Curtain, both Czechoslovakia and East Germany have tapped their rich supply of ores, and stepped up the training of their best minds in nuclear physics.

Similar data could be cited for Belgium, for Japan, for India, for Italy, and for West Germany. Within a few years, other countries should be able to accumulate the necessary industrial and scientific resources—countries of such varying political status as Poland, Yugoslavia, Finland, the Union of South Africa, Spain, Hungary, Argentina, and Austria. There is no evidence, moreover, that nuclear bombs developed by such nations as Sweden or Switzerland will not be sold on the world market, just as guided missiles and reactors for peaceful uses are sold commercially today. There is no evidence that a smaller or less developed nation could not secretly convert a reactor it receives for peaceful uses today to make plutonium for use in a bomb. On the contrary, the evidence indicates that those forty-two countries which will soon possess peaceful reactors will be one-half the distance to the development of nuclear weapons.

In short, many nations are potential members of the atomic club. Their intentions, to be sure, may not be to impair Western security —they may be seeking only increased prestige, or a reduction in expensive conventional forces, or a stronger voice in international councils, or more independence from big power decisions. But regardless of their present intentions, it is clear that this trend foreshadows developments that will alter every basic military and diplomatic premise of our time. It will radically change every fundamental concept which now prevails in our Departments of State and Defense.

Possibilities of accidental war will be enormously increased—the possibilities of a nuclear holocaust being initiated for irrational reasons by a fanatic or demagogue will be tremendously increased— so will the possibilities of nuclear blackmail by any nation that chooses to use its atomic armaments as a diplomatic tool or threat. It will make much more difficult and much less likely the chances for international agreement and controls on atomic weapons. The distinction between great powers and small powers will become less meaningful. To rest our hopes on a so-called balance of power will become impossible. And the security of this nation and the entire world will depend upon the daily events, the political stability, the motives, and the politics of unknown or little known leaders all over the globe.

If one thermonuclear bomb in the low megaton range were to be dropped on this nation—it would not matter whether the sender was responsible or fanatical, whether he was acting rationally or irrationally, deliberately or accidentally—it would still release more destructive energy upon this land than all the bombs dropped on Germany and Japan during World War II.

These developments should be of concern to everyone in Portland, to everyone in Washington and indeed to the entire country. They should be discussed, not for purposes of alarm, but for purposes of alert. For it is not too late. The "Nth country" problem is not yet an accomplished fact. France has not yet joined the nuclear club— Russia is not yet eager to share her atomic know-how with her satellites, or even with China—and the Geneva Conference on atomic testing and surprise attack, the other Geneva Conference, is still going on.

But its success will require new emphasis and a new effort on our part. The terrible dangers which are inherent in this situation have received very little public debate and attention—and they have apparently received very little top-level attention in Washington and other world capitals.

I do not say that a cessation of tests under international agreement provides the final answer. But it would place a major obstacle in the path of those nations which have not yet successfully conducted tests, and which would be unwilling to risk the tremendous investment necessary in weapons which could not be tested. And surely such an agreement would give reassurance to those of us who are concerned about the atmosphere we live in and the air our children breathe—for it is the same atmosphere and the same air in all nations, weak or powerful, rich or poor, on this side of the Iron Curtain or the other.

There is no serious scientific barrier to international agreement— despite increasing difficulties in problems of inspection and implementation. The only difficult barriers now are political and diplomatic. If we could mobilize the same talents and energy and resources to meet this challenge that we did to split the atom in the first place, then we should be able to persuade friend and foe alike that continued neglect of this problem will make all the world a loser— while its solution will make all the world a winner—and a better place with a better future for the children of every land.

5. Disarmament

WASHINGTON, D.C.
DECEMBER 11, 1959

No sane society chooses to commit national suicide. Yet that is the
fate which the arms race has in store for us—unless we can find a
way to stop it.

There is some argument as to just what proportion of our population would be destroyed in a missile-megaton war in the next decade.
But having recently attended hearings at which scientists and experts
were testifying—in that detached, statistical manner that scientists
have—about what would happen to this country and the world if war
should come, I am sorry to say that there is too much point to the
wisecrack that life is extinct on other planets because their scientists
were more advanced than ours.

Already our total destructive capacity is sufficient to annihilate
the enemy twenty-five times over—he has the power to destroy us
ten times. Between us we are in a position to exterminate all human
life seven times over. The nuclear load in only one of our B-52's
now in the air—at this minute somewhere above us or over the
Arctic—is said to be greater in terms of destructive power than all
of the explosives used in all of the previous wars in human history.
Yet today our hopes are still dim that any proposals for universal
disarmament will be agreed upon by either the U.S. or the U.S.S.R.
Disarmament remains a pious phrase which both sides invoke—but
which they will not implement together.

It is often said that arms are only a symptom of tension, not the
cause of it; and that, so long as situations such as Berlin exist, it will
be necessary to continue the arms race. But this is at best a half-
truth. Atomic and hydrogen weapons themselves have become a
major source of tension. Behind many political conflicts lie problems
of the military balance of power—problems rising from the need to
maintain troops or air bases or nuclear missile installations—problems that would not arise outside the context of the arms race.

The truth is that we are caught in a vicious circle comprised in
part of the arms race and in part of political conflict. For us, this
vicious circle of two great powers contending with each other for
sway over the destiny of man is compounded by the new dynamics of

an expansive world Communism, armed with revolutionary doctrines of class warfare and modern methods of subversion and terror. For the Kremlin, this struggle for the world is complicated by the contagious quality of freedom—by the ferment within the Communist empire for the freedom that all men want—by the powerful example and contrast that America and other free lands present to people suffering under Communist conformity. Yet both sides in this fateful struggle must come to know, sooner or later, that the price of running this arms race to the end is death—for both.

Some historic vicious circles have simply worn down and petered out in time. Toynbee keeps hopefully recalling that the cold and hot wars waged by a fanatic Islam and a crusading Christendom gradually transformed themselves into centuries of perpetual truce, although both parties retained their universal goals. Communism and the West, he suggests, may in time come tacitly to agree to coexist, even while each hopes and works for the extension of its way of life to the whole world.

The trouble with this cheerful picture is that the pace of events is much faster now—the logic of the present arms race seems to require more of a collision course than the slow changes wrought in medieval times. In the days of the crusades, it took months—sometimes years—of sailing by sea and marching overland for two worlds to collide. Today the deadly missiles with hydrogen warheads are only minutes away. For the first time since the War of 1812, the American people live on what would be the front lines of a world war. In 1814, forty British vessels outside Baltimore Harbor fired two-hundred-pound balls for twenty-five hours, "An awful spectacle to behold," Bishop John Carroll wrote. But it was nothing like the spectacle of a city going up in a nuclear cloud from one hydrogen bomb launched from one Soviet submarine. Today our cities are the bull's-eyes of the Soviet missile targets, just as their cities are the targets of our Strategic Air Force. To prevent this conflagration, some dramatic intervention is required to break the vicious circle of the Cold War and to start a constructive circle of confidence.

Since the circle of fear is fed both by the arms race itself and by the political conflicts between the West and the Communist world, real progress on either part of the problem—on either a political settlement of some important outstanding issue, or on atomic control and disarmament—might suffice to start a momentum toward peace, toward the kind of agreement to live and inhabit the same planet (even while disagreeing about other things) that Toynbee foresees.

In this formula, progress on either problem must lead to progress on the other if the source of the vicious circle is to be controlled. It is with this in mind that we must press forward now for any practical disarmament agreement within reach—not as a substitute for efforts to settle some of the great political divisions such as Germany, Korea, Vietnam, or China, but as a way of moving these and all other problems back from the brink of war. The way for these problems to be resolved—the only way now open—is through the peaceful processes of history that Toynbee describes. Our job is to bring those processes into play quickly, even though the ultimate resolution may take generations—or even centuries.

Some say that there is little point in negotiating with the Russians in these terms because they have never abided by any agreement and never will. But this is another way of saying that war is the unavoidable fate of mankind. Lenin used to say this, in the days before war meant the annihilation of whole peoples. Stalin blindly said it, even after the atomic bomb had been dropped on Japan. No American should say it. We who believe in human reason and in the possibilities of peaceful change should never lose hope that even a tough-minded Kremlin politician will see the light—or enough of the light to know that war, in the age of the hydrogen bomb, is no longer a rational alternative.

There are, I say, grounds for hope. We should certainly not neglect our armaments in the meantime. And we must not let our wishes father false thoughts—of unilateral disarmament, of disarmament without adequate controls, or without guarantees that all parties are in fact disarming. But we should not let our fears hold us back from pursuing our hopes. Disarmament talks historically fail when nations refuse to trust each other's intentions enough to take the first step. Even that first step must be subject to adequate inspection and enforcement. But this, too, requires a minimum of trust.

When I say "trust," I do not mean that we should for one moment think that the Kremlin has abandoned its aim of world domination or is ready to disband its present empire. Nor do I ask the Kremlin to think that we of the West have abandoned our concern for the people under Communist domination or our desire to promote the peaceful liberation of all people. But assuming we each maintain these objectives, we can also come to an understanding that peace is the precondition for any of these efforts. Naturally each side will assume his own success in the competition. Mr. Khrushchev has left no doubt of his self-confidence—and I am equally confident that, in conditions of peace, we can see freedom thrive and spread—even someday to Mr. Khrushchev's grandchildren. But trust we must—in each other's rational recognition of self-interest—in our mutual self-interest in survival.

The problem is to find a beginning. Archimedes is supposed to have said: "Give me a fulcrum and I can move the world." What we need is the first fulcrum in this situation. In the search for this we need to try every practical possibility.

It may be that an agreement on the control and limitation of nuclear tests will be the beginning. If the difficulties of detection and inspection prove insurmountable for the time being on underground or high-atmosphere tests, at least a beginning may be made with an agreement to suspend permanently low-atmosphere testing, which can be monitored adequately and which causes the worst fall-out. Perhaps a U.N. system of inspection to warn against surprise attacks will be acceptable as a start. Or the beginning might be an agreement to explore space jointly under United Nations auspices, perhaps through a world space agency.

Another dramatic step that might reverse the present pattern would be an agreement on general disarmament and demilitarization for some particular area of tension. The treaty of peace and the neutralization of Austria in return for the withdrawal of Soviet occupation forces may point to other applications of such a policy. The Middle East might be an area where a political settlement and disarmament could be fruitfully combined. The new treaty on Antarctica may show the way. Developing techniques of inspection and control in one such area could lead to the extension of these techniques to other areas, and eventually perhaps the world. Out of the experience of the emergency U.N. force sent to Suez could come the nucleus of the world policing forces necessary to ensure such demilitarized zones.

Peace may come through a combination of such beginnings, each small and insufficient in itself but together enough to provide the new momentum.

In this search for beginnings we must bring into play the imagination which our fears have in recent years paralyzed. The initiative taken by the new chairman of the Atomic Energy Commission, John McCone, is an example of the affirmative approach now required. So far it has met with an affirmative Soviet response. Mr. McCone and the United States scientific mission to the Soviet Union were shown far more of Soviet installations and laboratories for peaceful uses of atomic energy than anyone a year ago would have believed possible. And after the Soviet mission here, an initial agreement for co-operation in this field was reached, with far more extensive co-operation now being considered. Here is another beginning that would never have been possible if the negative, ever-suspicious spirit of Mr. McCone's predecessor had continued to prevail.

Even Mr. Khrushchev's all too general proposal for universal disarmament should be explored as a possible beginning, not shunted off as mere propaganda. The Soviet-American agreement and joint resolution in the U.N. Assembly to resume disarmament negotiations and to consider Mr. Khrushchev's proposal was a constructive response—one all too rarely seen. For the lesson to be drawn from Mr. Khrushchev's address to the U.N. was not the inadequacy of his plan —not his lack of specifics on the crucial questions of inspection and control. That was not news. The lesson rather was to be found in the great expectations raised throughout the world by the prospect of the Soviet leader proposing a far-reaching disarmament plan and in the considerable disappointment that his proposal did not go far enough.

It is for us now to meet these expectations with far-reaching new plans of our own, and not to disappoint the world by treating this problem merely as a matter of psychological warfare. We must design and propose a program that combines disarmament with the strengthening of the United Nations and with world development. We must propose the creation of new United Nations institutions of inspection and control and of economic development. And we must demonstrate our good faith by being prepared to make a beginning at any hopeful place along the broad front of present possibilities. So far we have lacked the vision to present a comprehensive program for the development of a world community under law and we have lacked the courage to try small beginnings. The legacy of these years of Cold War that Stalin forced upon us is that our policy-makers on too many levels and in too many fields have become narrow, cautious, and, in the literal sense, reactionary. It is time to stop reacting to our adversary's moves, and to start acting like the bold, hopeful, inventive people that we were born to be, ready to build and begin anew, ready to make a reality of man's oldest dream, world peace.

II
TWO CENTRAL
PROBLEMS

In Washington, as elsewhere, the urgent is often the enemy of the important. The need for decision and action on immediate crises too frequently seems to preclude the serious, careful study of fundamental and long-range problems that is so essential to foresighted leadership. Then the neglected problems of the future suddenly arise in their true importance and become the new urgencies to which we must quickly respond, generally with improvisations that are too little and too late.

One measure of the world crisis now upon us is that our basic, long-term problems are already dramatically confronting us and calling for urgent action. Feeling the need to assess the full facts of our changed military and economic situation, I attempted to think through the implications for American policy of both the threatening missile gap—caused by the Kremlin's rocket successes and our failures—and the increasing economic gap between the West and the underdeveloped world.

The resulting analyses and proposals that I presented to the Senate seem to me even more urgent and important now than when first given. The Russian pennant reaching the moon should raise our sights to both the great dangers and the great opportunities around us—to the great need to face and meet our central problems.

6. The Missile Gap

Mr. President, four hundred years ago the British crown and people realized with a sense of shock that they had lost Calais forever. Long considered an impregnable symbol of British supremacy in Europe, this last foothold of English power on the Continent was surrendered to the French in 1558. It is said that when Mary of England died, in the same year, the word "Calais" was engraved upon her heart—but that she was, in the words of *The Cambridge Modern History*, an eminent example "of the inadequacy of deep convictions and pious motives to guide the state aright." Once they had recovered from their initial panic, the British set about adjusting their thinking and their policies to the loss they had suffered. With their gateway to the Continent gone, they sought new power and influence in the seas. A navy was built, new trade routes promoted, a new maritime emphasis established; and when the Spanish Armada was defeated in 1588, the panic and pessimism that had followed the loss of Calais were forgotten as Britannia ruled the waves. The old power, the foundation for old policies, was gone—but new policies had brought a new power and new security.

The time has come for the United States to consider a similar change, if we, too, are to depend on something more than deep convictions and pious motives to guide the state aright. For we, too, are about to lose the power foundation that has long stood behind our basic military and diplomatic strategy.[4]

[4] Senator Kennedy's plea for realism in facing an imminent period of national peril caused a sensation in Congress. Senator Homer Capehart of Indiana, as Mr. Kennedy notes elsewhere in this book, threatened to have the galleries cleared on the ground that the speech was disclosing information inimical to the national interest. Actually, its statements as to the coming disparity between American and Russian strengths in long-range missiles were familiar to experts. Lieutenant General James Gavin, whom Mr. Kennedy quotes, had resigned from the army to present his views on this and other subjects to the public. His book, *War and Peace in the Space Age*, was soon being widely reviewed.

Mr. Kennedy's point that President Eisenhower's complacency over the deterrent power of our nuclear weapons was outdated, and that the "deterrent ratio" in the years 1960-1964 would probably be weighted heavily against us, has been supported by other careful students of the

33

That foundation—one of the key premises upon which our leaders of diplomacy, defense, and public opinion have based their policy thinking—has been, since Hiroshima, our nuclear power. We have possessed a capacity for retaliation so great as to deter any potential aggressor from launching a direct attack upon us. Spokesmen for both parties, in the Senate and elsewhere, have debated our preparedness upon the assumption that this "ultimate deterrent" would deter any Soviet attack. Our retaliatory power, said the President in his 1958 State of the Union message, is "the most powerful deterrent to war in the world today," offering any potential aggressor "the prospect of virtual annihilation of his own country." Possession of similar striking power by the Soviet Union has not altered this basic premise —it is instead described now as the result of a "nuclear stalemate," a point of mutual "saturation" or a "balance of terror."

The hard facts of the matter are that this premise will soon no longer be correct. We are rapidly approaching that dangerous period which General Gavin and others have called the "gap" or the "missile-lag period"—a period, in the words of General Gavin, "in which our own offensive and defensive missile capabilities will lag so far behind those of the Soviets as to place us in a position of great peril."

The most critical years of the gap would appear to be 1960-64.

This is not to say that during that period we will not retain a nuclear capacity sufficient to rain "virtual annihilation" upon the U.S.S.R. But in view of our unwillingness and inability to strike the first blow, the successful use of that capacity—and the prospects for success must be overwhelming to deter a Russian attack—actually depends upon the proper balance of six factors:

a. The striking power of the Soviet Union that could be brought to bear upon our retaliatory power in a surprise attack. In the years of

---

situation. George Kennan has argued that the very idea of nuclear deterrence must be questioned. If the use of a deterrent would mean national suicide—and a nuclear war would be precisely that—can it be considered a shield against a power which might stand a better chance of survival than we would? Another American expert, Raymond L. Garthoff, states in a book on *Soviet Strategy in the Nuclear Age* that the Russians are convinced that atomic weapons alone cannot win a war, and that simple and effective means of defense can be found against them. In other words, Russian fear of nuclear weapons would in certain circumstances not be a deterrent to Russian action. This might be particularly true in a period when the Soviet Union would enjoy a clearly superior fire power in missiles. Senator Kennedy's demand for hard thinking upon what may be a very hard period ahead of us could not have been more timely.—A.N.

the gap this will rest primarily upon their missiles—IRBM's and ICBM's.

b. The adequacy of American defenses to reduce the successes of that Soviet striking power. This will include our distant early warning system, antimissile missiles when available and other interceptor and defense devices.

c. The vulnerability of American retaliatory power to destruction by any Soviet weapons penetrating our defense. Exposed missile bases and planes wing-to-wing on the ground are prime examples of this factor; although in a sense it also covers our "destruction tolerance"— the amount of devastation we could endure and still fight back.

d. The retaliatory power of the United States, its size affecting the amount of such power remaining and available after the initial Soviet attack.

e. The adequacy of Soviet defenses to reduce the success of our retaliation.

f. The vulnerability of the Soviet Union and its tolerance of destruction, as a measure of what the Soviets will still be able and willing to do after our retaliation.[5]

In short, what might be called the deterrent ratio—in terms of a somewhat oversimplified mathematical formula—requires that the sum of (a), (e), and (c) be no greater than the sum of (d), (b), and (f)—if we are to have a stalemate. But as the missile striking

[5] Despite Premier Khrushchev's talk of peaceful coexistence, and the certainty of good observers that Russia does not want war, the Soviet military budget for 1960 was the same as for 1959, exceeding 96 billion rubles. Soviet spokesmen called attention to the "stabilization" of arms expenditures, declaring that inasmuch as the budget as a whole had risen, this meant a relative diminution. Perhaps it did. But the true scope of Russian spending for armaments remained, as always, a well-guarded secret, on which official statistics threw little light. What was certain was that the U.S.S.R. had made tremendous progress in military matters, and especially in the development of long-range missiles. The Soviet was also increasing her already great expenditures on science and technological inquiry.

Mr. Kennedy had repeatedly made clear his conviction that the United States should be ready to enter into any international conference which offered any prospect of promoting world peace. But in this speech he asked the country to face the fact that the time lay just ahead when it would negotiate from comparative weakness rather than comparative strength; to grasp the truth that the old assumption that America always had superior bargaining power at the diplomatic table was a false assumption. We could regain our position of strength not by pushing up national income, but only by sacrifice and laborious planning.—A.N.

power of the Soviet Union increases and our retaliatory power lags—
as the adequacy of our continental defense falls behind that of the
Soviets—as we fail to reduce sufficiently the vulnerability of our
attack installations and planes, as contrasted with the wide dispersal
of Soviet-Red Chinese power—and uncertain as we are about the
destruction tolerance of our people, whose political institutions
and way of life are not prepared by tradition for the devastation of
battle, again unlike the Soviets—then we must realize that the deterrent ratio during 1960-64 will in all likelihood be weighted very heavily against us.

These are not easy facts to face—and once faced, their implications are not easily comprehended. But the facts must be faced—and
soon. Our peril is not simply because Russian striking power during
the years of the gap will have a slight edge over us in missile power—
they will have several times as many: intermediate-range missiles to
destroy our European missile and SAC bases; and intercontinental
missiles to devastate our own country, installations, and Government;
and history's largest fleet of submarines, and possibly long-range super-
sonic jet bombers, to follow up this advantage. If by that time their
submarines are capable of launching missiles, they could destroy 85
per cent of our industry, forty-three of our fifty largest cities, and most
of the nation's population.

We shall have no such supply of missiles with which to retaliate—
particularly after our few exposed IRBM bases in Europe and the
Mediterranean are attacked. We shall rely to a great extent on
manned bombers—bombers which face a problem of sufficient alert
and sufficient dispersal to avoid decimation, particularly if current
Middle East trends should curtail our base operations in that area—
bombers that lack an adequate refueling system to penetrate Soviet
borders without some two to four refuelings from our inadequate
tanker supply.

Even then we shall encounter a Soviet air defense, and dispersal or
concealment of vulnerable power, far superior to our own—a margin,
according to some estimates, which the Soviets will be able to maintain at a level two to four times greater than our own. Indeed, our
own DEW system and other continental defense bulwarks—many of
which the Soviets will hope to knock out before or during the first
blow—were planned for manned bombers, and must be redesigned
and rebuilt before they are adequate for the missile age.

In short, the deterrent ratio might well shift to the Soviets so heavily, during the years of the gap, as to open to them a new shortcut to

world domination. A portion of their homeland would still almost inevitably be destroyed, no matter how great their defenses or how decimated our retaliatory power. And without doubt world opinion would not tolerate such an attack. But our experience with the illogical decisions of Adolf Hitler should have taught us that these considerations might not deter the leaders of a totalitarian state—particularly in a moment of recklessness, panic, irrationality, or even cool miscalculation.

Surely we realize that the possibilities of serious miscalculation of war by inadvertence, of having both sides caught in a course which would lead to an all-out war which neither originally contemplated, of the calling of a bluff or of the sudden spreading of a limited war, are very real possibilities, if we but recall the Soviet Union's miscalculations on Korea in 1950, our own miscalculation of the Red Chinese reaction in 1951, our near intervention at Dienbienphu in 1954, the Soviet threats of rocket war at the time of the Suez invasion in 1956, and the possibilities of massive intervention by both sides which the situation in Iraq would have posed this year, had that struggle continued for very long. For many years, now, we have been living on the edge of the crater. We know full well the lack of communications between ourselves and our adversaries, the mutual suspicion and hostility, the increased risks taken by the Soviets as their striking power grows. Let no one think, therefore, that a Soviet attack, inadvertent or otherwise, is impossible, because of the H-bomb damage which we would still hope to rain upon the Soviets.

The Soviets, moreover, will be as well aware as we of their advantage during the years of the gap. We cannot expect them to sit idly by, and make no profitable use of it, while we strive to catch up. If General Gavin is correct in estimating Russian lead time to be twice as short as ours—five years, as compared to ten—we may not even catch up in 1964, or thereafter. We cannot expect them to give us the same advantage—by sitting by until our missile power equals their own—that we gave to them during the years of our atomic monopoly.

But nuclear destruction is not the only way in which the Soviets will be able to use their advantages in striking power. War is not so much an objective of foreign policy, as an instrument—a means of securing power and influence, of advancing a nation's views and interests. In the years of the gap, the Soviets may be expected to use their superior striking ability to achieve their objectives in ways which may not require launching an actual attack. Their missile power will be the shield from behind which they will slowly, but surely, advance—

through Sputnik diplomacy, limited brush-fire wars, indirect non-overt aggression, intimidation and subversion, internal revolution, increased prestige or influence, and the vicious blackmail of our allies. The periphery of the Free World will slowly be nibbled away. The balance of power will gradually shift against us. The key areas vital to our security will gradually undergo Soviet infiltration and domination. Each such Soviet move will weaken the West; but none will seem sufficiently significant by itself to justify our initiating a nuclear war which might destroy us.

Throughout the years of the gap, a direct Soviet attack may be our greatest danger. But it is these other avenues of Soviet advance—with a thrust more difficult to interpret and oppose, yet inevitably ending in our isolation, submission, or destruction—which may well constitute the most likely threat.

Four hundred years ago, the English lost Calais. That event altered the course of British diplomatic and military policy, and changed the direction of British public opinion. The acceptance of the loss, and the adjustment of policy, were not easily or quickly accomplished; but they occurred eventually.

There is every indication that by 1960 the United States will have lost its Calais—its superiority in nuclear striking power. If we act now to prepare for that loss, and if, during the years of the gap, we act with both courage and prudence, there is no reason why we, too, cannot successfully emerge from this period of peril more secure than ever.

Unfortunately, our past reliance upon massive retaliation has stultified the development of new policy. We have developed what Henry Kissinger has called a Maginot-line mentality—dependence upon a strategy which may collapse or may never be used, but which meanwhile prevents the consideration of any alternative. When that prop is gone, the alternative seems to many to be inaction and acceptance of the inevitability of defeat. After all, once the Soviets have the power to destroy us, we have no way of absolutely preventing them from doing so. But every nation, whatever its status, needs a strategy. Some courses of action are always preferable to others; and there are alternatives to all-out war or inaction.

But the adjustment is made more difficult by our traditional failure to link our national strategy and our thinking to our military status. We have extended our commitments around the world, without regard to the sufficiency of our military posture to fulfill those commitments. Changes in our defense status are rarely reflected in our diplomatic policies, pronouncements, and planning. The State and Defense Departments negotiate with each other at arm's length, like so many Venetian envoys, without decisive leadership to break through the excess of bureaucratic committees, competition, and complacency. We think of diplomacy and force as alternatives to each other—the one to be used where the other fails—as though such absolute distinctions were still possible.

Today, we are approaching the years of the gap as though the situation were normal, and as though other assumptions were unchanged—or, in some quarters at least, as though the problem were one of arms alone. Nothing could be farther from the truth.

In the years of the gap, our threats of massive retaliation will lose most of their impact.

In the years of the gap, our exercises in brink-of-war diplomacy will be infinitely less successful.

In the years of the gap, every basic assumption held by the American public with regard to our military and foreign policies will be called into question. Among the assumptions to be invalidated will be the following ten, which probably are most fundamental to our thinking in the twentieth century:

1. American arms and science are superior to any others in the world.

2. American efforts for world-wide disarmament are a selfless sacrifice for peace.

3. Our bargaining power at any international conference table is always more vast and flexible than that of our enemy.

4. Peace is a normal relation among states; and aggression is the exception—direct and unambiguous.

5. We should enter every military conflict as a moral crusade requiring the unconditional surrender of the enemy.

6. A free and peace-loving nation has nothing to fear in a world where right and justice inevitably prevail.

7. Americans live far behind the lines, protected by time, space, and a host of allies from attack.

8. We shall have time to mobilize our superior economic resources after a war begins.

9. Our advanced weapons and continental defense systems, established at a tremendous cost and effort, will protect us.

10. Victory ultimately goes to the nation with the highest national income, gross national product, and standard of living.

All of these concepts will be altered or questioned in but a few years.

It is unthinkable that we approach the years of the gap with the same sense of normalcy, the same slogans and economics, the same assumptions, tactics, and diplomatic strategy.

Although other peoples have learned to live for years exposed to enemy attack, I realize that it is hard for us to accept the reality of our danger. I realize that we are reluctant to re-examine policies arduously reached, or to believe that these problems cannot be postponed. But it is precisely this substitution of our preferences for our responsibilities that has led us to the brink of the gap. Our missile lag is not the cause of the gap—it is but another symptom of our national complacency, our willingness to confuse the facts as they were with what we hoped they would be, to appeal at the same time to those who wanted a quick solution and those who wanted a less burdensome one. The people have been misled; the Congress has been misled; and some say with good reason that on occasion the President himself has been misinformed and thus misled.

Perhaps the most serious result of this complacency—and the one we must first reverse—was our willingness to place fiscal security ahead of national security. We tailored our strategy and military requirements to fit our budget—instead of fitting our budget to our military requirements and strategy. We facilitated the adoption of this popular course through a variety of appealing shibboleths proclaimed to the nation each year by the President:

> Maximum safety at minimum cost (1953 State of the Union).
> Sustained military capability at the lowest possible cost (1954 budget message).
> Our defenses have been reinforced at sharply reduced costs (1956 State of the Union).
> We cannot afford to build military strength by sacrificing economic strength (1954 budget message).
> Future defense costs must be held to tolerable levels (1957 budget message).
> Adequate military strength within the limits of endurable strain upon our economy (1953 State of the Union).

In recent years we have heard a good deal about an alleged quotation from Lenin, who is supposed to have stated that the destruction of the capitalistic world would come about as a result of overspending on arms. I would say that has probably been the most valuable quotation the Communists have had other than "Workers of the World, Unite." But the fact of the matter is that was not said by Lenin. However, this slogan, which has been spread before us during this decade, has caused us constantly to emphasize economic considerations rather than military considerations, and has been used as an authority for that policy. Although Lenin never stated it, I should think that in the future it would rank high among the slogans which had proved to be useful in the effort to destroy the capitalistic system.

There were many others. The rationale was simple:

> To build excessively . . . could defeat our purposes and impair or destroy the very freedom and economic system our military defenses are designed to protect (1956).
> Any program that endangers our economy could defeat us (1957).
> To amass military power without regard to our economic capacity would be to defend ourselves against one kind of disaster by inviting another (1953).

The fact of the matter is that during that period when emphasis was laid upon our economic strength instead of our military strength, we were losing the decisive years when we could have maintained a lead against the Soviet Union in our missile capacity. These were the vital years we lost, the years the locusts have eaten, and it is quite obvious we obtained economic security at the expense of military security, and that this policy will bring us into great danger within the next few years.

I have never been very persuaded by this argument. It has always seemed to me that the converse was much more persuasive—that to emphasize budgetary limitations without regard to our military position was to avoid an inconvenient effort by inviting the disaster that would destroy all budgets and conveniences. Surely our nation's security overrides budgetary considerations—the President himself indicated this was true in times of war. Then why can we not realize that the coming years of the gap present us with a peril more deadly than any wartime danger we have ever known? And most important of all—and most tragically ironic—our nation could have afforded, and can afford now, the steps necessary to close the missile gap.

But our task now is not to fix the blame for the past, but to fix a course for the future.

Our attention is logically and necessarily directed first at the short-range military steps necessary to keep the deterrent ratio from shifting still further to the Red side and to lessen their advantage, if possible. Here other Senators have distinguished themselves in thoughtful addresses or committee action—including in particular the majority leader (Mr. Johnson), the junior Senator from Missouri (Mr. Symington), and the junior Senator from Washington (Mr. Jackson).

More air tankers to refuel our SAC bombers and more air-to-ground missiles to lessen the need for their deep penetration of Soviet territory are among the first steps to be taken while we expedite our longer-range ICBM and IRBM developments, and our progress on atomic submarines, solid fuels, the Polaris, and the Minuteman. Our continental defense system, as already mentioned, must be redesigned for the detection and interception of missile attacks as well as planes.

It should be obvious from our Lebanon experience that we lack the sea and airlift necessary to intervene in a limited war with the speed, discrimination, and versatility which may well be needed to keep it limited—and without weakening our ultimate retaliatory power. We need to reverse what General Gavin describes as the "critical cut" in our military manpower begun in 1954.

Finally, if we do not take care, we will create a second gap—between the date when our present ready weapons are obsolescent and the date when our ballistic missiles are operational in any sufficient quantity. To prevent this short-term gap, and to make certain that we have ended the missile lag by 1964, when we shall have mass production, we hope, of the Minuteman solid-fuel missile, may well require a complete re-examination of our traditional systems of evaluating, budgeting, researching, assigning, developing, and procuring weapons.

But discussions of new armaments are not enough—and too late to halt the gap. The gap will begin in 1960. And while stepped-up defense efforts are essential to insure its close in 1964 and thereafter, and to lessen its impact in between, the years of the gap demand something more than a purely military answer.

A Maginot-line reliance upon the military answer of massive retaliation has frustrated policy discussions to date, as mentioned—we must now be prepared to demonstrate that we have other courses besides military action and no action at all. For absence of power no more dictates an absence of policy than the presence of power. On the contrary, ancient man survived the more powerful beasts about him because his wisdom—his strategy and his policies—overcame his lack of power. We can do the same. We dare not attempt less, nor do we dare rely wholly upon those same policies in effect during the years of our retaliatory lead.

What is the fundamental approach to formulating a strategy from a basically but only temporarily disadvantageous position? It is first, of necessity, to work for a real peace—for a reduction of armaments, a reduction of tensions, and a reduction of areas of dispute. The goal of universal disarmament—at least in the area of nuclear weapons and long-range ballistic missiles—takes on an urgency not heretofore demonstrated by American negotiators who felt they held most of the trump cards. We must redouble our efforts in that regard—and the work of the Senate Disarmament Subcommittee, headed by the distinguished junior Senator from Minnesota (Mr. Humphrey), has made a major contribution in illuminating areas where our efforts might be redoubled.

But that failing—as well it might, once the Soviets are in the driver's seat, though we must never stop trying—the question again arises as to what basic strategy we employ during the years of the gap.

The best and most recent example is that provided by the Soviets themselves during the years of their gap—when American might was superior. While we would not imitate the Communists per se, they demonstrated the classic strategy of the underdog—and soon we will be the underdog. It is basically a strategy of making the most of all remaining advantages and making the most of the enemy's weaknesses —and thus to buy the time and opportunity necessary to regain the upper hand. This will require not only strong leadership in Washington but also expert ambassadors in the field—men equal to the best of any other nation, who are skilled in the needed techniques of probe and prudence, and whose judgments and reports are more reliable than some of those which misled us in Indochina and other difficult areas in years gone by.

Twentieth-century America is not accustomed to this underdog strategy—although it was expertly practiced by our Founding Fathers in time of peace as well as war. And we can practice it now.

Consider for a moment the advantages we retain even after our retaliatory lead is lost:

We retain an economic and industrial advantage, of little use once a bomb is dropped, but of considerable use now in building situations of strength and good will in such key areas as India and Tunisia. There is no need to waste this advantage in a drawn-out recession— and the Congress has an important opportunity to utilize this advantage in an action this week on the Development Loan Fund— the best hope for nations seeking the capital necessary to outstrip their population increases.

We retain an ideological advantage, better equipped than any nation in the world to export the revolutionary ideas of the Declaration of Independence, and thus lead, not frustrate, the nationalist movement against imperialism of any variety, East and West. Particularly after our recent excursion in the Middle East, we are regarded in too many parts of the world as an enemy of popular rule—when we had every right to enjoy the cleanest, strongest reputation in this regard of any nation on earth.

We retain a geographical advantage, essential to adequate dispersal and warning systems, and to the encouragement of local resistance to the Red tide. Although, as Mr. Dulles has said, we cannot make popularity our goal, we must shape our attitudes and procedures in a way that will not cost us our geographical advantage. We do not retain that advantage simply through paper alliances with the reactionary, unpopular governments which have no indigenous support; and recent events in the Middle East should also have taught us that, to maintain that geographical advantage, no commitment at all is better than one which we cannot or should not honor, which the local populations did not request, which our allies do not support, and which is politically or militarily unfeasible.

How well we learned that lesson, to be more precise and to compare strength, may soon be tested in the case of Quemoy and Matsu. I do not think there is greater folly than to leave our commitment in that area as vague as the Secretary of State has left it. If the Chinese should assume we are not going to come to the defense of Quemoy and Matsu, and it is the intention of the United States to come to the aid of those islands, we could find ourselves embroiled in a struggle which could lead to a major political action and perhaps to disaster for all of us, East and West.

As we approach the years of the gap, the U.S.S.R. will also retain weaknesses for us to probe—chief among them being the Achilles' heel of the satellite nations. The Congress and Administration must reverse those policies, last affirmed by a one-vote margin in June, which hamstrung our flexibility in attempting to wean the satellites from the Soviets, and to drive new wedges into each new crack in the Iron Curtain.

There is no point now in consolidating the Red bloc with our talk of massive retaliation—now we must seek ways of dividing it.

In short, to sound the alarm is not to panic—it is not to sell America short. It gives the enemy no encouragement he did not already possess. But the sound of the alarm does warn us that time is running out—that no matter how complex the problems, how discouraging the prospects, or how unpopular the decisions, these facts must be faced.

Complacency or hysteria will not help. Sustained and informed constructive effort will help—not to provide all the answers for the future, but to help assure us that there will be a future.

In Gibbon's volumes on *The Decline and Fall of the Roman Empire* he stated that the Romans maintained the peace by a constant preparation for war and that they indicated to the enemies on their periphery they were as little disposed to endure injury as to offer it. I do not say we should only prepare for war. But we should certainly use all elements of national policy—economic, diplomatic, and military—in order to prepare us for the most serious test in our nation's history, which will be impending in the next five years.

No Pearl Harbor, no Dunkirk, no Calais is sufficient to end us permanently if we but find the will and the way.

In the words of Sir Winston Churchill in a dark time of England's history: "Come then—let us to the task, to the battle and the toil— each to our part, each to our station. . . . Let us go forward together in all parts of the [land]. There is not a week, nor a day, nor an hour to be lost."

7. *The Economic Gap*

IN THE SENATE
FEBRUARY 19, 1959

Mr. President, the attention of the Congress and the American people in recent weeks has been turned—and properly so—to the forthcoming "missile gap." I wish to speak today about a gap which constitutes an equally clear and present danger to our security.

Unlike the missile gap, the gap to which I refer will not reach the point of critical danger in 1961. That point has been reached now.

Unlike the missile gap, the gap to which I refer is not even on the surface being reduced by the combined efforts of our executive and legislative branches. It is, on the contrary, consistently ignored and steadily widening.

Unlike the missile gap, the gap to which I refer gives rise to no speculation as to whether the Russians will exploit it to their advantage and to our detriment. They are exploiting it now.

I am talking about the economic gap—the gap in living standards and income and hope for the future—the gap between the developed and the underdeveloped worlds—between, roughly speaking, the top half of our globe and the bottom half—between the stable, industrialized nations of the north, whether they are friends or foes, and the overpopulated, underinvested nations of the south, whether they are friends or neutrals.[6]

It is this gap which presents us with our most critical challenge today. It is this gap which is altering the face of the globe, our

[6] The means by which the United States can accomplish much more than it has yet done to narrow the gap between the have and the have-not nations have often been pointed out; but as Senator Kennedy declared in this speech, the Eisenhower Administration has signally failed to act upon them. It could make long-term loans for development at low interest rates, for American charges for money have been materially higher than Russian charges. In countries like Thailand and Pakistan it could reduce the proportion of money spent on military aid, and increase that on economic aid. It could adopt more liberal trade policies. It could encourage American businessmen to be a little more tolerant of state enterprises in various Asian countries. The American press gave this speech an unusually warm endorsement.

The facts behind Mr. Kennedy's argument are as impressive as they are simple. The United States occupies only 6 per cent of the world's surface, yet it produces half of the manufactures of the globe, and a third of all its commodities. The life expectancy of Americans is twice as great as that of the people of India. Even in 1949, according to United Nations statistics, Americans had an average income of $1,440, a figure since then much exceeded; the earnings of an Indonesian in that year averaged $27. The terrific gap on the economic side is matched by an almost equal gap on the social and cultural side. While increasingly every American youth can count on a high school education, and about three and a half millions are now getting a higher education, the masses of Asia and Africa still stagger under the burden of illiteracy, ignorance, and superstition.

The frantic desire of the underdeveloped areas of the world to catch up and to improve their lot to the point where it is endurable naturally engenders envy of more fortunate lands. If these lands, the United States at their head, do not strenuously help struggling countries, envy will turn to hatred. The lagging peoples look to America and Britain, to Russia and China, for lessons in lifting themselves from their unhappy condition. For obvious reasons they find more applicable instruction in the recent progress of the Communist lands, which themselves started from a low level, than in that of the great democracies. It is important that they should find more sympathy, understanding, and practical assistance from the United States than they have thus far obtained. Soviet aid to China in gifts, credits, and technical advice is estimated at a figure higher than American aid to all Asiatic nations. Mr. Kennedy's argument is as important as it is eloquent.—A. N.

strategy, our security, and our alliances, more than any current military challenge. And it is this economic challenge to which we have responded most sporadically, most timidly, and most inadequately.

Since the truce negotiations in Korea began eight years ago, it should have been obvious that our greatest danger was no longer military. Since the Russians began their aid and trade penetration of the underdeveloped world some five years ago, it should have been obvious now that if India were to fall, if Latin America turned away, and if the Middle East slid behind the Iron Curtain, then no amount of missiles, no amount of space satellites or nuclear-powered planes or atomic submarines could ever save us.

And yet our response to this economic gap has never equaled our obligation or our opportunity. The problem is neither regional nor temporary—it is global and long-range. Our response has sometimes been wasteful in expenditure and grandiloquent in rhetoric—but it has never been global and long-range.

We have reacted *ad hoc* to a crisis here and a crisis there, year by year, region by region. When the Latin Americans throw rocks at the Vice President, there is finally talk of a Latin-American loan fund. When a friendly monarch is threatened in the Middle East, money is dispersed helter-skelter while there is brave but brief talk about an Arab development fund.

Let there be pressures from a North African nation and there is talk of economic aid to meet that crisis in that nation at that time. Let there be a foreign exchange crisis in India threatening all democratic hope in India and free Asia as a whole—and we bail the Indians out, at an inadequate level, for one year only.

This policy of using money on a crisis basis, from year to year, wherever difficulty arises, is expensive and ineffective. It is wasteful of our funds. It fails to stimulate effective long-range planning and effort by the recipients. It denies us the opportunity to impose meaningful standards for the use of our aid or significant requirements as to what they must do to match it. There is no follow-through, no consistency, no attempt to match our effort to their need and our resources. And so, among the nations of the world, the rich grow richer as the poor grow poorer—with less capital and more people and fewer hopes. It is this kind of atmosphere which increases the appeal of a narrow nationalism and dictatorship, which argues that economic interdependence with foreign nations is ominous.

The United States of America, the richest nation on earth, has not given the poorer nations new hope. But it is an unfortunate fact that the Soviet Union and particularly China have attracted the attention of the underdeveloped world to another, and seemingly quicker, route to closing the gap. Communist China's "great leap forward" was the primary event of 1958. We may discount her official figures—which claim to have doubled both agricultural and steel production—but they are based on a hard substance of fact, and they carry credibility in other nations.

China and India are roughly comparable in terms of their historic stages of economic growth and in resources; but China's rate of economic growth in 1958 was at least three times as high as India's. Especially in agricultural development and food production, where India's performance has been sagging, the Chinese record carries great appeal to underdeveloped Asian nations uncertain of which economic route they should follow. A top Ceylonese official was quoted earlier this year as expressing unrestrained admiration for Red Chinese economic achievements.

Within the last year the Chinese have produced their first automobile. Within the next year they may have launched their first earth satellite. Even more seriously, they may well begin to take their place among the select company of nuclear powers. This has been accomplished in part with the nearly $3 billion in credits which China has received from the Soviet Union since 1950, and the over two hundred major industrial projects to which the Soviet Union has given technical and machine assistance. But perhaps more significant for the future is the fact that China has become a major trading nation— not only in Southeast Asia, where she is gradually supplanting Japan, but also in the growing trade movements to Europe and Africa. Peking has used its position to launch a trade price war which supplements impressively the foreign economic offensive which the Soviet Union launched three years ago. Indian primary products such as manganese ore and oil seed, for example, now suffer heavily as a result of China's price competition.

In a year when China may well have increased her over-all food production by one-half, Indian food production rose only by a few bare percentage points. Last year India produced only slightly more than sixty million tons of food grains, yet the minimum annual need for India at the start of her Third Five-Year Plan two years from now will be eighty million tons. For the first time in modern history a government appears to have found a way—however brutal its human defects—to solve the problems of large peasant underemployment and labor surplus. The mobilization of the unemployed mass of

Chinese rural workers through economic communes, cottage industry, small pig-iron schemes, and all the rest is an achievement whose political and intellectual impact in less developed areas is bound to be immense.

We know that in a nation of stable population which is in the process of economic take-off a program of investment of at least 8 per cent of national income is necessary, for an annual growth of 2 per cent. But more typically these nations are also areas of great population growth. In countries with annual population increases of 2 to 3 per cent such as India, it requires an additional 6 to 8 per cent of investment if national growth is not to be offset by the rise in population. During the past year India has had a national growth rate of only 3 per cent and 2 per cent of this is largely dissipated by population increases. Two years ago India was reaching a national growth rate of nearly 5 per cent but the cutbacks in her Plan and bad harvests have blighted this achievement.

In short, to nations in a hurry to emerge from the rut of under-development, Communist China offers a potential model. The year 1958 was their "round." As their trade and aid offensive mounted, as their own example proved more attractive, our trade and aid programs faltered and our economy stood still—with our recession cutting the prices received for commodities the underdeveloped nations must sell, while our inflation continued to boost the prices they paid for our machinery.

But 1959 could and should be our "round," our year. We have, in this Congress, in these next few months, a moment of opportunity which may never come again. If we act now, on the right scale, in the right way, we may reverse the ever-widening gap—we may diminish the threat of a Communist takeover, and increase the chances of a peaceful evolution in India and other uncommitted, less developed areas. This can be the beginning of their economic downfall —or of their economic "take-off," enabling them to get ahead of their exploding population, to stabilize their economies and to build a base for continuing development and growth. Whichever answer emerges will shape for a generation to come the destiny of the world and the security of our nation. And which answer emerges is in large measure for this Congress to decide.

In recent years, the scale of our effort in foreign economic policy has been based upon what the Administration considered to be the requirements of the domestic budgetary and political situation.

It is time now for that effort to be based upon the requirements

of the international economic situation—and our own national security. Let us see exactly what is needed, when it is needed, how much
of it must come from this country and how much it will cost.

And then let us enact the program that will do the job. To do less
than is needed is just as wasteful as to do more than is needed. To
put it off is just as dangerous as refusing to do it at all.

By what means do we attack this problem? If we are to mobilize
our efforts and our resources to conquer this problem before it
conquers us, what must we do? There are several desirable steps to
be taken—and one urgent one.

We can—and should—achieve a better balance between military
and economic assistance and a more constructive use—including
local economic development—of that military assistance. In some
areas there are substantial untapped potentials for economic development purposes if local military forces can be guided on to constructive
civilian tasks—public works, community construction, irrigation
works, bridges—which will provide not only military training and
preparation for local combat, but also a ferment for local progress.
Such a redirection to constructive military purposes can help to re-
orient the goals and objectives of foreign military leaders toward
domestic development and away from external adventure. But this
is not enough.

We can—and should—take up the more imaginative proposals
offered to break the log jam restricting our use of surplus farm crops
abroad, to ease the food crisis in such nations as India and Pakistan
without impairing the markets of such friends as Canada and Argentina. We are blessed with abundance, yet we are unable to make
it more than a marginal asset in world leadership. We must expand
the range of our agricultural aid and integrate it more closely with
other foreign aid decisions. But this is not enough.

We can—and should—formally dedicate the year 1959 to the concept of International Development—ease trade barriers and Export-
Import Bank restrictions—work out international commodity agreements—expand technical assistance programs—encourage greater private investment—and take a series of other steps previously suggested
on this floor and elsewhere. It is almost exactly a decade since the
world emerged from its immediate postwar problems of reconstruction
and confronted the long-run issues of growth. It is exactly ten years
since President Truman enunciated Point Four. There is a decade's
experience to survey, successes and failures to be identified, experi-

ences to be summarized and exchanged, technical and scientific problems to be isolated and subjected to concentrated efforts at breakthrough. Even more, there are forward commitments to be made and plans developed for the decade which lies before us. But all this is not enough.

The heart of any solution must be a substantial, long-term program of productive loans to underdeveloped areas from a fully capitalized central fund, capable of working with either independent nations or regional groupings.

This is not a new concept or proposal. The need for it is not new —I make no claim to being the first to describe it. On the contrary, the tool for which we are looking is already in existence—the Development Loan Fund.

But the hard facts of the matter are that the Development Loan Fund has never fulfilled the barest intentions, much less the long-range visions, of its architects here in the Senate. It has totally failed to fill the need for long-term capital—because it has never been given either a long term or very much capital. It has never become a going bank. It has never been permitted to take hold of any major foreign development effort such as India's. It has never given less developed nations a real incentive to present programs and activities of highest promise for future economic growth.

Instead the Development Loan Fund is in real danger of becoming just another lending institution without distinctive criteria or functions. It has tended to consider only conventional loan applications for particular projects without regard to their significance to the recipient's long-range over-all economic development.

This is not only wholly inadequate to meet the crisis of the economic gap—it is also wholly contrary to the purpose of the program. The Senate Foreign Relations Committee originally intended a long-term fund capitalized at least $1 billion a year. The Administration enthusiastically urged a large scale and duration. But when it came to appropriating the actual funds, neither the Congress nor the Administration lived up to its earlier promises.

The Development Loan Fund has been forced to get by from year to year without enough funds to get very thoroughly under way. Practically all of its initial $700 million has been virtually committed, with a backlog of more than $1.7 billion in requests which have passed the first screening. Action is still awaited on more than $½ billion in still other applications which meet the Development Loan Fund criteria. As a solution the Administration's supplemental request for $225 million will not go very far for very many projects in very many countries. Neither will the $700 million and one more year of authorization requested in the President's budget.

There may be partisan approval for threatening to balance the budget by cutting this now hopelessly inadequate sum. There may be popular approval for standing by this meaningless figure, regardless of world developments. But there is only one responsible course which responsible citizens can approve. This Congress must take it.

Giving the Loan Fund continuity over a period of years will increase its effectiveness in a number of respects. In the first place, the leadership of the underdeveloped countries will not commit their political energies to development unless they see some prospect that the outside resources will be available over a period of years. In the second place, the Development Loan Fund has not been in a position to impose the kind of criteria of effective parallel effort by the recipient country for fear that if appropriations were not committed by the end of the fiscal year they would no longer be available. We can give recipients a strong incentive to meet serious conditions for the granting of loans only if we are in a position to hold the prospects of loans open over a period of time. Thus, continuity would actually increase the efficiency of loan administration. Finally, continuity would greatly increase the incentive effect on countries slow to mobilize their own resources by providing the example of a few successful cases of countries which have responded.

Congress must obtain a clear and comprehensive picture of the necessary missions to be performed by the Development Loan Fund in narrowing this critical economic gap—and the amount of funds and time necessary to fulfill those missions. We must then provide those funds for that length of time.

The alternative is chaos, not economy—a continuing of *ad hoc* crisis expenditures—a further diffusion and dilution of our effort— a series of special cases and political loans—an overreliance on inflexible, hard loans through the Export-Import and World Banks, with fixed-dollar repayment schedules that retard instead of stimulating economic development—a lack of confidence and effort in the underdeveloped world—and a general pyramiding of overlapping, standardless, incentiveless, inefficient aid programs. The cost of wasted effort, the cost of salvage after the damage has been done, and the cost of our lost security will be more than we can afford. But the cost of doing the job right is not more than we can afford. It may not be cheap or easy or popular—but we cannot afford to do less.

Revitalizing the Development Loan Fund is the most important step we can take to assure the Indians and others of our readiness to stand behind effective long-range economic development. It is also the most effective step we can take to give other governments in Asia and the Middle East, many of whom are now balanced precariously in deciding whether to channel their energies and resources around the tasks of economic growth or around military build-up and divisive conflict, new incentive and inspiration. The Development Loan Fund cannot be a magic solvent of all of India's difficulties, or those of the underdeveloped world in general. There are no such solutions. The gap is large. The barriers are great. The political and ideological dilemmas are many.

But I am equally confident that this nation can recover the initiative, that we can give to a doubting world the realization that we, and not Russia and China, can help them achieve stability and growth. We cannot be content merely to oppose what the Kremlin may propose, nor can we pretend that the East-West conflict is the only basis for our policy. Above all, we must not resolve these difficult issues of foreign aid by perpetual postponement and compromise. There are times when it is far better to do the right thing as a result of debate and sacrifice than the wrong thing as a testimonial to national unity.

In short, it is our job to prove that we can devote as much energy, intelligence, idealism, and sacrifice to the survival and triumph of the open society as the Russian despots can extort by compulsion in defense of their closed system of tyranny. We can give a convincing demonstration that we have not a propaganda or crisis interest but an enduring long-term interest in the productive economic growth of the less developed nations. We can finally make it clear to ourselves that international economic development is not, somehow, a nagging responsibility, to be faced each year in the context of giveaways and taxes—but a vast international effort, an enterprise of positive association, which lies close to the heart of our relations with the whole Free World and which requires active American leadership.

As a nation, we think not of war but of peace; not of crusades of conflict but of covenants of co-operation; not of the pageantry of imperialism but of the pride of new states freshly risen to independence. We like to look, with Mr. Justice Holmes, beyond the vision of battling races and an impoverished earth to catch a dreaming glimpse of peace. In the words of Edmund Burke, we sit on a "conspicuous stage," and the whole world marks our demeanor. In this year and in this Congress we have an opportunity to be worthy of that role.

III
AREAS
OF TRIAL

Our frontiers today are on every continent. "Where liberty is, there is my country," said Benjamin Franklin. "Where Liberty is *not*, there is mine," said Tom Paine. In the second half of the twentieth century the original American spirit embodied by our Founding Fathers is meeting its greatest test. For our future and that of the rest of the people of the world are inseparably bound together, economically, militarily, politically.

In the last eight years the question of our relationship with the people of the world has come up in the form of particular crises in particular places: in South Asia, in Eastern Europe, in the Middle East, in Africa, in Latin America. Some of these critical areas are quiet for the moment—although there are still dangers and opportunities in each—but the lessons that we learned or should have learned may serve as guides to the future. For the issues in each were of a fundamental and recurring character; the failure of United States policy in each case seems to have the same causes; and the need for an imaginative and constructive American response to the revolutionary demands of a fast-changing world remains.

My main effort, as shown by the sections that follow, has been to try to call attention to some of these situations, and to get action on them, before they came to a head. Unfortunately, this has not been an era of American initiative. In most cases all the advance warnings, including mine, have been ignored. The crisis has then come, shaped by others in the worst possible terms for us and for any peaceful and democratic solution. And what is worse, we have continued to repeat our mistakes.

Fortunately, these are all still areas of trial. The lost opportunities for creative leadership cannot be recalled, but by understanding the harsh logic of events we can make the most constructive use of the time that is left.

8. Indochina and Vietnam

Indochina presents a clear case study in the power of the anticolonial revolution sweeping Asia and Africa. What has happened also demonstrates that national independence can lead to genuine resistance to Communism. It is a long, sad story with a hopeful chapter, but the end not in sight.

On a trip to Asia in 1951 I saw firsthand that in Indochina we had allied ourselves with a colonial regime that had no real support from the people. The flower of the French Army was being spent in a jungle war that had been going on since 1946. As T. E. Lawrence of Arabia wrote, "war upon rebellion" is "messy and slow, like cutting soup with a knife." I called for American support of genuine independence and self-determination for the Indochinese people. Only by such a course, I urged, could we hope to build strong indigenous strength that would stop Communism and move toward democracy.

In 1953, with the situation further deteriorating, with American aid to the French effort in Indochina amounting to over one billion dollars, with the *New York Times* reporting that the United States would be paying for at least 40 per cent of the cost of the war, I moved in the Senate for the adoption of an amendment to the Mutual Security Act requiring that our aid should, so far as feasible, "be administered in such a way as to encourage through all available means the freedom and independence desired by the peoples of the Associated States, including the intensification of the military training of the Vietnamese." The war would never be successful, I stated on the Senate floor in an address giving the history of the protracted struggle in Indochina, unless large numbers of the people of Vietnam were won over from their sullen neutrality and open hostility. This could never be done, I said, unless they were assured beyond doubt that complete independence would be theirs at the conclusion of the war.

The amendment was defeated upon the assurance of the Administration that we would work toward Indochinese freedom. But we continued to hesitate, the successive French grants of limited independence to the people of Vietnam continued to be too little and too late, and the military threat grew. Finally, with the siege of Dienbienphu, seeing that all of Southeast Asia might fall, the United States considered direct military intervention. The Chinese and Rus-

sians indicated in turn that we would have to expect their further intervention.

Not only was there a risk of world war, but, even if the struggle
could be geographically confined, the precondition for any effective
local military solution—a full grant of Indochinese independence,
fully backed by Western power—had not been established. Nor were
those calling for, or threatening, or bluffing about direct United States
involvement in this war linking this fateful step with the essential
step toward Indochinese freedom. In this uncertain situation, with
our intentions still unclear, with the French military position crum-
bling, with world peace at stake, we and the other parties involved
agreed to negotiate in Geneva.

Judging that the moment had come when either we would finally
and effectively support Indochinese independence as a prerequisite of
salvaging anything from the debacle or we would be left with the
terrible choice betweeen complete surrender of Indochina to Communism or a disastrous war, I again on the Senate floor presented the
case for a change of policy.

IN THE SENATE
APRIL 6, 1954

Mr. President, the time has come for the American people to be
told the blunt truth about Indochina.[7] Two basic alternatives are
being discussed.

The first is a negotiated peace, based either upon partition of the
area between the forces of the Vietminh and the French Union,

[7] The speech here given was made in a time of serious crisis. For eight
years a bloody war had been raging in what was once French Indochina,
and when 1954 began it was further from a settlement than ever. A great
French army, some 80,000 strong, was busy fighting Communists who
were steadily reinforced from China, and who were thrust back at one
point only to advance at others. General de Lattre de Tassigny won victo-
ries but lost campaigns. As spring came on in 1954 the French, under the
critical gaze of the whole world, were about to lose Dienbienphu, their last
great stronghold. Their puppet emperor, Bao Dai, was clearly on the way
out. All the northern part of this rich country was in Communist hands,
and in the south guerrillas made life outside the large cities unsafe. The
danger that other nations, including the United States, would be drawn
into the conflict, steadily increased. Indeed, the State Department flirted
with the perilous idea of sending forces to strengthen the French—an idea
which public opinion sharply rejected.

Americans had a special interest in the struggle because French in-

possibly along the 16th Parallel; or based upon a coalition government in which Ho Chi Minh is represented. Despite any wishful thinking to the contrary, it should be apparent that the popularity and prevalence of Ho Chi Minh and his following throughout Indochina would cause either partition or a coalition government to result in eventual domination by the Communists.

The second alternative is for the United States to persuade the French to continue their valiant and costly struggle; an alternative which, considering the current state of opinion in France, will be adopted only if the United States pledges increasing support. Secretary Dulles' statement that the "imposition in Southeast Asia of the political system of Communist Russia and its Chinese Communist ally . . . should be met by united action" indicates that it is our policy to give such support; that we will, as observed by the New York Times last Wednesday, "fight if necessary to keep southeast Asia out of their hands"; and that we hope to win the support of the free countries of Asia for united action against Communism in Indochina, in spite of the fact that such nations have pursued since the war's inception a policy of cold neutrality.

Certainly, I, for one, favor a policy of a "united action" by many nations whenever necessary to achieve a military and political victory for the Free World in that area, realizing full well that it may eventually require some commitment of our manpower.

But to pour money, matériel, and men into the jungles of Indochina without at least a remote prospect of victory would be dangerously futile and self-destructive. Of course, all discussion of "united action" assumes the inevitability of such victory; but such assumptions are not unlike similar predictions of confidence which have lulled the American people for many years and which, if continued, would present an improper basis for determining the extent of American participation.

Moreover, without political independence for the associated states, the other Asian nations have made it clear that they regard this as a war of colonialism; and the "united action" which is said to be so desperately needed for victory in that area is likely to end up as uni-

---

volvement weakened the common front against Communism in Korea and Europe. It was clear that the British had set the right example in their generous grant of freedom to neighboring Burma, and that France should follow it. Senator Kennedy's speech was a much-needed warning to Americans of the perils in the situation, and a strong exhortation to France to take the only way out.—A.N.

lateral action by our own country. Such intervention, without participation by the armed forces of the other nations of Asia, without the support of the great masses of the peoples of the associated states, with increasing reluctance and discouragement on the part of the French—and, I might add, with hordes of Chinese Communist troops poised just across the border in anticipation of our unilateral entry into their kind of battleground—such intervention would be virtually impossible in the type of military situation which prevails in Indochina.

This is not a new point, of course. In November of 1951, I reported upon my return from the Far East as follows:

> In Indochina we have allied ourselves to the desperate effort of a French regime to hang on to the remnants of empire. There is no broad, general support of the native Vietnam Government among the people of that area. To check the southern drive of communism makes sense but not only through reliance on the force of arms. The task is rather to build strong native non-Communist sentiment within these areas and rely on that as a spearhead of defense rather than upon the legions of General de Tassigny. To do this apart from and in defiance of innately nationalistic aims spells foredoomed failure.

Every year we are given three sets of assurances: first, that the independence of the associated states is now complete; second, that the independence of the associated states will soon be completed under steps "now" being undertaken; and, third, that military victory for the French Union forces in Indochina is assured, or is just around the corner, or lies two years off. But the stringent limitations upon the status of the associated states as sovereign states remain; and the fact that military victory has not yet been achieved is largely the result of these limitations. Repeated failure of these prophecies has, however, in no way diminished the frequency of their reiteration, and they have caused this nation to delay definitive action until now the opportunity for any desirable solution may well be past.

The hard truth of the matter is, first, that without the wholehearted support of the peoples of the associated states, without a reliable and crusading native army with a dependable officer corps, a military victory, even with American support, in that area is difficult, if not impossible, of achievement; and, second, that the support of the people of that area cannot be obtained without a change in the contractual relationships which presently exist between the associated states and the French Union.

I realize that Secretary Dulles cannot force the French to adopt any course of action to which they are opposed; nor am I unaware of the likelihood of a French military withdrawal from Indochina, once its political and economic stake in that area is gone. But we must realize that the difficulties in the military situation which would result from a French withdrawal would not be greatly different from the difficulties which would prevail after the intervention of American troops without the support of the Indochinese or the other nations of Asia. The situation might be compared to what the situation would have been in Korea, if the Japanese had maintained possession of Korea, if a Communist group of Koreans were carrying on a war there with Japan—which had dominated that area for more than a century—and if we then went to the assistance of the Japanese, and put down the revolution of the native Koreans, even though they were Communists, and even though in taking that action we could not have the support of the non-Communist elements of the country.

That is the type of situation, whether we like it or not, which is presented today in connection with our support of the French in Indochina, without the support of the native peoples of Indochina.

In Indochina, as in Korea, the battle against Communism should be a battle, not for economic or political gain, but for the security of the free world, and for the values and institutions which are held dear in France and throughout the non-Communist world, as well as in the United States.

Events proved me wrong in one respect. Vietnam was partitioned, the price of years of Western folly. But my fear that Ho Chi Minh and his Communists would ultimately come to dominate all Indochina has not yet come to pass. I should have had more faith in my own propositions about the potential power of free Asian nationalism. For one result of the Geneva settlement was that, too late for her own good, but perhaps not too late to save the day for a good part of Indochina and for Southeast Asia, France granted full and complete independence to Vietnam, Laos, and Cambodia. Then, at last, in what everyone thought was the hour of total Communist triumph, we saw a near miracle take place. Despite the chaos, despite the universal doubts, a determined band of patriotic Vietnamese around one man of faith, President Diem, began to release and to harness the latent power of nationalism to create an independent, anti-Communist Vietnam. Today that brave little state is working in friendly and free association with the United States, whose economic and military aid has,

in conditions of independence, proved to be effective. The following
address on America's stake in Free Vietnam was made during the
period when that miracle was being worked but when many Americans
still could not believe what their eyes saw.

CONFERENCE OF THE AMERICAN FRIENDS
OF VIETNAM
WASHINGTON, D. C.
JUNE 1, 1956

It is an ironic and tragic fact that this conference is being held at
a time when the news about Vietnam has virtually disappeared from
the front pages of the American press, and the American people have
all but forgotten the tiny nation for which we are in large measure
responsible.[8] This decline in public attention is due, I believe, to
three factors:

1. First, it is due in part to the amazing success of President Diem
in meeting firmly and with determination the major political and
economic crises which had heretofore continually plagued Vietnam.

2. Secondly, it is due in part to the traditional role of American
journalism, including readers as well as writers, to be more interested
in crises than in accomplishments, to give more space to the threat
of wars than the need for works, and to write larger headlines on the
sensational omissions of the past than the creative missions of the
future.

3. Third and finally, our neglect of Vietnam is the result of one
of the most serious weaknesses that has hampered the long-range

[8] Exceptional interest attaches to this speech; the vision which it em-
bodies has been amply justified by events. When in the summer of 1954
Vietnam was partitioned between Communist North and Nationalist
South, most people feared that aggressive Red forces would soon sweep
over the whole country. But the faith of friends like Senator Kennedy was
actually well founded. The United States had the wisdom to grant South
Vietnam about $500 million in various forms of assistance—military aid,
help to refugees, and the improvement of agriculture, industry, education,
and public health. The little republic truly became what Mr. Kennedy
calls it, a proving ground of democracy. It has produced in its President,
Ngo Dinh Diem, one of the true statesmen of the new Asia. Peace and
order have been restored, food is abundant, the economic life is troubled
only by inflation, and education is improving. With current economic aid
of about $185 million, Vietnam is a country of which the West may feel
proud, and which it should continue to protect.—A.N.

effectiveness of American foreign policy over the past several years—and that is the overemphasis upon our role as "volunteer fire department" for the world. Whenever and wherever fire breaks out—in Indochina, in the Middle East, in Guatemala, in Cyprus, in the Formosan Straits—our firemen rush in, wheeling up all their heavy equipment, and resorting to every known method of containing and extinguishing the blaze. The crowd gathers—the usually successful efforts of our able volunteers are heartily applauded—and then the firemen rush off to the next conflagration, leaving the grateful but still stunned inhabitants to clean up the rubble, pick up the pieces, and rebuild their homes with whatever resources are available.

The role, to be sure, is a necessary one; but it is not the only role to be played, and the others cannot be ignored. A volunteer fire department halts, but rarely prevents, fires. It repels but rarely rebuilds; it meets the problems of the present but not of the future. And while we are devoting our attention to the Communist arson in Korea, there is smoldering in Indochina; we turn our efforts to Indochina until the alarm sounds in Algeria—and so it goes.

Of course Vietnam is not completely forgotten by our policy-makers today, but the unfortunate truth of the matter is that, in my opinion, Vietnam would in all likelihood be receiving more attention from our Congress and Administration, and greater assistance under our aid programs, if it were in imminent danger of Communist invasion or revolution. Like those peoples of Latin American and Africa whom we have very nearly overlooked in the past decade, the Vietnamese may find that their devotion to the cause of democracy, and their success in reducing the strength of local Communist groups, have had the ironic effect of reducing American support. Yet the need for that support has in no way been reduced. (I hope it will not be necessary for the Diem Government—or this organization—to subsidize the growth of the South Vietnam Communist party in order to focus American attention on that nation's critical needs!)

Much more needs to be done. Informational and propaganda activities, warning of the evils of Communism and the blessings of the American way of life, are not enough in a country where concepts of free enterprise and capitalism are meaningless, where poverty and hunger are not enemies across the 17th Parallel but enemies within their midst.

I shall not attempt to set forth details of the type of aid program this nation should offer the Vietnamese—for it is not the details of that program that are as important as the spirit with which it is offered and the objectives it seeks to accomplish. We should not attempt to buy the friendship of the Vietnamese. Nor can we win their hearts by making them dependent upon our handouts. What we must offer them is a revolution—a political, economic, and social revolution far superior to anything the Communists can offer—far more peaceful, far more democratic, and far more locally controlled. Such a revolution will require much from the United States and much from Vietnam. We must supply capital to replace that drained by centuries of colonial exploitation; technicians to train those handicapped by deliberate policies of illiteracy; guidance to assist a nation taking those first feeble steps toward the complexities of a republican form of government. We must assist the inspiring growth of Vietnamese democracy and economy, including the complete integration of those refugees who gave up their homes and their belongings to seek freedom. We must provide military assistance to rebuild the new Vietnamese Army, which every day faces the growing peril of Vietminh Armies across the border.

This is the revolution we can, we should, we must offer to the people of Vietnam—not as charity, not as a business proposition, not as a political maneuver, nor simply to enlist them as soldiers against Communism or as chattels of American foreign policy—but a revolution of their own making, for their own welfare, and for the security of freedom everywhere. The Communists offer them another kind of revolution, glittering and seductive in its superficial appeal. The choice between the two can be made only by the Vietnamese people themselves.[9] But in these times of trial and burden, true friendships stand out. As Premier Diem recently wrote a great friend of Vietnam, Senator Mansfield, "It is only in winter that you can tell

[9] Since this speech was made, the Vietnamese have made their choice in the way that Senator Kennedy hoped they would. So have the people of Laos and Cambodia. A British expert, Stanley Mayes, who toured Southeast Asia in 1959, writes that "Communist reverses have been more resounding than Communist successes," and that "Communist aggression has not paid dividends in Southeast Asia; hence the switch now to subversion." In Malaya, too, which the British freely gave independence, the Communists have been routed; although at one time they had put 11,000 fighters in the field for jungle warfare, the middle of 1959 found their forces reduced to 800, and public sentiment overwhelmingly against them. Communist pressures on the Vietnamese continue. But, wrote Vermont Royster, editor of the *Wall Street Journal*, when visiting them in 1959, "These are not only delightful people; they are more energetic and determined than most in Southeast Asia." And Ngo Dinh Diem has an impressively able staff of advisers, mainly American and English.—A.N.

which trees are evergreen." And I am confident that if this nation demonstrates that it has not forgotten the people of Vietnam, the people of Vietnam will demonstrate that they have not forgotten us.

9. Algeria

Incredible as it seemed, in view of the fresh lessons of Indochina, history immediately began repeating itself in Algeria. When not only France but the United States showed no signs of facing reality and coming to terms with Algerian nationalism, I felt it necessary to issue the strongest warning one man could give, to our French allies, to the United States Government, and to the American people. The friends of the West in Africa and the Middle East, such as Prime Minister Bourguiba of free Tunisia, were imploring us to cease driving North Africa into the flames of Arab xenophobia and anti-Westernism. In the wake of the ruthless Soviet "pacification" of Hungary it seemed to me essential that the Western house be swept clean of its own lingering imperialism.

Criticism was to be expected, for I was criticizing a firmly entrenched policy. But my views were the result of following and studying for a number of years the sorry latter-day course of Western colonialism, and particularly French colonialism. The future freedom of all North Africa, and perhaps all of Africa, seemed to me to require a change of policy by both the United States and France.

It was heartening that in the storm of criticism that ensued, Senator Humphrey addressed the Senate, associating himself with my remarks, supporting the "soundness" of the case I had made, calling it "a service to the cause of American foreign policy, of human freedom, and national independence for people who long for it." Senator Humphrey rightly stressed that "Our views are expressed not as anti-French, but as a recognition of what is taking place in the twentieth century."

Fortunately, after the Algerian tragedy had deepened until it became intolerable for the people of France and the French in Algeria, and after the Fourth Republic had fallen under the weight of the burden, President de Gaulle accepted the heavy responsibility of leading France away from its proud imperial past to a dignified acceptance of twentieth-century necessity.

Whether his offer to the Algerians of a "peace of the brave" and of a later free choice of independence (presumably with some kind of partition), integration as an equal part of France, or free association within the French Union has come too late in the day, we cannot yet say. If the United States had done its part to precipitate such an offer earlier, the picture probably would be far brighter. In any event, the uprising of the French extremists in Algeria in 1958, the actions of President de Gaulle in 1959, and the continuing war today have given continued pertinence to the basic analysis I presented in July, 1957.

IN THE SENATE
JULY 2, 1957

Mr. President, the most powerful single force in the world today is neither Communism nor capitalism, neither the H-bomb nor the guided missile—it is man's eternal desire to be free and independent. The great enemy of that tremendous force of freedom is called, for want of a more precise term, imperialism—and today that means Soviet imperialism and, whether we like it or not, and though they are not to be equated, Western imperialism.

Thus the single most important test of American foreign policy today is how we meet the challenge of imperialism, what we do to further man's desire to be free. On this test more than any other, this nation shall be critically judged by the uncommitted millions in Asia and Africa, and anxiously watched by the still hopeful lovers of freedom behind the Iron Curtain.

I am concerned today that we are failing to meet the challenge of imperialism—on both counts—and thus failing in our responsibilities to the Free World. I propose, therefore, as the Senate and the nation prepare to commemorate the 181st anniversary of man's noblest expression against political repression, to begin a two-part series of speeches, examining America's role in the continuing struggles for independence that strain today against the forces of imperialism within both the Soviet and Western worlds. My intention is to talk not of general principles, but of specific cases—to propose not partisan criticisms but what I hope will be constructive solutions.

There are many cases of the clash between independence and imperialism in the Soviet world that demand our attention. One, above all the rest, is critically outstanding today—Poland.

There are also many cases of the clash between independence and imperialism in the Western world that demand our attention. But again, one, above all the rest, is critically outstanding today—Algeria.

I shall speak this afternoon of our failures and of our future in Algeria and North Africa—and I shall speak of Poland in a later address to this body.[10]

Mr. President, the war in Algeria confronts the United States with its most critical diplomatic impasse since the crisis in Indochina—and yet we have not only failed to meet the problem forthrightly and effectively, we have refused even to recognize that it is our problem at all. No issue poses a more difficult challenge to our foreign policy-makers—and no issue has been more woefully neglected. Though I am somewhat reluctant to undertake the kind of public review of this case which I had hoped—when I first began an intensive study of the problem fifteen months ago—that the State Department might provide to the Congress and people, the Senate is, in my opinion, entitled to receive the answers to the basic questions involved in this crisis.

I am even more reluctant to appear critical of our oldest and first ally, whose assistance in our own war for independence will never be forgotten and whose role in the course of world events has tradi-

[10] No speech on foreign affairs by Mr. Kennedy attracted more attention at home and abroad. Algeria, with a million French and nearly nine million Moslems, had seen a fierce Nationalist outbreak in 1954 grow into a great and desolating war. The National Liberation Front, with aid from Morocco and Egypt, had thrown into the field forces which steadily increasing French armies could not control. Even able French leaders like the Socialist Guy Mollet and the Radical Pierre Mendès-France proved unable to cope with the situation. The French *colons* in Algeria and the French military leaders fighting there tended to take an intransigent line which separated them from the more moderate position of most citizens of metropolitan France; the loyal Moslems and the Moslems in revolt were bitterly opposed to each other. In this confused situation the conflict became deplorably cruel, marked by atrocities, massacres, and tortures on both sides. The value of France as a partner in NATO, as Senator Kennedy pointed out, was half destroyed by the struggle; for half a million French troops in the end were pinned down, and French treasure had to be poured out in an endless stream. There was danger, too, that one of the successive government crises would end in a coup by some extremist of fascist type. "It is sad," wrote André Philip, a former cabinet member and professor of law at the Sorbonne, "to see such a great nation, rich in every form of culture, old and new, slowly strangling itself in this unresolved conflict." To such liberal voices Mr. Kennedy wished to give encouragement.—A.N.

tionally been one of constructive leadership and co-operation. I do not want our policy to be anti-French any more than I want it to be antinationalist—and I am convinced that growing numbers of the French people, whose patience and endurance we must all salute, are coming to realize that the views expressed in this speech are, in the long run, in their own best interest.

American and French diplomats, it must be noted at the outset, have joined in saying for several years that Algeria is not even a proper subject for American foreign policy debates or world consideration—that it is wholly a matter of internal French concern, a provincial uprising, a crisis which will respond satisfactorily to local anesthesia. But whatever the original truth of these clichés may have been, the blunt facts of the matter today are that the changing face of African nationalism, and the ever-widening by-products of the growing crisis, have made Algeria a matter of international, and consequently American, concern.

The war in Algeria, engaging more than 400,000 French soldiers, has stripped the Continental forces of NATO to the bone. It has dimmed Western hopes for a European common market, and seriously compromised the liberalizing reforms of OEEC, by causing France to impose new import restrictions under a wartime economy. It has repeatedly been appealed for discussion to the United Nations, where our equivocal remarks and opposition to its consideration have damaged our leadership and prestige in that body. It has undermined our relations with Tunisia and Morocco, who naturally have a sense of common cause with the aims of Algerian leaders, and who have felt proper grievance that our economic and military base settlements have heretofore required clearance with a French Government now taking economic reprisal for their assistance to Algerian nationalism.

It has diluted the effective strength of the Eisenhower Doctrine for the Middle East, and our foreign aid and information programs. It has endangered the continuation of some of our most strategic airbases, and threatened our geographical advantages over the Communist orbit. It has affected our standing in the eyes of the Free World, our leadership in the fight to keep that world free, our prestige, and our security; as well as our moral leadership in the fight against Soviet imperialism in the countries behind the Iron Curtain. It has furnished powerful ammunition to anti-Western propagandists throughout Asia and the Middle East—and will be the most troublesome item facing the October conference in Accra of the free nations of Africa, who hope, by easing the transition to independence of other African colonies, to seek common paths by which that great continent can remain aligned with the West.

Finally, the war in Algeria has steadily drained the manpower, the resources, and the spirit of one of our oldest and most important allies—a nation whose strength is vital to the Free World.

No, Algeria is no longer a problem for the French alone—nor will it ever be again. And though their sensitivity to its consideration by this nation or the U.N. is understandable, a full and frank discussion of an issue so critical to our interests as well as theirs ought to be valued on both sides of an Atlantic alliance that has any real meaning and solidarity.

This is not to say that there is any value in the kind of discussion which has characterized earlier United States consideration of this and similar problems—tepid encouragement and moralizations to both sides, cautious neutrality on all real issues, and a restatement of our obvious dependence upon our European friends, our obvious dedication nevertheless to the principles of self-determination, and our obvious desire not to become involved. We have deceived ourselves into believing that we have thus pleased both sides and displeased no one with this head-in-the-sands policy—when, in truth, we have earned the suspicion of all.

It is time, therefore, that we came to grips with the real issues which confront us.

Instead of contributing our efforts to a cease-fire and settlement, American military equipment—particularly helicopters, purchased in this country, which the natives especially fear and hate—has been used against the rebels. Instead of recognizing that Algeria is the greatest unsolved problem of Western diplomacy in North Africa today, our special emissary to that area this year, the distinguished Vice President, failed even to mention this sensitive issue in his report. Instead of recognizing France's refusal to bargain in good faith with Nationalist leaders or to grant the reforms earlier promised, our Ambassador to the U.N., Mr. Lodge, in his statement this year as previously, and our former Ambassador to Paris, Mr. Dillon, in his statement last year, both expressed firm faith in the French Government's handling of the entire matter. I do not criticize them as individuals, because they were representing the highest Administration policy.

Naturally the French were delighted with Ambassador Dillon's statement. Premier Mollet expressed his nation's pleasure at having the United States "at her side at this moment." *Le Monde* described it as "a victory of the pro-French camp in the State Department over the champions of anticolonialism and appeasement of the Arabs." But the leader of the national Algerian movement, under house arrest in France, expressed his dismay that the United States had departed from its democratic tradition to ally itself with French colonialism and to favor "the military reconquest of Algeria at the expense of the self-determination of peoples."

Similarly, when in 1955 the U.N. steering committee was asked to place the issue on the agenda of the General Assembly, and our Ambassador to the U.N. insisted that Algeria was so much an integral part of the French Republic that the matter could not properly be discussed by an international body, an Algerian spokesman commented that his people were "at a loss to understand why the United States should identify itself with a policy of colonial repression and bias contrary to American political traditions and interests."

The General Assembly, as the Senate will recall, overruled the committee's decision and placed the question of Algeria on the agenda, causing the French delegates to walk out of the Assembly, the United States again voting against discussion of the issue. Two months later, of course, the matter was dropped and the French returned. In the 1956-57 session the United States again labored to bring about a compromise resolution postponing U.N. consideration for at least a year until the French had settled the matter as they saw fit.

This is not a record to view with pride as Independence Day approaches. No matter how complex the problems posed by the Algerian issue may be, the record of the United States in this case is, as elsewhere, a retreat from the principles of independence and anticolonialism, regardless of what diplomatic niceties, legal technicalities, or even strategic considerations are offered in its defense. The record is even more dismal when put in the perspective of our consistent refusal over a period of several years to support U.N. consideration of the Tunisian and Moroccan questions.

I realize that no magic touchstone of "anticolonialism" can overcome the tremendous obstacles which must confront any early settlement giving to the Algerians the right of self-determination, and which must distinguish them from the Tunisians or Moroccans. But let us consider the long-range significance of these objections and obstacles, to determine whether our State Department should remain bound by them.

First. The first obstacle is the assertion that Algeria is legally an integral part of metropolitan France and could no more be cut loose than Texas could be severed from the United States, an argument used not only by France but by American spokesmen claiming concern over any U.N. precedent affecting our own internal affairs. But this objection has been largely defeated by the French themselves, as I shall discuss in a moment, as well as by the pace of developments which have forced Algeria to become an international issue, as I have already pointed out.

Second. The second hurdle is posed by the unusually large and justifiably alarmed French population in Algeria, who fear for their rights as French citizens, their property, and their lives, and who compare their situation to that of American colonists who drove back the native Indians. Their problem, in my opinion, is one deserving of special recognition in a final settlement in Algeria, but it does not reduce the necessity to move forward quickly toward such a settlement. On the contrary, the danger to their rights and safety increases the longer such a settlement—which in the end is inevitable —is postponed.

Third. The next objection most frequently raised is the aid and comfort which any reasonable settlement would give to the extremists, terrorists, and saboteurs that permeate the Nationalist movement, to the Communist, Egyptian, and other outside anti-Western *provocateurs* that have clearly achieved some success in penetrating the movement. Terrorism must be combated, not condoned, it is said; it is not right to "negotiate with murderers." Yet once again this is a problem which neither postponement nor attempted conquest can solve. The fever chart of every successful revolution—including, of course, the French—reveals a rising temperature of terrorism and counterterrorism; but this does not of itself invalidate the legitimate goals that fired the original revolution. Most political revolutions—including our own—have been buoyed by outside aid in men, weapons, and ideas. Instead of abandoning African nationalism to the anti-Western agitators and Soviet agents who hope to capture its leadership, the United States, a product of political revolution, must redouble its efforts to earn the respect and friendship of Nationalist leaders.

Fourth. Finally, objection is raised to negotiating with a Nationalist movement that lacks a single cohesive point of leadership, focus, and direction, as the Tunisians had with Habib Bourguiba, or as the Moroccans certainly had after the foolish and self-defeating deposition of Sultan Ben Youssef in 1953—now Mohammed V of Morocco. The lack, moreover, of complete racial homogeneity among the African Algerians has been reflected in cleavages in the nationalist forces. The Algerians are not yet ready to rule their own country, it is said, on a genuine and permanent basis, without the trained leaders and experts every modern state requires. But these objections come with ill grace from a French Government that has deliberately stifled educational opportunities for Algerian natives, jailed, exiled, or executed their leaders, and outlawed their political parties and activities. The same objections were heard in the cases of Tunisia and Morocco—where self-government has brought neither economic chaos, racial terrorism, nor political anarchy; and the problem of the plural society, moreover, is now the general, and not the exceptional, case in Africa.

Should we antagonize our French allies over Algeria? The most important reason we have sided with the French in Algeria and North Africa is our reluctance to antagonize a traditional friend and important ally in her hour of crisis. We have been understandingly troubled by France's alarmist responses to all prospects for negotiations, by her warning that the only possible consequences are political and economic ruin, "the suitcase or the coffin."

Yet, did we not learn in Indochina, where we delayed action as the result of similar warnings, that we might have served both the French and our own causes infinitely better, had we taken a more firm stand much earlier than we did? Did that tragic episode not teach us that, whether France likes it or not, admits it or not, or has our support or not, their overseas territories are sooner or later, one by one, inevitably going to break free and look with suspicion on the Western nations who impeded their steps to independence? In the words of Turgot: "Colonies are like fruit which cling to the tree only till they ripen."

I want to emphasize that I do not fail to appreciate the difficulties of our hard-pressed French allies. It staggers the imagination to realize that France is one nation that has been in a continuous state of war since 1939—against the Axis, then in Syria, in Indochina, in Morocco, in Tunisia, in Algeria. It has naturally not been easy for most Frenchmen to watch the successive withdrawals from Damascus, Hanoi, Saigon, Pondicherry, Tunis, and Rabat. With each departure a grand myth has been more and more deflated. But the problem is no longer to save a myth of French empire. The problem is to save the French nation, as well as free Africa.

Mr. President, no amount of mutual politeness, wishful thinking, nostalgia, or regret should blind either France or the United States to the fact that, if France and the West at large are to have a continuing influence in North Africa—and I certainly favor a continuation of French influence in that area—then the essential first step is the independence of Algeria along the lines of Morocco and Tunisia. If concrete steps are taken in this direction, then there may yet be a French North Africa. Short of this step, there will inevitably only be a hollow memory and a desolate failure. As Mr. David Schoenbrun, in his recent excellent volume *As France Goes*, cogently argues:

> France must either gamble on the friendship of a free North Africa or get out of North Africa completely. It should be evident after the Egyptian fiasco that France cannot impose her will upon some 22 million Africans indefinitely. Sooner or later the French will have to recognize the existence of an Algerian state. The sooner, the cheaper in terms of men, money, and a chance to salvage something from the wreckage of the French Union.

Indeed, the one ray of hope that emerges from this otherwise dark picture is the indication that the French have acknowledged the bankruptcy in their Algerian policy, however they may resent our saying so, by legislating extremely far-reaching and generous measures for greater self-government in French West Africa. Here, under the guidance of M. Felix Houphouet-Boigny, the first Negro cabinet minister in French history, the French Government took significant action by establishing a single-college electoral system, which Algeria has never had, and, by providing universal suffrage, a wide measure of decentralized government and internal self-control. Here realistic forward steps are being taken to fuse nationalist aspirations into a gradual and measurable evolution of political freedom.

The strong pro-Western bent in Tunisia and Morocco today, despite beguiling offers from the Communist East, is a tribute to the leadership of such men as Prime Minister Bourguiba, whose years in French confinement never dimmed his appreciation of Western democratic values. Fortunately for the United States and France, and in spite of—not because of—our past records, neither Tunisia nor Morocco has a natural proclivity toward either Moscow, Peking, or Cairo today. But it is apparent, nevertheless, that the latter constitute possible alternate magnets if the Western nations become too parental or tyrannical. In Tunisia, the political opposition to Premier Bourguiba, led by the self-exiled Sala ben Youssef, is clearly seeking to mobilize the support of the Egyptian and Russian Governments. In Morocco the more reactionary and traditional forces, which could come to power if the present Western-minded Government fails, seem to be groping for support in Cairo, and probably Moscow as well, and we in this country are finally fully aware of the fact that Russia possesses an effective repertoire of economic inducements and political tricks; that Egypt appeals persuasively, in the name of African nationalism, for unity against the West; and that Red China offers nations emerging from a colonial state a ready answer on how to achieve quickly the transition from economic backwardness to economic strength.

United States policies in these areas—to provide an effective alternative to these forces, who aided Tunisian and Moroccan independence while we remained silent—cannot be tied any longer to the French, who seek to make their economic aid and political negotiations dependent upon the recipient's attitude toward Algeria. We cannot temporize as long as we did in 1956 over emergency wheat to Tunisia. We cannot offer these struggling nations economic aid so far below their needs, so small a fraction of what we offered some of their less needy, less democratic, and less friendly neighbors that even so staunch a friend as Premier Bourguiba was forced to reject Ambassador Richards' original offer—just as he had rejected an offer of Soviet aid more than thirty times as great. In Morocco, too, our aid has fallen short of the new nation's basic needs.

We must, on the other hand, avoid the temptation to imitate the Communists by promising these new nations automatic remedies and quick cures for economic distress—which lead only too readily to gathering disillusionment. But we can realistically contribute to those programs which will generate genuine economic strength as well as give relief from famine, drought, and catastrophe. The further use of agricultural surpluses, and the new revolving loan fund making possible long-term planning and commitment, should be especially well suited to the requirements of Morocco and Tunisia, which have moved beyond the point of most underdeveloped states but not yet attained the strength of most Western economies.

Another step which we can take immediately, of the highest priority yet small in cost, is to step up considerably the number of young people of North Africa who have so far come to the United States for higher education and technical training, and to increase our own educational and training missions in that area. The building up of a national civil service, a managerial talent, and a pool of skilled tradesmen and professionals is an immediate prerequisite for these countries—and the addition of even a few trained administrators, engineers, doctors, and educators will pay off many times over in progress, stability, and good will.

In these days, we can help fulfill a great and promising opportunity to show the world that a new nation, with an Arab heritage, can establish itself in the Western tradition and successfully withstand both the pull toward Arab feudalism and fanaticism and the pull toward Communist authoritarianism.

The lessons of Tunisia and Morocco, like the lesson of Indochina before them, constitute, I hope, the final evidence of the futility of the present French course in Algeria and the danger of the present frozen American posture. Prompt settlement is an urgent necessity—for North Africa, for France, for the United States, NATO, and the Western world. Yet what are the elements of "settlement" put forward from time to time by the French, in which we have placed our faith? They are three: first, military reconquest or pacification; second, social and economic reform; and third, political union with France.

I respectfully suggest that these three elements represent no settlement at all, that the continual emphasis upon them is only postponing, not hastening, the day of final reckoning. Permit me to examine each point briefly.

First is the French insistence upon pacification of the area, in reality reconquest, before further talks proceed, a policy which only makes both settlement and a cease-fire less likely. For it encourages the Nationalists to assume that they can play a game of endurance in which the patience and tenacity of French politicians will finally snap as they did regarding Indochina in 1954. The so-called pacification policy of M. Lacoste does consist of more imaginative measures than simple military repression, since it attempts to combine the elimination of rebel and terrorist activity in individual localities with measures of social reform and reconstruction. But the rebellion is now too contagious to be treated by pacification methods, even if the French could afford to increase substantially the manpower already poured into the area, and despite the steady stream of optimistic French communiqués.

For, as General Wingate wisely pointed out in the last war, "Given a population favorable to penetration, a thousand resolute and well-armed men can paralyze for an indefinite period the operations of a hundred thousand," and this is precisely what has happened in Algeria. The French tend to look at the Algerian rebel problem in terms of a military chessboard, when in fact each identifiable rebel has behind him the silent or half-articulate support of many other Algerians. Thus, nearly half a million valiant French soldiers face an enemy with no organized forces, no acceptable strategy, no military installations, and no identifiable lines of supply. They themselves fight not with the zeal with which they defend their own liberty but fight in vain—and it has throughout history been in vain to curb the liberty of another people.

Second, the French have continued to tell the U.N. of their present and proposed economic and social reforms in Algeria, promising a better life for all if they can ever end the fighting. It is true that the French have finally opened up greater employment opportunities for the Moslems, have expropriated some land for redistribution, and have made some efforts to increase wages of agricultural workers. But the tardiness of these reforms and the narrow-mindedness of the French minority in Algeria, which over more than twenty years defeated the reform efforts of the few liberal ministers, have permitted the wave of nationalism to move so far, and to take root so deeply, that these palliative efforts are too little and too late for a situation of now convulsive proportions. We must, I am afraid, accept the lesson of all nationalist movements that economic and social reforms, even if honestly sponsored and effectively administered, do not solve or satisfy the quest for freedom. Most peoples, in fact, appear willing to pay a price in economic progress in order to achieve political independence.

Third and finally, the French conception of settlement has stubbornly adhered to the concept of Algerian incorporation within France itself. This area, it should be recalled, was taken by the French only a little more than a century ago—the southern desert area has always been governed from Paris like a crown colony—and although the populous and fertile northern coastland was legally made a part of France in 1871, native Algerians were not made French citizens until 1947. Even then, that move was made to cement French control rather than to grant equality, for at the same time a system of electoral representation in the French National Assembly and Algerian Assembly was established giving equal power to two strictly separated electoral groups—one consisting of over seven million Algerians and

the other consisting of some one million French colonials. Only 75,-
000 African Algerians had full voting rights—and only thirty seats
from Algeria, mostly filled by French politicians, were elected to the
French National Assembly.

The result of this gap between word and deed, and the continued
reluctance of the French to permit more than spasmodic and slight
reforms at the expense of vested interests in France and Algeria, has
been to alienate most sections of Algerian opinion so that assimilation
is now a fruitless line of effort. There has been a progressive increase
in the number of African Algerians, once committed to a program of
integration with France, who have recanted and joined the movement
of independence (the most notable instance being that of Ferhat
Abbas, one of the ablest Nationalist leaders, who long argued for the
assimilationist approach and did not wholly despair of such a settlement until shortly before 1956, when he joined the National Liberation Front).

Nationalism in Africa cannot be evaluated purely in terms of the
historical and legal niceties argued by the French, and thus far accepted by the State Department. National self-identification frequently takes place by quick combustion which the rain of repression
simply cannot extinguish, especially in an area where there is a common Islamic heritage and where most people—including Algeria's
closest neighbors in Tunisia, Morocco, and Libya—have all gained
political independence. New nationhood is recorded in quick suc-
cession—Ghana yesterday, Nigeria perhaps tomorrow, and colonies
in Central Africa moving into dominion status. Whatever the history
and lawbooks may say, we cannot evade the evidence of our own
time, especially we in the Americas whose own experiences furnish
a model from which many of these new nations draw inspiration.

And thus I return, Mr. President, to the point at which I began
this analysis. The time has come when our Government must recognize that this is no longer a French problem alone and that the time
has passed where a series of piecemeal adjustments, or even a last attempt to incorporate Algeria fully within France, can succeed. The
time has come for the United States to face the harsh realities of the
situation and to fulfill its responsibilities as leader of the free world
—in the U.N., in NATO, in the administration of our aid programs
and in the exercise of our diplomacy—in shaping a course toward
political independence for Algeria.

It should not be the purpose of our Government to impose a solution on either side, but to make a contribution toward breaking the

vicious circle in which the Algerian controversy whirls.

Nor do I insist that the cumbersome procedures of the U.N. are necessarily best adapted to the settlement of a dispute of this sort. But direct United Nations recommendation and action would be preferable to the current lack of treatment the problem is receiving; and in any event when the case appears on the U.N. agenda again the United States must drastically revise the Dillon-Lodge position in which our policy has been corseted too long.

Moreover, though the resolution which was adopted at the last session in general gave backing to the French efforts to localize the dispute, there was nonetheless a proviso—a proviso which served to put France on a probationary status and warn that measurable progress would have to be shown by the next meeting of the Assembly. We have now come nearly to the halfway point of this interim period, and the situation has only further deteriorated. To prevent a still more difficult situation in the fall session, our State Department should now be seeking ways of breaking the present stalemate. And I am asking this body, as it has successfully done before in cases of Indonesia and Indochina, to offer guidance to the Administration and leadership to the world on this crucial issue.

I am submitting today a resolution which I believe outlines the best hopes for peace and settlement in Algeria. It urges, in brief, that the President and Secretary of State be strongly encouraged to place the influence of the United States behind efforts, either through the North Atlantic Treaty Organization or good offices of the Prime Minister of Tunisia and the Sultan of Morocco, to achieve a solution which will recognize the independent personality of Algeria and establish the basis for a settlement interdependent with France and the neighboring nations.

This resolution conveys my conviction that it should not be impossible to break a deadlock in a matter of such close concern to NATO and to mediatory forces in the rest of North Africa. The governments of Tunisia and Morocco, neither members of the Arab League and each concerned to continue Western connections, provide the best hope and, indeed, they furnished such help, as already noted, last summer and early fall. Two weeks ago M. Bourguiba again made an appeal for an Algerian solution within an over-all French-oriented North African federation. Even the Indian Government, often assumed to be spokesman of nationalism for nationalism's sake, offered last summer to act as a possible intermediary in a solution which would grant political independence to Algeria but confirm special protections for French citizens and to place Algeria in a special economic federation with France.

Neither reasonable mediators nor reasonable grounds for mediation are impossible to find. The problem in Algeria is to devise a framework of political independence which combines close economic interdependence with France. This is not an illusory goal. Algerian Nationalist leaders are mostly French-speaking; Algeria has an inherent interest in continued economic and cultural ties with France as well as in Western aid generally. But these natural links with France will ebb away if a change is not soon made. Last November, when Algeria was under U.N. consideration, Premier Bourguiba expressed the anguish which afflicts the responsible Nationalists of North Africa on the Algerian question:

> The vote of free Tunisia will be against France, but it would be a mistake to believe that we are happy about this conflict. I had hoped sincerely that Tunisia would be a bridge between the Occident and the Orient and that our first independent vote would have been in favor of France. Although that has proved to be impossible I still cannot bring myself to despair, for the first time in my life, of the wisdom of the French people and their government. The day may perhaps yet come, if the government of the Republic acts swiftly enough, when French civilization will be truly defended in world council by the leaders of a French North African Confederation.

The United States must be prepared to lend all efforts to such a settlement, and to assist in the economic problems which will flow from it. This is not a burden which we lightly or gladly assume. But our efforts in no other endeavor are more important in terms of once again seizing the initiative in foreign affairs, demonstrating our adherence to the principles of national independence and winning the respect of those long suspicious of our negative and vacillating record on colonial issues.

It is particularly important, inasmuch as Hungary will be a primary issue at the United Nations meeting this fall, that the United States clear the air and take a clear position on this issue, on which we have been vulnerable in the past. And we must make it abundantly clear to the French as well as the North Africans that we seek no economic advantages for ourselves in that area, no opportunities to replace French economic ties or exploit African resources.

If we are to secure the friendship of the Arab, the African, and the Asian, we cannot hope to accomplish it solely by means of billion-dollar foreign aid programs. We cannot win their hearts by making them dependent upon our handouts. Nor can we keep them free by selling them free enterprise, by describing the perils of Communism or the prosperity of the United States, or limiting our dealing to military pacts. No, the strength of our appeal to these key populations—and it is rightfully our appeal, and not that of the Communists—lies in our traditional and deeply felt philosophy of freedom and independence for all peoples everywhere.

IN THE SENATE
JULY 8, 1957

Mr. President, the reaction to my remarks both at home and abroad has further strengthened my conviction that the situation in Algeria is drifting dangerously, with the French authorities reluctant to seek a fresh approach, and our American authorities refusing to recognize the grave international implications of this impasse. No amount of hopeful assertions that France will handle the problem alone, no amount of cautious warnings that these are matters best left unmentioned in public, and no amount of charges against the motives or methods of those of us seeking a peaceful solution can obscure the fact that the Algerians will someday be free. Then, to whom will they turn—to the West, which has seemingly ignored their plea for independence; to the Americans, whom they may feel have rejected the issue as none of our affair while at the same time furnishing arms that help crush them; or to Moscow, to Cairo, to Peking, the pretended champions of nationalism and independence?

And who, by that time, will be leading the Algerians—the moderates with a pro-Western orientation with whom negotiations might still be conducted now, or the extremists, terrorists, and outside *provocateurs* who inevitably capture such a movement as the conflict drags on? Finally, what will such a settlement in Algeria at some distant date mean to France then? Will it not mean the loss of all her economic, political, and cultural ties in North Africa which could still be salvaged in a settlement today? Will it not mean that France will have suffered a weakened economy, a decimated army and a series of unstable governments only to learn once again—as she learned too late in Indochina, Tunisia, and Morocco—that man's desire to be free and independent is the most powerful force in the world today?

When the roll is called on Algeria this fall in the United Nations, as it must inevitably, we in this nation will be forced to face this issue publicly. If no reasonable proposal for settlement has by then been put forward by the French and encouraged by the West, will we be able to say to the General Assembly in all sincerity that progress has been made? Will we again vote against the anticolonial bloc that controls the world balance of power? Or will we finally take back from the Soviets the leadership that is rightfully ours of the world-wide movement for freedom and independence?

We dare not overlook, in our concern over legal and diplomatic niceties, the powerful force of man's eternal desire to be free and independent. The world-wide struggle against imperialism, the sweep of nationalism, is the most potent factor in foreign affairs today. We can resist it or ignore it, but only for a little while; we can see it exploited by the Soviets, with grave consequences; or we in this country can give it hope and leadership, and thus improve immeasurably our standing and our security.[11]

[11] At the end of this speech Senator Kennedy offered a resolution that the United States support an international effort to seek peace in Algeria. This resolution was given wide publicity in France as in the United States.

In national elections late in 1958, the French people gave the de Gaullist party, or Union for the New Republic, a sweeping victory with 118 seats in the National Assembly. It and its allies held an easy parliamentary majority. Incidentally, they gave the Communists a severe defeat. Among the many problems which de Gaulle faced, the Algerian question easily took first place, and he grappled with it courageously. A series of increasingly generous utterances culminated in a declaration on September 16, 1959, that almost took rank with the great Labourite decision by which Britain gave freedom to India.

De Gaulle gave the Algerians a solemn promise that if they accepted his plan, within four years a referendum would permit them to choose among three courses. They could accept assimilation, with full equal rights, into the French Republic, and be "Frenchified"; or they could have complete internal autonomy in Algeria, leaning upon French aid and direction in such matters as foreign affairs, defense, and economic development; or they could have complete independence, though France would keep control of the Sahara oil fields and the port facilities serving them. This offer at once captured world opinion. The Provisional Government of the Algerian Republic announced that it was ready to enter into talks with the French Government to discuss the political and military conditions of a cease-fire, and the conditions and guarantees of self-determination. This was the kind of solution contemplated by Senator Kennedy's resolution.—A.N.

10. Poland and Eastern Europe

In the light of the tragic failure of the Hungarian revolution, of the earlier short-lived uprising in Eastern Germany, and of the changes in Poland following the Poznań riots and the subsequent peaceful rise to power of the anti-Stalinist leader, Gomulka, in October, 1956, the need for formulating a new American policy toward Eastern Europe was apparent.

The test case for the possibilities of peaceful change within the Communist world and for a new American policy in Eastern Europe is still Poland. The following talk, given one month after the preceding talk on Algeria, was Part Two of my discussion of the worldwide struggle against imperialism. While the popular desire for independence is much the same everywhere in the world, the remnants of imperialism in the West cannot be equated with the far more formidable problem of a Soviet empire whose military and economic power is growing. The reasons for the amendment to the Battle Act that I propose below and the action the Senate has taken on it have been discussed in Chapter 3 above.

IN THE SENATE
AUGUST 21, 1957

Mr. President, just as the challenge of Western imperialism is most critically confronting us in Algeria and North Africa, so, too, does the challenge of Soviet imperialism confront American foreign policy today in one critical area in particular—Eastern Europe and Poland.

The Soviets, of course, regard their actions in Eastern Europe much as the French regard their actions in Africa—as none of our affair. Our own Department of State and diplomatic officials are also likely to regard Congressional discussion of these vital world issues as a trespass upon their private domain.

I am strongly persuaded that the inadequacies of current American foreign policies and programs concerning Poland and Eastern Europe require their public review and re-examination by the Senate, the Congress, and the people of the United States—not to assign the blame for our past failures, but to explore what steps might be taken to increase the future effectiveness of our foreign policy in this area.

I realize that it is not difficult to make a popular speech on Poland and Eastern Europe. It is easy to denounce the "treachery" of Yalta;

to call upon the enslaved millions to cast off their chains; to decry Soviet brutality and greed; and to predict eventual deliverance of those nations now held captive behind the Iron Curtain. If necessary, it can even be easy to favor American aid—to be delivered only to those satellite nations that become truly independent, or that join an anti-Russian alliance, or that abandon national Communism—or to be limited to emergency relief or surplus foods, with its distribution in each village carefully supervised by American observers to guarantee its delivery to the needy and the starving alone.

But such a speech, however plausible it may seem in its oratorical or political context, only makes it more difficult to take the hard decisions and real risks necessary in any effective policy for Eastern Europe. We are reluctant to take risks in this dangerous age; we are reluctant to make hard and unpopular decisions in this popular democracy. But the complex problems of Eastern Europe—the area which at one and the same time represents a great Western setback and a great Western hope—will never be solved with an excess of caution or an avoidance of risk.

It is baffling beyond words to review that so-called "Liberation" policy which this Administration has proclaimed and on which it has taken patent rights. In several speeches in 1952 Mr. Dulles sought to shed light on a new "Liberation" policy which would replace the supposed sterilities of "Containment." For example, in a prepared address before a learned gathering in Buffalo on August 27, 1952, Mr. Dulles elaborated a three-pronged program for the freeing of the Iron Curtain satellites. In this speech he emphasized that the Voice of America and other agencies should "stir up" the resistance spirit of peoples behind the Iron Curtain and make certain that they have the assurance of our "moral backing." He went on to say that resistance movements would spring up among patriots who "would be supplied and integrated via air drops and other communications from private organizations like the Committee for Free Europe." Finally, he underscored his now familiar thesis that the Communists would disintegrate from within and that the Russians, "preoccupied with their own problems, would cease aggressive actions" and eventually give up and go home "realizing that they had swallowed more than they could digest."

Four years later, on October 29, 1956, the distinguished Vice President announced confidently at Occidental College that the Soviet "setback" in Poland and Hungary proved the "soundness" of the Administration's "Liberation" policy. A little more than two weeks later on November 14 the President, in a prepared preface to his press conference, spoke of our sympathy for the suffering people of Hungary: "Our hearts have gone out to them and we have done everything it is possible to, in the way of alleviating suffering." "But," he continued, "the United States doesn't now, and never has, advocated open rebellion by an undefended populace against force over which they could not possibly prevail." One needs little imagination to appreciate the feeling of frustration which overcame the people of Eastern Europe to hear that the United States had never meant the obvious implications of its "Liberation" policy.

It is all very well to talk of "liberation" or "peaceful evolution." But until we formulate a program of concrete steps as to what this nation can do to help achieve such goals, we are offering those still hopeful partisans of freedom behind the Iron Curtain nothing but empty oratory.

I respectfully suggest that the last comprehensive review of our policies with respect to the satellite areas by the Secretary of State failed to provide the specific steps necessary to implement his rhetorical goal of "liberation." In that address of April 23 in New York, Mr. Dulles outlined, as I analyzed his speech, six steps as constituting our approach to liberation:

1. "Provide an example which demonstrates the blessings of liberty," and "spread knowledge of that around the world," through our information and cultural exchange programs.
2. "See to it that the divided or captive nations know that they are not forgotten" through such means, for example, as sponsoring a U.N. resolution condemning Soviet intervention in Hungary.
3. "Never make a political settlement at their expense."
4. "Revere and honor those who as martyrs gave their blood for freedom . . . but do not . . . incite violent revolt."
5. "Make apparent to the Soviet rulers [that] our real purpose" in liberation is peace and freedom and not the encirclement of Russia with hostile forces.
6. "Encourage evolution to freedom . . . and when some steps are made toward independence . . . show a readiness to respond with friendly acts . . . see to it that the divided or captive nations know . . . that a heartfelt welcome and new opportunity await them as they gain more freedom."

This policy, if it can be called a policy, is easily stated and even more easily implemented. It requires practically no risk, no cost, no thought, and very little explanation. Its contents are neither new nor tangible—and its results in terms of helping liberate Eastern Europe are speculative, to say the least.

The key to our present policy, I believe, is found in the sixth and final item I quoted from the Secretary's address. We will "show a readiness to respond with friendly acts," with "a heartfelt welcome and new opportunity"—whatever that may mean—only "as they gain more freedom . . . [and] steps are made toward independence," not before. No suggestion is made as to what we might do, in the way of positive and concrete diplomacy, to help them take those steps and gain that freedom.

I believe it is this *status quo* policy which has stultified all discussion of new proposals for the area—the terms under which withdrawal of Soviet troops from Eastern Europe might be arranged, Hungary neutralized or Germany united, proposals which merit more careful analysis than they have been given. It is this approach of broad generalizations and platitudes that treats all European satellites alike, without regard to anti-Russian and anti-Slav traditions (as in Rumania), higher rates of industrialization and living standards (as in Czechoslovakia), and other distinguishing characteristics that lend themselves to individual approaches. And finally it is this attitude— of merely waiting and hoping—that caused us to be caught wholly unprepared for the events in Poland and Hungary last October.

I shall limit my discussion today to Poland[12]—because that is the area of both our greatest failures and our greatest hope, and the area

[12] The hearts of all Western peoples were wrung in November, 1956, by the brutal use of Soviet troops to crush a popular rebellion which had broken out in Hungary. Russian machine guns mowed down angry crowds, Russian agents deported thousands to the U.S.S.R., Russian officers violated safe-conduct guarantees to seize Imre Nagy and later executed him, and Russian force installed a new puppet regime under Janos Kadar in Budapest. But at the same time the Poles fared better in their thrust for greater freedom. Wladyslaw Gomulka, who had been thrown into jail as a Titoist in 1951, became head of the Polish Communist party in October, and in that position dominated the government of the so-called republic. He represented national aspirations, and lost no time in declaring to a crowd of a half-million in Warsaw that "every country has the right to be independent and sovereign." If Poland continued to be Communist, it would be under a Polish Communism. Preparations began for celebrations of one thousand years of national life, and other expressions

most urgently demanding a re-examination of our current policies. I make no claim to Poland as a typical example of Eastern Europe. On the contrary, it would be dangerously erroneous to assume that our policies and programs for that area may be applied generally behind the Iron Curtain. But the nature and success of our relations with Poland—like a wind, good or ill, that blows through the only open window in a vast and crowded prison—will vitally affect the future, the hope or despair, of every satellite country.

The most important fact about Poland today is that it is different, however easy it may be to dismiss it as just another Communist country. To be sure, it is still in many outward appearances a Communist regime. There are many magnetic pulls toward the Soviet orbit; Russian soldiers still patrol in the country; anti-Western sentiments in the U.N. are supported by Polish representatives. But it is essential that we look deeper than the labels of Communism. Terrorism and thought control have very much diminished; public opinion, very markedly anti-Communist and always anti-Soviet, is influential; and at least a precarious working accommodation has been reached with the Catholic Church in Poland under Cardinal Wyszynski. Visitors in Poland note practically no Red flags and feel little of the inquisitorial pressure that has characterized most of the Iron Curtain countries. We must be very careful not to miss the internal realities of the Polish scene while looking at the outward and legal forms.

Moreover, Mr. President, there has been an increasing decentralization of agriculture. The denationalization and decentralization of industry has not been nearly as effective, but in April the Polish Parliament approved a new budget and economic plan to slacken the rate of heavy industrial expansion and raise the living standards. And perhaps most telling of all, the Polish Government last fall turned for the first time toward the West—for friendship, for increased trade, and for American credit and economic assistance.

This economic assistance was made urgent by the cruel and corrosive results of Communist mismanagement, inefficiency, and exploitation. Absentee Soviet centralization and nationalization resulted only

---

of deep national feeling were numerous. In the hard circumstances under which Poland had to live, her policy toward Russia had to be prudent and restrained, but there was no question as to the nature of popular feeling.

Senator Kennedy, who had visited Poland and talked with her journalists, professors, and political leaders, could speak with authority on the subject.—A.N.

in lower productivity, widespread raw material deficits, both labor shortages and surpluses, and increasing uselessness and obsolescence of machinery. At the moment, the unemployment problem is assuming critical proportions. This provides melancholy testimony as to the ability of a directed Communist economy to cure dislocations, maintain planning goals, and allocate raw materials—supposedly the peculiar virtues of a socialist state. The attempt to force a heavy industrialization and rearmament program too rapidly upon an economy milked dry by Soviet demands resulted in drastic shortages of consumer goods and housing, spiraling inflation, and a raging black market. It is no wonder that, without decent living standards, adequate housing or fuel, and ravaged by tuberculosis and other diseases, the Polish people turned rumbling discontent into a violent roar at Poznań, and finally last October insisted upon the new anti-Stalinist regime of Mr. Gomulka.

But it is not my intention today to dwell on Soviet brutality or Polish bravery—for I am sure this body is well aware of both—but to examine instead the response of our own foreign policy-makers to the Polish crisis and our preparedness to meet this problem.

The adequacy of that response ought to be reviewed by the Congress now, even after the Polish loan agreement has been concluded—not for purposes of distributing credit or blame, but for purposes of revising our policies and statutes for the future. In my opinion, revision will definitely be in order—for the loan agreement of last June for American aid to Poland can unfortunately be summed up in only five words—too little and too late.

I do not mean to say that that agreement was worse than no agreement at all, that it will accomplish nothing, or that it should be regarded as a waste of American funds and a mistake in American diplomacy. But I do say that this inadequate agreement, coming at such a late date, after months of haggling, indecision, and delay, fell so short of our earlier boasts and our earlier promises that it failed to obtain for either our country or the people of Poland the full benefits for the cause of independence which such an agreement might have achieved.

Permit me to explain further what I mean when I say that this agreement is "too little." American aid under the new agreement will be helpful, to be sure. The Poles, without doubt, appreciate it and will make good use of this assistance and Mr. Khrushchev has indicated that he is not happy about it. But let us compare the assistance contained in this agreement with the needs of the Polish people embraced in their original request, a request which a bolder, more imaginative American foreign policy might have met more closely.

The Polish mission originally requested a total of over $300 million worth of aid, to prevent mass unemployment, discontent, sabotage, and either a recurrence of violence and revolt doomed to be crushed or a return to complete economic subservience to the Soviet Union. We agreed to less than one-third of the amount requested.

Perhaps most desperate of all their needs was the Polish request for one million tons of wheat and other grains—to end compulsory deliveries of grain by the Polish farmers, a chief cause of discontent; to prevent skyrocketing prices from spreading hunger and starvation in the cities; and to reduce reliance upon the irregular supplies of the Russians. One million tons of grain would have provided the Polish Government with an adequate reserve against another bad crop year, and with enough grain for use on the domestic market as a means of holding down inflation and abolishing the compulsory deliveries—a major step in transforming the former Stalinist pattern of the Polish economy, and a genuine incentive for greater farm production. But these plans are now less certain—for we agreed to only one-half of the amount requested.

The next most urgent request was for at least 100,000 tons of our surplus cotton. The Polish textile industry, one of the nation's most important, employing one-sixth of the labor force, is operating far below capacity, with many mills shut down and thousands out of work, despite a crying need for cloth—and unless their needs for cotton can be met, experts have warned, the industry will be chronically restless and completely dependent on the Soviets. But we agreed to only one-half of the amount requested.

The next Polish request was for upward of $30 million in coalmining machinery. Coal is a mainstay of the Polish economy, constituting 40 per cent of its export trade—and yet their equipment is so outmoded and run-down that productivity is actually below its rate of twenty years ago. New machinery in new mines could do wonders in putting the Polish economy back on its feet without dependence on the U.S.S.R.—but we agreed to less than one-seventh of their request on this item.

Finally (in addition to a request for surplus fats, oils, and soybeans), the Poles were interested in obtaining $70-$100 million worth of American farm machinery, fertilizer, and seeds to increase the output of the gradually decollectivized Polish farms. Once Poland was the breadbasket of East Central Europe—now there is not enough grain to supply bread for her own people. Here again, this nation had a dramatic opportunity to demonstrate to other Iron Curtain countries that courage in turning away from complete Soviet domination, and looking to the West for aid, could mean a better life for the farmer and the consumer. But we failed to grant a single dollar of this request.

I say, therefore, that our final offer was too little to match the striking opportunity that has been ours to seize. Mr. Gomulka is grateful for the help, and he needs it badly—but considering the risk undertaken by his Government in turning to the West for aid, I can only repeat my statement that our action was too little and too late. The failure by the United States to deliver on the implied promises of Mr. Eisenhower's October speech, widely advertised through the Voice of America and other U.S. information media, has brought much disappointment to anti-Soviet Poles and greatly weakened their authority. The frustration of hopes has unquestionably strengthened the anti-Gomulka faction in the Central Committee, which argues that American aid is largely verbal and propagandistic. The pro-Soviet faction in the Central Committee contends that United States assistance is too erratic and meager to provide the catalyst for long-term economic development. We must make every effort to avoid a further disenchantment with the United States and a heightened acceptance of fraudulent Soviet promises.

Why do I say "too late"? Let us review the record of events following the dramatic "Polish Revolution" of last October. On October 20, President Eisenhower promptly pledged the United States to offer economic aid to Poland because of our mission to "expand the areas in which free men and free government can flourish"; and the official Polish newspaper *Trybuna Ludu* commented editorially that "we are in favor of assistance with no political strings attached." The Polish Government thereupon advised the United States that it would be interested in concluding a loan agreement. But other than a reiteration on December 18 by Secretary Dulles of our willingness to "give assistance to Poland which would assist it to maintain its growing independence," the American Government took no further steps. Finally, the welcome mat was haltingly extended in February after four precious months had gone by; and negotiations began here on February 26. Then, while the Gomulka regime teetered on a dangerous tightrope between a new bloody, fruitless revolt and a return to

Soviet domination, we offered delay and indecision, and we extended an offer of aid so small the Polish delegation dared not return home with it. On May 26, as negotiations continued to drag, a news dispatch from Warsaw reported that the Poles were forced once again to ask Moscow for increased economic help. "Long before now," the report went on, "the Poles had hoped to be receiving United States economic assistance that would have made it unnecessary to turn to their mighty Eastern neighbor again. A sense of frustration and dismay has been gathering strength for weeks in Poland over the failure to complete the Polish-United States negotiations in Washington." Finally, after nearly four more precious months had passed, a partial agreement was signed in June.

The need to set our economic relations with Poland in a fresh perspective is further underscored by the fact that the survival of the Gomulka regime is more and more dependent on economic progress and specific achievements. Mr. Gomulka's early successes rested primarily upon a political ascendancy and a political detachment from the U.S.S.R. Inevitably these successes will fade into the background and popular anticipation of economic improvement will have to be met. The Polish story is but one more lesson illustrating the close harness in which political and economic development occur in the modern world. A political convalescence has no durability unless it is invigorated by economic therapy.

There were two fundamental reasons for the failure to meet fully Poland's needs and our opportunities. The first was a pervading doubt as to whether aid to this Communist state was a wise policy after all. The distinguished minority leader (Senator Knowland), I know, has strongly criticized such a policy, and its controversial nature convinced the Administration that it should not request Congress for the specific statutory authority necessary to make the loan complete. The negotiations dragged on while the risks were weighed—and they were very real risks. There was the risk that we would be doing nothing more than aiding the prestige of a Communist regime that all too often praised the Soviet Union and criticized the West; strengthening the Communist bloc; relieving pressure on the Soviets; and permitting the U.S.S.R. to divert to armaments those resources devoted to staving off Polish discontent. Others warned that extensive American aid to Red-occupied Poland might serve only as a pretext for violent Soviet intervention, permanently crushing the Gomulka Government and completely wasting any American investment.

No, I do not say that there are no real risks in aiding the Gomulka

Government. But I do say that the United States had an even greater responsibility, as leader of the Free World, to take those risks, to meet this opportunity and this challenge. Any other course would have either forced a suffering nation into a fruitless revolt—or forced the Polish Government to become hopelessly dependent once again on Moscow completely on Moscow's terms. Any failure on our part to help Poland today is only encouraging the Polish Stalinists—who have already considerably exploited the delay in our loan negotiations —in their anti-Western propaganda; and it is very possibly causing the collapse of the present, more independent Government. Other satellites, we may be sure, are watching—and if we fail to help the Poles, who else will dare stand up to the Russians and look westward?

If, on the other hand, we take these risks, through a more adequate program of loans and other assistance, and provide a dramatic, concrete demonstration of our sympathy and sincerity, we can obtain an invaluable reservoir of good will among the Polish people, strengthen their will to resist, and drive still a further wedge between the Polish Government and the Kremlin. For the satellite nations of Eastern Europe represent the one area in the world where the Soviet Union is on the defensive today, the tender spot within its coat of iron armor, the potential source of an inflammation that could spread infectious independence throughout its system, accomplishing from within what the West could never accomplish from without.

Poland may still be a satellite government—but the Poles, as I have said many times, are not a satellite people. To deny them help because they have not been able to shake off total Communist control would be a brutal and dangerous policy, either increasing their dependence on Russia, driving them into the slaughter of a fruitless, premature revolt, or causing them to despair of ever regaining their freedom.

It is difficult to believe the latter could ever come about. I was in Poland less than two years ago. I saw firsthand not only the total repression which gripped that country in contrast with the gradual increases in freedom we have witnessed since last October; but I saw, too, that the Polish people of the mid-twentieth century would never in their hearts accept permanent status as a Soviet colony. Indeed, the people of Poland—because of their religious convictions and strong patriotic spirit, because of their historical hatred of the Russians— are perhaps better equipped than any people on earth to withstand the present period of persecution, just as their forefathers withstood successive invasions and partitions from the Germans and the Austrians and the Russians for centuries before them, and just as theirs was the only country occupied by Hitler that did not produce a quisling.

But time works against the people of Poland. If the Poles come to believe that we in the West, with all of our advantages and wealth, care little about their problems and are unwilling to risk going to their assistance even economically, then even their courageous struggle to preserve the spirit of independence may fail.

The second reason for the final American loan agreement being too little and too late was the inflexibility of our various foreign aid statutes in dealing with a nation in Poland's unique position between Moscow and the West. The Battle Act, which is the pertinent law governing this aspect of our foreign aid under the Mutual Security Act, and the Agricultural Surplus Disposal Act recognize only two categories of nations in the world: nations "under the domination or control" of the U.S.S.R. or the world Communist movement—and "friendly nations." They make no recognition of the fact that there can be shades of gray between these blacks and whites—that there are and will be nations such as Poland that may not yet be our allies or in a position to be truly friendly, but which are at least beginning to move out from Soviet domination and control.

Thus, in order for American surplus cotton and wheat to be sent to Poland as a part of this loan, it was necessary for Secretary of State Dulles to make the highly arguable finding that Poland is not "dominated or controlled" by the U.S.S.R. and is a "friendly nation"—a finding which was vulnerable on its face to criticism and ridicule from the opponents of Polish aid. In order for the rest of the loan to go through, the Administration was forced to resort to still another legal artifice to get around the Battle Act, transferring to the Export-Import Bank for loan purposes money from the President's unrestricted Foreign Aid Contingency Fund under Section 401 of the Mutual Security Act—an action which brought with it a $30-million limitation on the amount going to any one country in any fiscal year. Moreover, part of the local currencies resulting from sales of agricultural surpluses are often loaned back to the recipient nation for economic development projects—but this presumably cannot be done in Poland's case because of the Battle Act.

We may, by resorting to these artificial—though self-defeating—

devices, have avoided for a time the responsibility of openly ventilating this problem in the Congress and the larger forum of public opinion. But the issue cannot be long smothered. The existing agreement may need additional legislative implementation—a new and more adequate Polish loan undoubtedly will be requested in the near future—and while the Gomulka Government falters and all of Eastern Europe watches its performance and our response, Congress and the Administration must face up to this issue directly.

For these reasons, I am introducing today a bill to amend the Battle, Surplus Disposal, and Mutual Security Acts which would make unnecessary these strained interpretations to sell or loan surplus foods for local currencies to countries in Poland's situation; which would permit regular Export-Import Bank loans, guarantees of private loans, and presumably regular Foreign Aid Development loans under the Mutual Security Act; and which would thus recognize that nations in neither the completely friendly nor completely dominated categories may be in a situation where American aid—surplus sales, development loan, commercial loan, technical assistance—might well, if the President so determined on a selective basis, be in the interest of the national security of the United States.

Specifically, this bill would authorize such assistance

> whenever the President shall determine that there is an opportunity thereby—
> (1) to assist the freedom-loving peoples of any such nation to achieve greater political, economic, and social freedom and well-being; or
> (2) to enable such freedom-loving peoples to strengthen their capacity to maintain a sovereign national government increasingly independent of outside domination and control, and thus to promote world peace and to strengthen the national security of the United States by expanding the areas in which free men and free governments can flourish.

Finally, what other steps might be taken to help the Poles short of civil or international war?

1. Perhaps the next most important step we could take would be an increase of people-to-people contacts, of cultural, scientific, and educational exchanges, of reciprocal visits by delegations representing every aspect of life in the two countries. In addition to improving our propaganda activities, let us also break through the long isolation from the Western world, imposed upon the Polish people by

the Soviets with films, records, and a true picture of life in the West. I emphasize true, for it has repeatedly been shown that cheap sensationalism, public relations gimmicks, and the propagation of unrealizable promises and hopes only injure our prestige. Though no information program can be perfectly attuned to political needs or address itself to all potential audiences, it is probably true that the British, working with a much smaller budget, have very often had better effect in radio broadcasts to East Europe—especially in their transmission of simple, unadorned, and factual news broadcasts.

There has been some progress made already in unofficial student-teacher exchanges through the generosity and foresight of the Ford and Rockefeller Foundations. These are beginnings, which the Congress, acting within the framework of the Smith-Mundt Act, could further consolidate to demonstrate our readiness to take advantage of a unique opportunity to strengthen our ties with the Polish. This kind of "aid" is not costly, and yet is rewarding—especially in Poland, where the younger generation and university students and teachers have been singularly brave and resistant to Communist pressures. In no small measure, the Polish revolution is an intellectual revolution fed by the infusion of Western ideas, books, and principles of conduct.

2. Secondly, we may strengthen ties by an expansion of trade,[13] visible and invisible, between our countries. American exports are only a fraction of their prewar level. Other than Polish hams and coal-tar derivatives, we have done very little to encourage those

[13] As a commentary on Senator Kennedy's statements, the observations of Adolph Sturmthal, after a visit to Poland in 1959, published in the *New Leader* of November 23, have special pertinency. Mr. Sturmthal is professor of international labor relations in Roosevelt University. He writes that in international affairs the Poles know they must accept Russian leadership; in domestic affairs they look to the United States as a model. The demonstrative reception given to Vice President Nixon, a man quite unknown except as a representative of America, proved that. "For the common man in Poland," Sturmthal was told, "the United States is just one step this side of paradise." The peasantry sorely needed mechanical equipment and other improvements for farming. The city workers were faced by shortages on every hand, so that housewives spent untold hours searching for common necessities; the intellectuals looked to the West for cultural nourishment.

Freedom in Poland, flanked on one side by the Soviet Union and on the other by Grotewohl's East Germany, holds a precarious position. Mr. Sturmthal agreed with Senator Kennedy that no country could do so much to strengthen it as the United States.—A.N.

imports which might be most suitable for our markets. The Poles have indicated their desire to accelerate considerably the flow of commerce between our two countries—and I am confident that some of these wishes can be fulfilled. One very practical step we could take would be to lift the bars—as the Canadians have done—against Polish ships and liners coming to our ports. At a later date it may be possible to certify a Polish airline for transatlantic air service. These are very practical moves which would have a bracing effect on Polish dollar income, fill a general consumer need with ever-enlarging international travel, and encourage people of Polish extraction to make visits to Poland.

There are also "exports" which the United States might make to Poland through private capital investment, possibly with governmental sponsorship. One suggestion which has been under discussion is American sponsorship and financing of a housing district in Warsaw, preferably illustrating also some of the best features of our contemporary architecture and urban planning. We have seen in Berlin how the Germans with Western help have undertaken some large building and construction programs which not only fill vital needs but also offset the impressive showpiece façade of Russian rebuilding in the Stalinallee of East Berlin. In Warsaw, too, we could counter the gaudy and hated Soviet Palace of Culture with such a municipal project.

3. Third, we should explore further the possibilities of offering a program of technical assistance to the Gomulka Government. Such a policy is obviously subject to some of the same risks as economic assistance, but it also offers even greater possibilities for enlarging the independent personality of the Polish nation. I feel certain that ways can be found to help the Poles acquire expert help, especially for agriculture and the management of medium-sized industry.

4. Fourth, the United States should consider some humanitarian relief to repatriates who are still, twelve years after the war, returning from Russia. This is more in the nature of emergency, short-term aid to tide over some of these persons who are finding it very difficult to locate jobs and shelter. All in all there are about 300,000 returning, of whom 20,000 to 25,000 were members of the Polish underground, whom General Eisenhower in September, 1944 rightfully called "fellow combatants."

5. Fifth, we must think more clearly and make more specific preparations for effective action in case of another outbreak of

violence or Soviet intervention in Eastern Europe. The dangers of such a crisis persist in Poland, where anti-Russian sentiment and continued political and economic discontent make Mr. Gomulka's efforts at gradualism very hazardous indeed. It could recur in Hungary—or East Germany—or Rumania, or elsewhere in Eastern Europe. The West cannot be caught again, as it was during the Berlin riots of June, 1953, or last fall in Poland and Hungary, without co-ordinated policies or machinery to meet such a crisis.

For on last October 21, Mr. Dulles, during an era of Republican campaign pacificism, veered to an extreme position when he wrote off completely any possibility of the use of American military means in East Europe, thus inviting Soviet intervention. I suggest that Mr. Dulles and his party, who have often condemned the previous Secretary of State for his January, 1950 speech on the Far Eastern perimeter and Korea, might usefully ponder Mr. Dulles' much more sweeping remarks of last October in regard to East Europe. At the very minimum, it would be desirable at once to create a permanent U.N. observation commission, ready to fly at a moment's notice to any spot where an advance toward freedom is menaced by Soviet intervention. The recent and classic U.N. Commisson report on Hungary, though in the nature of a post-mortem, indicates how world opinion could be rallied if such an investigation could be made on the spot and simultaneously with the rupture of a nation's independence.

6. Finally, we must view the Polish problem in its wider European setting. Though chances for a general European and German settlement are not at the moment bright, we must not foreclose possibilities when they present themselves. New policies and proposals for troop withdrawals, disarmament, and neutralization must receive our careful consideration. Moreover, the effect of our present policies —our failure to outlaw genocide, the inadequacy of our assistance to refugees, escapees, and repatriates—must be re-examined.

Especially, we cannot honestly overlook the close connections between our policies toward Germany and those toward Poland. Though I agree in very wide measure with the policies of our Government toward Germany under both Democratic and Republican Administrations, there is, I think, a danger that the very unanimity of support which they have enjoyed makes them a little too rigid and unyielding to changing currents in European politics. The United States has had every reason to rejoice in the statesmanship of

Chancellor Adenauer and the impressive leadership he has given in shaping the new German democracy. But I do think that the United States, in assessing this achievement, has in its public statements and in the more informal workings of its diplomacy unduly neglected the contribution of the democratic opposition, the German Socialists, whose resistance to Communism has been stalwart and who may someday become a part of a German Government with whom we shall be allies. Especially in Eastern Europe, it has not been to our interest to make pariahs of the German Social Democrats.

Chancellor Adenauer on August 4 gave public voice to the rising realization that there will soon have to be an exchange of recognition between Western Germany and Poland, despite the unfortunate fact that all the countries of Eastern Europe recognize also the Communist regime of Eastern Germany. There is already substantial trade between Western Germany and Poland, and we should seek to clarify the benefits of an exchange of political recognition between the two countries.

I realize that this raises some collateral issues of great complexity —particularly the question of the Polish western borders and the German eastern territories which the Potsdam Agreement passed under Polish administration. This question, perhaps more than any other, serves to create gravitational pulls in Poland toward Russia. It is not possible or proper to freeze the legal status of these territories until there has been a final peace conference. The German Foreign Minister, Dr. von Brentano, asserted last December 14 that this was an issue which could be worked out "in a European spirit" and that there are possibilities for negotiation. Our former High Commissioner in Germany, John McCloy, a distinguished Republican who ably served the United States and the cause of the new Germany, has likewise pointed to the danger of failing to determine the future of these territories. This is not a matter on which the United States should impose a settlement, but we can encourage the many reasonable voices in all parties who have recognized the need in Germany to press toward an accommodation of this dispute. Fortunately, with full employment and a sustained prosperity in Western Germany, this is a matter which is less charged with emotional asperities than it was some years ago. It is certainly within the interests of the United States to adopt an attitude which accepts no settlement which has not been recognized by a free Polish nation. To say this is not, of course, to gloss over the fact that many Germans have suffered in these territories and that many expellees—especially the older ones—have not found happiness or even a tolerable existence in their new homes.

Finally, it is obvious that we should, where possible, avoid the minor irritants which can be magnified into national affronts. A small recent example was an action of the State Department in changing methods of issuing passports. Although perhaps meaningless to us, it was provoking to the Poles when the State Department altered the way in which the birthplace of persons born in the Eastern territories is indicated. For nearly twelve years after the war, a person born in Breslau or Stettin was identified as having been born in "Poland." This year the identification was changed to "Germany" (under Polish administration). Whatever the reasons for such an action, it only plays—at this date—into the hands of the U.S.S.R.

There is, Mr. President, no single passkey to freedom in this program, no easy solution by which Poland can gain its freedom effortlessly or by simple counting on the internal erosion of the Soviet Union. Action and foresight are the only possible preludes to freedom. And there are, I repeat, obvious risks. There is a sardonic saying of a Polish exile that we might recall: "I wish," he said, "that Poland would become the world's business rather than the world's inspiration." We have too long covered a nakedness of policy with lofty phrases, which call attention to the glory of Poland, but hardly offer signposts to her salvation. Recent dispatches from Warsaw have made it all too clear that the brave people of Poland are still, even under present conditions, in a prison—however more tolerable their jailers may have become. But are we to ignore their needs because they cannot escape by one leap or by picking one lock? Is this an excuse for inaction? Have we forgotten the words:

> I was
> Hungry, and you gave me to eat;
> Naked, and you covered me;
> Sick, and you visited me;
> I was in prison, and you came to me.

11. The Reconstruction of NATO

PALM BEACH, FLORIDA
DECEMBER 15, 1959

Among all the situations which have been permitted to deteriorate
in recent years, few are more distressing than the deterioration in
relations among members of the North Atlantic Community.

The Common Market nations have been at cross-purposes with
Great Britain and the others in economic policy. Strong and dis-
ruptive differences have emerged over negotiations with the Soviet
Union concerning Berlin. France has underlined its uneasiness about
the special intimacy of the United States and Great Britain with respect to atomic weapons by asking the withdrawal of American
nuclear weapons and their instruments for delivery from French
bases, and by pressing on with the manufacture of atomic weapons.
And beyond these specific matters, there is a widespread uneasiness
that the North Atlantic Alliance is no longer fulfilling its purpose of
harmonizing and protecting the common interests.

This situation has arisen for two reasons. First, it is because of
the remarkable economic and political recovery of the nations of
Western Europe. They have acquired a momentum they have not
known since 1914 at least; and with this momentum has come a
new confidence and a new determination that the North Atlantic
Alliance must be an alliance among equals. The relationships that
grew up in the immediate postwar years—when the United States
was virtually alone in a position to bear the economic and military
burdens of the alliance—can no longer serve.

The second reason for this situation is that the problems confronting the members of the North Atlantic Community have
radically altered. The Russian threat is now a missile threat as well as
the threat of Russian divisions mounted in East Germany. The
principal links to the Middle East, Asia, and Africa are no longer
colonial links; the problem is what kind of relationship shall exist
between the older industrialized nations and the newer independent
states. Financially, the position of the dollar has altered as trade has
expanded and the Western European nations have gained in their
competitive position. The "dollar problem" is quite different than
it was a decade ago.

American policy has failed to lead the way in reshaping the agenda and common policy of the North Atlantic Community around these new issues. American policy has clung to the formulas and the attitudes of 1953; and while the other members of the North Atlantic Alliance have gained in strength, without American leadership they have been incapable of bringing their energies and resources to bear on the new agenda. While our partners are stronger now than they formerly were, the American role in the North Atlantic Alliance remains a decisive role.

But what are we to do to bring the Alliance back to a sense of unity and common purpose? The essence of the task is to lead the way in a new program of common action on the major issues which confront the Alliance. There is every reason to believe that in such a setting the matters which now divide and threaten the Alliance will diminish in importance and in their power to divide.

What items belong on this new agenda?

First, we must look again at the strictly military agenda of the North Atlantic Community. So long as the arms race continues—so long as we face the problem of continuing to make irrational the Soviet use of nuclear weapons—the Western European nations must be given an enlarged role in this effort. European capabilities in research and development could make an important contribution to the common defense; and we must consider whether it is wise to maintain a situation in which information is denied to our friends which we know for certain is available to our potential enemies, and which places a premium on our allies developing at great expense nuclear capabilities which in themselves are of limited military significance. We should face the fact that the fundamental purpose of the French atomic bomb is not to increase French capabilities but to increase its stature in the Alliance. The French bomb is aimed toward Washington rather than Moscow. This is an odd way to run an alliance.

In addition, it is time for the North Atlantic Alliance as a whole to consider whether its nonnuclear forces are adequate either for the effective deterrence of limited war or to provide an adequate security force should a break-through be achieved in the international control of nuclear weapons.

The second item on the agenda is the creation of a joint policy of loans and technical assistance to the underdeveloped areas. There is no item of action more important to the Free World than the prompt creation of an enlarged flow of capital and technical assistance, in which the United States, Canada, Western Europe, and Japan would share. On the American side, I believe the proposal of the Senate Foreign Relations Committee last year was about on the right scale. We proposed an American soft loan flow of about one billion and a half a year for five years. The other industrialized nations of the Free World should, in my view, increase their contribution by about the same amount in long-term aid.

These long-term loans should be woven into a common program along with other existing sources of aid and technical assistance: including private lending, food surpluses, and international loans. With resources of this kind we could, I believe, meet all the legitimate demands for economic assistance of Free Asia, the Middle East, Africa, and Latin America, and establish the basis for a new noncolonial relationship between the more advanced and less advanced nations of the world.

The third item on the agenda is the reserves problem. The expansion in world trade has proceeded at a pace which is outstripping the Free World's production of gold, and the dollar has been forced to bear a disproportionate burden as a reserve currency. It is time that we considered in common a method for economizing international reserves which would exploit the new strength of the pound and the Continental currencies. Such action ought to be accompanied by new efforts to lower tariffs and to remove the obstacles to American imports which grew up in the immediate postwar years when the dollar was a scarce currency. Action along these lines on a Free World basis would put the conflict between the common market and the "Outer Seven" in perspective. It would also permit us to define in good order—and without panic—what further steps, if any, the United States ought to take to deal with its balance of payments problem.

A fourth item on the agenda ought to be a common policy for the exploration of space. Although space exploration has certain military implications, these are a minor component. Primarily the exploration of space is an action of science and of human adventure. It ought to be placed on an international footing as soon as possible. Certainly our friends in the North Atlantic Community ought to share in it, and we ought to explore also with the Russians whether this is not one of those activities which we might not conduct together rather than in competition.

I am confident that if, with vigorous American leadership, the North Atlantic Community would get to work on this four-point agenda, we would quickly see that the underlying foundations for unity are still there, and are, in fact, stronger than ever.

12. Quemoy and Matsu

Although the forces of Chiang Kai-shek hold Quemoy and Matsu, they are in effect, by laws of geography, hostages held by Mao Tse-tung. The political and military reasons for defending Formosa do not apply to these two little islands just off the shore of Communist China. Instead, our commitment there gives the Peking Government an ever-ready occasion to put on the pressure, to take it off, to bring us to the brink of war, then to please the world by withdrawing the immediate threat. With the Chinese revolution now apparently going through an aggressive and irrational Stalinist phase, it is a dangerous mistake to leave such a temptation standing. In the interest of world peace the lines of non-Communist resistance must be clearly drawn and drawn in the right places.

The recurring problem of these offshore islands should by now have led through negotiation to our disentanglement. But nothing has happened to remedy the situation since we were last drawn to the brink over these islands; and the lessons I drew from this in 1958 still seem valid and necessary.

TULSA, OKLAHOMA
SEPTEMBER 16, 1959

No crisis created by the lack of decisive leadership under this Administration compares with the constant state of crisis which confronts us around the world. The current crisis is that which confronts us in the Formosa Strait.

It is difficult, perhaps, to pass judgment on an Administration policy which seems to change daily, and with respect to events which are also undergoing constant change. But what we can and should do is to consider as fairly and frankly as we can the lessons which this crisis teaches us for the future—the guideposts which we hope will govern our conduct when a similar crisis arises, either under this Administration during the next two years or under a Democratic Administration after 1960. It seems to me that there are four basic lessons to be learned from our present difficulty in the Formosa Strait:

First, let us remember in the future that control over the issue of war or peace should always remain in our own hands. Newspaper accounts at the time of the latest Red Chinese offer quoted American spokesmen in Formosa as saying it was largely up to the Chinese Nationalists as to whether our convoys would continue. An earlier report had quoted another spokesman as expressing concern over our necessary involvement, if the Nationalists chose to attack the mainland and the Reds retaliated against Formosa. Still another dispatch quoted Chiang Kai-shek himself expressing distaste over American negotiations in Warsaw. When the recent speeches of Mr. Dulles and Mr. Herter indicated a possible softening in our stand on Quemoy and Matsu, it was necessary for our Ambassador on Formosa to reassure the Chiang Government that there was no change. When there was talk here of neutralization or demilitarization of Quemoy and Matsu, the Generalissimo insisted that there would be no neutralization and no demilitarization. And he indicated that he, and he alone, would decide whether to attack Communist installations and supply lines on the mainland.

Here is a real example of how control of events—even the critical issues of war and peace—can pass from our own hands. For there is a real possibility that the tail in this case will wag the dog—that, in the event of Chiang's attack upon the mainland and a Communist retaliation upon Formosa, we will be dragged into a war—possibly an atomic war, probably a world war—at a time and place *not* of our own choosing, in an argument over two islands *not* essential to our security, and by an action of Chiang Kai-shek *not* initiated with our consent.[14]

---

[14] Senator Kennedy's warning was fully substantiated by the facts. Chiang Kai-shek repeatedly spoke of "a return to the mainland," and plainly regarded Quemoy and Matsu not so much as a first line of defense for Formosa as the potential staging-ground of an attack on Communist China. In such plans of conquest he would be only too glad to make America a cat's-paw. In the late summer of 1958, a year before Mr. Kennedy's speech, Communist forces had put Quemoy under a strong artillery barrage. Secretary Dulles was so alarmed that he declared that it had been "rather foolish" to set such large Nationalist forces on Quemoy and Matsu, and that it would be wise to take them off if a cease-fire could be arranged. Later he forced Chiang Kai-shek into accepting a statement that any liberation of China was to be accomplished by Sun Yat-sen's principles, "and not by force." Mr. Kennedy was emphasizing the danger of involvement in an alien and totally unnecessary war which Mr. Dulles himself had recognized.—A.N.

The American people want to be the masters of their own policy. Whatever they may think our policy in the Far East should be, they want it to be decided here, in this country, by the American people and their elected representatives. We want the question of peace or war for America to be decided by the Congress as the Constitution provides—not by Generalissimo Chiang Kai-shek.

Secondly, let us remember in the future that foreign policy is neither successfully made nor successfully carried out by mere pronouncements—and that the use of such terms as appeasement, Far Eastern Munich, and national unity does not in itself constitute a policy.

The American people, in my opinion, do not want either appeasement or war, if either can be avoided through peaceful negotiations. Neither do they want to become bogged down in an armed conflict over two offshore islands less distant from the Chinese mainland than your airport is from this city—islands which are not essential to the defense of Formosa, islands which in themselves are indefensible—for such a war would bring us neither allies, valuable territory, nor the support of world opinion.

I do not think that any of us support a policy of appeasement. I think all of us would support the President in his determination that Communist domination of the Far East must never be permitted—and that our commitments to protect Formosa, South Korea, Japan, and the Philippines must be honored. The demands of national unity and national security call upon each of us to stand firm in a moment of crisis.

But that does not mean that the announced policies of any one man, be he the President or the Secretary of State, are sufficient to commit the willing efforts of the American people to an atomic war which they neither want nor understand. The repeated calls for national unity, the repeated assertions that such unity exists, the attempt by Mr. Nixon to silence those who would admit that public opinion is negative, all this cannot and should not conceal the present actual disunity over our policy in the Formosa Strait—a disunity which is not limited to any one party, but which finds critics within the defense establishment itself, within both parties, and among all Americans.

I might mention in this regard, in making my present position clear, that I was one of fourteen Senators in 1955 who supported an amendment to the Congressional resolution sought by the President —an amendment which would have specifically excluded Quemoy and Matsu from its jurisdiction. I did not regard that as appeasement then—I do not regard it as appeasement now.

Third, let us strive in the future to draw our lines of commitments in such a way—and around such areas—as will insure to us, in the event of an attack, the support of peace-loving nations all over the world in honoring those commitments. Even now, we are uncertain of any support from our allies or the United Nations in the event of a Red Chinese attack on these offshore islands and American intervention in that area. To become bogged down in such a conflict, without allies, without the support of world opinion, might well be a disaster far worse than any we have heretofore known. The United Nations offers the best possibilities for a real solution to this crisis by means of some process of trusteeship, demilitarization, or neutralization of Quemoy and Matsu.

Fourth and finally, let us remember in the future that we are only asking for trouble when we extend our commitments around the world without regard to the sufficiency of our military posture to fulfill those commitments.

In the Formosa Strait today, we are faced with another possibility of fighting a local brush-fire war after six years of steady deterioration in our capacity to fight local brush-fire wars. And this insufficiency of our military posture is even more striking in the matter of our defensive and deterrent strength in view of the rapidly approaching "missile gap."

When I spoke of these matters on the Senate floor last month, Senator Capehart and other members of his party responded with outraged indignation. They talked of clearing the Senate galleries and closing the Senate doors for a "star chamber" session. They talked, despite the fact that Defense Department spokesmen had publicly confirmed these facts long ago, about our giving information to the enemy and alarming the American people. They talked about our undermining confidence in the President and "selling America short."

But this is not a time to keep the facts from the people—to keep them complacent. To sound the alarm is not to panic but to seek action from an aroused public. For, as the poet Dante once said: "The hottest places in hell are reserved for those who, in a time of great moral crisis, maintain their neutrality."

No, my friends, it is not we who are selling America short—not those of us who believe that the American people have the capacity to accept the harsh facts of our position and respond to them. But

I will tell you who is selling America short. It is the little men with little vision who say we cannot afford to build the world's greatest defense against aggression—it is those who say we cannot afford to bolster the Free World against ravages of hunger and disease and disorder upon which Communism feeds. The men who lack confidence in America are the men who say our people are not up to facing the facts of our missile lag—who say they are not up to bearing the cost of survival.

These are the men who are selling America short—who have substituted fear for faith in our future—who are caught up in their own disbeliefs and doubts about our ability to build a better America.

13. The Middle East

The Middle East today is a monument to Western misunderstanding. During the last eight years the West has ignominiously presided over the liquidation of its power in the whole region, while the U.S.S.R. has gained important footholds. American policy has wavered and wobbled as much, if not more, than any other Western country.

The situation was not improved by the dramatic announcement of an Eisenhower Doctrine which treated the Middle East as an American province to be defended against external aggression when, in fact, the indigenous Arab nationalist revolution and internal Communist subversion were the crucial factors. However, in 1957 the Senate had no choice but to approve the Administration's resolution on the Eisenhower Doctrine, for repudiation of the President would have blunted our warning to the Soviets and dismayed those few friendly Middle Eastern nations who favored this approach.

While stating that the resolution should never have been introduced and that it offered solutions neither to the immediate crises of Gaza and Aqaba nor to the long-range crises of Communist subversion, arms traffic, Suez, refugees, boundaries, and other issues in the continuing Arab-Israeli dispute, I argued in the Senate against the move to cut from the resolution all provisions for assistance to these countries. In fact, the total amount of economic and technical aid received by all eight Arab states in the five years before 1957 was only about $73 million. Israel had received about $237 million. Both of these sums were very small compared with over $2 billion in aid to Greece alone, roughly $2.5 billion up to then in Korea (not counting the war), and nearly $2 billion on Formosa. The amount under debate for the entire Middle East was less than the amount we were spending for similar purposes each year—mostly in economic aid—in either Vietnam, Korea, or Formosa alone. It was not an unprecedented sum with which to bolster the economic and political stability of a great and critical region.

But the main problem was and is understanding the driving forces and central needs of the region as a whole and devising an appropriate farsighted American policy. The statements that follow try to take a measure of the whole situation and to raise our sights to the full dimensions of the challenge.

EASTERN OREGON COLLEGE OF EDUCATION
LA GRANDE, OREGON
NOVEMBER 9, 1959

Our mistakes in the Middle East, it seems to me, were primarily mistakes of attitude. We tended to deal with this area almost exclusively in the context of the East-West struggle—in terms of our own battle against international Communism. Their own issues of nationalism, of economic development, and local political hostilities were dismissed by our policy-makers as being of secondary importance.

This is not to say that we were necessarily wrong in saying that Communism was their greatest enemy—but we were wrong in believing that we could convince them that it was. We were wrong in believing that what was so clear to us could be made equally compelling to other peoples with problems very different from our own— people with a much lower standard of living, a much greater pride in neutrality and a much more recent history of foreign exploitation. The Arabs knew that their lands had never been occupied by Soviet troops—but that they had been occupied by Western troops—and they were not ready to submerge either their nationalism or their neutrality in an alliance with the Western nations.

We made other grave errors in the Middle East. We overestimated our own strength and underestimated the force of nationalism. We failed to perceive when we had lost control of events—and failed to act accordingly once it became clear. We gave our support to regimes instead of to people—and too often we tied our future to the fortunes of unpopular and ultimately overthrown governments and rulers.

We believed that those governments which were friendly to us and hostile to the Communists were therefore good governments—and we believed that we could make unpopular policies acceptable through our own propaganda programs. Without question some of these governments were good governments—genuinely devoted to the welfare of their people and the development of their economies—but logic and fact are not the same as what people believe. The mutilated body of Iraqi Premier Nuri As-said, to cite one vivid example, hanging from a Baghdad lamp post a year ago last July, became the symbol of what happened to our policy in Iraq.

Is it not ironic that today—after considerable expenditure, turmoil, Communist gains and Western defeats—we are striving to achieve for the Middle East the very status of neutrality on which we turned our backs some three years ago?

In short, from here on out, the question is not whether we should accept the neutralist tendencies of the Arabs, but how we can work with them. The question is not whether we should recognize the force of Arab nationalism, but how we can help to channel it along constructive lines.

The mistaken attitudes of the past—our previous misconceptions and psychological barriers—must all be junked—for the sake of the Arabs and for our own sake as well. Where our approach was once trite and traditional, it must now be imaginative, progressive, and practical. Above all, it must recognize things as they are and not just as we would have them be for our convenience. We must talk in terms that go beyond the vocabulary of Cold War—terms that translate themselves into tangible values and self-interest for the Arabs as well as ourselves.

It is not enough to talk only in terms of guns and money—for guns and money are not the basic need in the Middle East. It is not enough to approach their problems on a piecemeal basis. It is not enough to merely ride with a very shaky *status quo*. It is not enough to recall the Baghdad Pact or the Eisenhower Doctrine—it is not enough to rely on the Voice of America or the Sixth Fleet. These approaches have failed.

But if we can learn from the lessons of the past—if we can refrain from pressing our case so hard that the Arabs feel their neutrality and nationalism are threatened—if we can talk with them in terms of their problems, not ours—then I am convinced that the Middle East can become an area of strength and hope. Let us make clear that we will never turn our back on our steadfast friends in Israel, whose adherence to the democratic way must be admired by all friends of freedom. But let us also make clear throughout the Middle East that we want friendship, not satellites—and we are interested in their prosperity as well as ours. To do this job, to do it right, requires a combination of imagination and restraint which we have thus far not demonstrated in the Middle East. But the time to do so is now.

ANNUAL BANQUET OF THE HISTADRUT ZIONIST ORGANIZATION
BALTIMORE, MARYLAND
NOVEMBER 27, 1956

While we, along with the leaders of our nation and the world, are concerned tonight with the daily developments in the Middle East, I think my comments should be directed toward a longer-range view of the situation.[15] It would be worth while for all of us now while negotiations proceed to examine the problems that will still be present once hostilities have ceased, borders have been redrawn, and alliances rebuilt.

[15] Senator Kennedy's expression of sympathetic interest in Israel, and analysis of Near Eastern problems, was delivered at an anxious moment —all moments in the Near East being more or less anxious. The last British troops left Egypt in June, 1956, after more than seventy years in guarding the Suez Canal and other duties. Then on July 26 President Nasser suddenly nationalized this great artery. The step caused intense resentment in Britain, France, and other countries, and Secretary Dulles termed it a blow to international confidence. Meanwhile relations between Israel and her Arab neighbors had reached a stage of extreme tension. Blows and counterblows were constantly being exchanged across the borders of Israel and Syria, Israel and Jordan, and Israel and Egypt; in the U.N. the Security Council early in the year had unanimously condemned Israel for a raid into Syria which had resulted in numerous deaths, and a little later had sent Secretary General Dag Hammarskjold to the area to try to obtain an improvement in armistice arrangements. While he was on his way Israeli artillery fire slew more than fifty people in the Gaza district of Egypt, chiefly Arab refugees, and Egypt retaliated by sending "fedayeen" or guerrilla squads deep into Israeli territory. Communist nations were busy helping Egypt to rearm, and piling up such large military stores there that Great Britain, Canada, and France sent large counterbalancing shipments of arms to Israel.

The region was in such an alarming state of turmoil, and the possibilities of serious trouble were so numerous, that Mr. Kennedy's appeal for tolerance and enlightened relations among different ethnic groups was much needed.—A.N.

Much in the Middle East, of course, is the same as it was a generation ago; much will remain the same: the special importance of the Middle East to the great religions of the world, Jewish, Moslem and Christian; the economic interests of Britain and France in the area, present today as they were a generation ago; the traditional rivalries between the various Arab blocs, between the Saudis and the Hashimites, between the Nile and the Euphrates-Tigris valleys, between northern Arabs and southern Arabs, rich states and poor.

But let us consider the new trends and developments which have altered the character and significance of the Middle East and its problems, and with which we will be reckoning long after the present crisis has ended. There are, it seems to me, seven such facts.

1. First is the highly strategic position occupied by the Middle East in the world's political, ideological, and military battles. Located midway between the giants of the East and the West, and populated by millions not yet firmly committed to either, the Middle East has consequently assumed an importance in the Cold War out of proportion to its size, strength, and previous significance.

2. The second permanent factor in the Middle East of which we must never lose sight is oil. The dependence of the world upon Middle Eastern oil and its transportation through the Suez Canal has been made abundantly clear. Whatever political and military settlements are made, whatever tensions are lifted and problems solved, we must remember that Europe's dependence upon these oil supplies will continue—and continue indefinitely, regardless of our developments in atomic energy.

3. The third fact which will remain once the dust of the present battle has settled and the smoke has cleared away will be the unprecedented success of Soviet penetration in the Middle East. Charles Malik, the Lebanese diplomat and philosopher, has written that "Moscow probably has never in history had the direct or indirect influence it now enjoys in the Near East. . . . This Communist penetration is the most important phenomenon in the Near East at present, and the interpretation or adjustment of every other situation should be made with this matter in view." Much of this is apparent to us in this country in the statements of Arab and Communist leaders, in the delivery of Communist arms to the area and in the exchange of trade missions and trade agreements. Much of it, however, we are less aware of and alert to—the steady penetration of Communists into key positions in Middle Eastern governments,

newspapers, trade unions, and other organizations; the steadily climbing circulation of Communist literature in contrast to anti-Communist publications; the steadily growing acceptance by Middle Eastern people of the Soviets as their friend and benefactor, a leader in their fight against Western domination and a sympathizer in their struggle with Israel. All of these and a host of other items have increased the strength of Communism among the Arab nations while the Western nations, divided and suspected, have steadily lost influence and prestige in the area.

4. Fourth, we must never consider the problems of the nations of the Middle East apart from the economic and social conditions which surround them. Life in the Middle East, it has been said, is a perpetual fight against the desert, and always the desert has won in the past—with poverty and illiteracy and disease and underdevelopment dominating an area where only a few enjoy the benefits of great oil and land holdings. Indeed, the increase in outside capital poured into the area to exploit its oil and other resources has only aggravated the problems of unequal distribution of wealth and inadequate development of human resources. These are problems with which the new nations of the Middle East must struggle for the next generation; and no amount of nationalistic oratory can create the scientific and technological revolution necessary to raise the standard of living of their people. Nor is such a revolution easily purchased by oil royalties. It requires the closest association and assistance of either Western Europe, who is mistrusted, or the Soviet Union, or the United States. This decision will be a continuing one facing our nation and the nations of the Middle East for many years after the close of the present hostilities.

5. Another factor is the rise of Arab nationalism, the revolt in the Middle East against Western colonialism. In Morocco, Algeria, and Tunisia; in Jordan, Yemen, Iraq, Saudi Arabia, and Aden; and in Egypt and throughout the entire area, the desire to be free from direct or indirect Western influence has become a powerful and sometimes violent force. Policies of repression have only fanned the flames of discontent; and the close ties between this nation, home of the Declaration of Independence, and the great colonial powers have caused Arab spokesmen to warn our State Department that the nations of the Middle East were beginning to regard America as a supporter of colonialism. In recent weeks, particularly with respect to the present crisis, we have proclaimed our independence from our traditional allies on issues affected by the colonialism-nationalism

struggle, but it is not yet clear that we have recognized this factor to be the most powerful, dynamic force for good or evil in the Middle East today.

6. A sixth factor, related to but separate from the growing force of Arab nationalism, has been the emergence of Egypt as the leader of the Arab bloc, the champion of Arab unity, and the chief provocator against the West. The explanation involves more than the personality of Mr. Nasser. Its roots are in the history of Egypt's bitter relations with the British, in the influence of Egypt and its university in the Moslem world, and in a series of more recent Western actions in the area which Egypt regarded either as an affront or a threat to its prestige. It is doubtful, therefore, that any change in government or personnel could insure Egyptian friendship for the West or diminish Egyptian power in Middle Eastern affairs during the next generation.

7. Seventh, the character of the Middle East will be shaped for generations to come by one more factor which was not present a generation ago—the State of Israel. It is time that all the nations of the world, in the Middle East and elsewhere, realized that Israel is here to stay. Surrounded on every side by violent hate and prejudice, living each day in an atmosphere of constant tension and fear, Israel is certain to survive the present crisis and all future crises; and all negotiations between the United States and Arab nations should accept that fact.

The future of the Middle East will be based upon the interrelation of these seven factors. We now realize that there is no problem in the Middle East in which the security of the United States is not involved and to the solution of which we do not have some responsibility. But we shall fulfill those responsibilities with lasting benefits for ourselves and the world only if we develop a Middle Eastern policy of our own; and only if we base that policy upon a long-range point of view—upon the interlacing and interaction of the above facts and factors.

THE 1957 BROTHERHOOD YEAR OBSERVANCE OF THE
NATIONAL CONFERENCE OF CHRISTIANS AND JEWS
CLEVELAND, OHIO
FEBRUARY 24, 1957

Brotherhood, tolerance, enlightened relations between members of different ethnic groups—these are, after all, simply an extension of the concept upon which all free organized society is based. Some call this concept comity. Some find it in the Golden Rule, others in Rousseau's "social contract." Our Declaration of Independence calls it "the consent of the governed." The ancient Romans called it *"civitatis filia,"* or civic friendship.

It is upon this principle and practice, by whatever name it may be called and regardless of what form it takes, that free societies function, governments operate, and orderly, amicable relations between civilized human beings go on. For although the continued presence of sanctions is a necessary part of any legal structure, we depend, in the last analysis, not upon our police force and our jails for the preservation of law and order, but upon voluntary observance and self-restraint. We all pay taxes without a court order (with a few notable exceptions); comply with laws we dislike; and respect the rights and privileges of others even when those rights and privileges necessarily interfere with our own.

The family also functions on this same basis of comity. Sanctions are available in the home, too, as I recall—but obviously a child is not to be beaten into observing every customary rule of conduct from morning to night. On the contrary, we take it for granted that such observance comes as a matter of course.

What is true in the relations of the family at home can be equally true, I believe, in the family of nations. Without some super-sovereign, some police force, some guaranteed enforcement and punishment, most scoffers say, there can be no such thing as international law and order. But such an attitude fails to recognize that comity, not sanctions, is the basis of law and order among free equals.

It seems to me that this nation would do well to bear in mind this concept of *civitatis filia* as we consider the tense and troubled situation in the Middle East. For it is unfortunate, I think, that our chief concern has been with sanctions and hostilities, with troop authorizations and constitutional powers. In the Senate we have spent nearly two months debating the President's Middle East Resolution. I have supported that resolution in Committee and will vote for it on the floor. But once it is passed, signed, and proclaimed to the world, we will still not be one step nearer than we were two months ago to a solution of the real problems of the Middle East— including access to Suez and the Gulf of Aqaba, homes for Arab refugees, permanent national boundaries, development of the River Jordan resources, political and economic instability, and an end to

continuous border raids and tension. For the resolution we have
been debating has absolutely nothing to do with those problems. It
offers guns and money—but guns and money are not the Middle
East's basic need.

Similarly, the invocation of sanctions by the United Nations, or
the adoption of denunciatory resolutions, upon which the world's
attention is presently concentrated, will not—regardless of their
effect on the immediate crisis in that area—contribute anything to a
long-range solution of the major problems of the Middle East. The
U.N. must, of course, take prompt and effective action to meet
aggression—but let no one be deceived into believing that the
Middle East crisis will be over once Israeli troops are pulled back and
the Suez Canal cleared. Little is to be accomplished by merely
restoring the muddled and frictional situation out of which the
present crisis came.

What we clearly need in the Middle East, and need quickly, in my
opinion, is a final entente, a permanent settlement of all major
problems which reasonable men and nations can accept—a settlement, in short, based not on armed truce but on comity, accepted
not out of fear but out of civic friendship.

Such a settlement cannot and need not give any nation all she
would like—each side will have to make concessions. But recall, if
you will, the Webster-Ashburton Treaty of 1842 between the United
States and Canada—how unpopular it was on both sides of the line;
how both Mr. Webster and Lord Ashburton were denounced for
sacrificing the rights of their people. (Indeed, Webster and Ashburton finally convinced the Senate and Parliament respectively, it
is said, only after each had used a different map to pretend that he
had in reality cheated the other.) And yet the peace and prosperity
to both countries flowing from that much abused settlement for more
than a century have been worth several thousand times as much as
the value of all the territory that was in dispute.

I am convinced that if Arab, Israeli, and world leaders can once
agree in a spirit of civic *filia*, and endure the obloquy from home that
was endured by Webster and Ashburton, a permanent settlement
can be reached in the Middle East which will be worth, in terms of
peace and prosperity for both sides, in terms of men and money
devoted to something more constructive than war, many million
times the value of all the disputed points that keep them apart.

It is not enough to say, as our own officials have repeatedly said,
that we are willing to discuss long-range solutions once all other

current problems have been met. For the two are not unrelated. In Indochina and elsewhere Western nations have in the past taken this attitude of delaying discussions for a permanent settlement until after hostilities cease—only to discover that the absence of such an agreement aggravated the hostilities until finally a settlement had to be reached after needless harm to our cause had been done. We have the responsibility now to deal with basic causes of conflict as well as the conflict itself. We have the responsibility now to approach the problem as a whole, not on a piecemeal basis—to let Israel, Egypt, and all the world know that we look for a solution ending all outstanding differences, not simply Egypt's current grievances against Israel.

I do not wish to oversimplify endlessly complex problems, or load unnecessary burdens upon our troubled diplomatic officials. But I respectfully urge that the Government of the United States—through its Department of State, its United Nations delegation, and perhaps through a Presidential declaration of a status equal to the less long-range declarations on the Gulf of Aqaba and Communist aggression—promptly set forth, after consultation with Arab, Israeli, and other world leaders, a specific and comprehensive formula for a permanent Middle East settlement—a settlement to be offered and accepted in a spirit of civic friendship—a settlement based not upon force of arms or fear of men, but upon common sense and comity.

Permit me to suggest some of the principles and procedures which I believe to apply.

First, let us consider the problem of the Suez Canal. In our concern over its obstruction we have very nearly forgotten what started the dispute in the first place. Whether Egypt's rights flow from sovereignty, suzerainty, or dominion is not as crucial as an accommodation by both Egypt and all user nations, by which the canal will be in full operation, benefiting Egypt through the revenues it provides and benefiting the world by offering free and open transit to the ships of all nations without discrimination or political interference. The canal can be enlarged and deepened to make its continued operation even more profitable to Egypt. The dues and charges on canal passage can be mutually agreed upon; the proportion of net income to be allotted to further canal maintenance and development can be mutually agreed upon; and all unresolved disputes concerning the canal in the future can be referred for impartial arbitration. Discussions can begin with a clean slate, not on the basis of legal fictions or ancient treaties or aggressive threats, but on the basis of mutual benefits and comity.

Secondly, let us consider the inseparable problems of national boundaries and aggression. Instead of devoting our efforts to determining what kind of arms balance at what level will maintain existing armistice lines, permanent boundaries must be fixed, not necessarily along the present lines. This is not an unprecedented problem —the United States and Canada, as mentioned, and scores of other neighbors, have successfully settled such boundary disputes time and time again, including those that had caused or seemed certain to cause an outbreak of war. I would recommend consideration in this regard of the familiar device of an International Boundary Commission, staffed by impartial experts in geography, economics, and history as well as diplomacy and international law, men who can draw reasonable, practicable lines that both sides can live with, ignoring sentimental claims and giving neither side all it seeks.

Once such boundaries are determined, the United Nations and the United States could sponsor a security guarantee or exchange of treaties formally fixing those lines, and preventing their alteration by force. Such a solution would immediately reduce not only tensions but the need for armaments expenditures both in Israel and the Arab states. The same treaties fixing boundaries could renounce the use or threat of force for aggressive purposes, and provide for progressive limitations of armaments. A Special U.N. Commission on Arms Traffic could be established to prevent outside nations, Communist or otherwise, from renewing the Middle East arms race; and a more permanent United Nations force could police the area, much as it is now, until all threats to peace have vanished. The mutual benefits flowing to the entire area—in terms of a higher standard of living, new economic development, and an end to constant fear and slaughter—would be immeasurable.

Third, let us consider the problems of Arab Palestinian refugees. Their impoverished and tragic existence in makeshift camps near Israel's borders offers a constant source of national antagonism, economic chaos, and Communist exploitation of human misery. Stopgap solutions are frequently offered—and there is talk of forcing either Israel or the Arab states to take all of them. But let us apply the spirit of brotherhood and comity. Let those refugees be repatriated to Israel at the earliest practical date who are sincerely willing to live at peace with their neighbors, to accept the Israeli Government with an attitude of *civitatis filia*. Those who would prefer to remain in Arab jurisdiction should be resettled in areas under control of governments willing to help their Arab brothers, if assisted and enabled to earn their own living, make permanent homes, and live in peace and dignity. The refugee camps should be closed. Those who suffered actual losses of property or bank accounts in flight should be compensated by Israel. New water utilization and arable land projects should be instituted to assist their resettlement in Arab countries.

All of this will require financial assistance. Israel will need assistance in making compensation payments; the Arab states will need assistance in developing land and water projects. The means for such assistance I shall mention in a moment. But I want to stress again the mutual benefits that flow from a settlement of comity— the removal of an obstacle to peace, the dispersal of a threat to Israel, the elimination of a condition depressing Arab wages and living standards, the development of Arab resources.

Fourth, what about economic and resource development and assistance? Mutual economic benefit is the key I have stressed with respect to Suez, boundaries, disarmament, and refugees. But these benefits are not limited to the Middle East alone. The entire world, and certainly the United States, will obtain considerable economic advantage in the prevention of war and the end of an armaments race in that area. Thus all nations, led by our own, should be willing to invest the funds necessary to attain this goal.

I would propose, therefore, a Middle East Regional Resources Fund, under the auspices of the United Nations and the World Bank, for assisting in the stimulation, initiation, and financing through loans and grants of resource development and other projects in the area. Soil projects could include harnessing the waters of the Nile for the benefit of the Sudan, Ethiopia, and Uganda as well as Egypt; coordinated development of the resources of the Jordan River Valley for the benefit of Israel and the three Arab states through which it flows; the development of arable land and irrigation projects for the resettlement of refugees; a loan to Israel to help her make compensation payments to refugees; and a Middle Eastern Nuclear Center, similar to the Asian Nuclear Center already proposed, which could bring untold benefits in energy utilization to former deserts and wastelands. These projects would be developed and administered under the auspices and control of the nations in the region, who would also participate in their financing wherever feasible (and many of these nations are not poor), much as our states participate in Federal grant programs which assist and stimulate them to greater action. The burdens would once again be shared—the benefits would once again be mutual.

The problems I have discussed here—Suez, boundaries, arms, refugees, and economic development—are all closely interrelated. It is to be expected that one or both sides will find objections to one or more of the solutions outlined. But I am convinced that as a permanent "package," there is no single obstacle to the achievement of a comprehensive Middle East solution, based upon comity and common sense. It is time for this nation to take the lead in seeking such a solution, instead of devoting all of our efforts to warnings and debates about temporary, symptomatic crises that cannot be ended apart from the whole pattern.

14. Israel

Israel is the bright light now shining in the Middle East. We, and ultimately Israel's neighbors, have much to learn from this center of democratic illumination, of unprecedented economic development, of human pioneering and intelligence and perseverance.

In 1939 I first saw Palestine, then an unhappy land under alien rule, and to a large extent then a barren land. In the words of Israel Zangwill: "The land without a people waited for the people without a land." In 1951, I traveled again to the land by the River Jordan, to see firsthand the new State of Israel. The transformation that had taken place was hard to believe.

For in those twelve years, a nation had been born, a desert had been reclaimed, and the most tragic victims of World War II—the survivors of the concentration camps and ghettos—had found a home.

The survival and success of Israel and its peaceful acceptance by the other nations of the Middle East is essential, as the following talk tries to make clear.

GOLDEN JUBILEE BANQUET OF B'NAI ZION
NEW YORK CITY
FEBRUARY 9, 1959

It is heartening to spend an evening where the focus is set on works of peace and social improvement.[16] For the years of crisis, through

[16] Israel celebrated its tenth anniversary of independence with due pomp and ceremony in 1958. Its relations with its neighbors were quieter;

which we have been passing for more than two decades, have left no more bitter heritage than the homelessness and landlessness of millions. Your works constitute one of the great social achievements of our time, combining the highest idealistic vision with the greatest practical vigor. And what work could be more heart-warming or more enduring than the great forest at Jerusalem. Your children and grandchildren when they visit Israel will find your monument.

There have always been skeptics scoffing at the possibility of making deserts bloom and rocky soils productive. In this regard, our own history as a nation and Israel's have many parallels—in the diversity of their origins, in their capacity to reach the unattainable, in the receptivity to new ideas and social experimentation.

In this country, throughout much of the nineteenth century, warnings were repeatedly proclaimed that mid-America and its plains beyond the 100th Parallel could never be settled and made productive. One writer, traveling from Illinois to Oregon in 1839, spoke of the Great American Desert "burnt and arid . . . whose solemn silence is seldom broken by the tread of any other animal than the wolf or the starved and thirsty horse which bears the traveler across its wastes." The sterility of the plains, and their implacable resistance to civilizing influence or settlement, were themes of major writers, such as Francis Parkman in *The Oregon Trail* or Washington Irving in his *Astoria*. At best, these writers argued, a kind of nomadic existence could be salvaged from the mid-American land mass, from these "bare" and "wasted" plains with their "level monotony."

But on the Great American Plains—as decades later in the great Palestinian plains and valleys—determined settlers learned the truth of the epigram that "Rain follows the plow." By 1881 a great Western town builder and scientist, Charles Dana Wilber, was saying: "In this miracle of progress, the plow was the advance messenger—the unerring prophet—the procuring cause."

Egypt had been chastened by Israeli successes in the Sinai campaign, and Iraq and Lebanon underwent revolutions this year. But Israel, as Senator Kennedy points out, had much to celebrate besides a mere tenth anniversary. This year it opened a 150-mile road over most difficult terrain between Elath on the Gulf of Aqaba and Beersheba, and dedicated a nuclear research institute as a branch of the Weizmann Institute. Continued immigration lifted its population above the two-million mark. Under the wise guidance of Prime Minister Ben Gurion, and with the unprecedentedly generous aid of the Jewish people all over the world, the little republic had become a shining example to other Near Eastern lands of the possibilities of enlightened progress.—A.N.

These words sound deep resonances in the minds and memories of those who have observed the gradual Zionist fulfillment in Israel. History records several such break-throughs—great efforts to which spiritual conviction and human endurance have combined to make realities out of prophecies. The Puritans in Massachusetts, the Mormons in Salt Lake City, the Scotch-Irish in the Western territories were all imbued with the truth of the old Jewish thought that a people can have only as much sky over its head as it has land under its feet.

The Jewish National Fund, which for forty-seven years foreshadowed the existence of an independent Jewish state, and assembled long in advance a perpetual trust in land for the Jewish people, symbolizes this magnificent achievement. Just as our own West has sustained progress against the impacts of serious farm depressions, crop failures, credit crises, and droughts, so, too, Israel has had to exist on narrow margins of survival, in a constant climate of hostility and outside danger. Yet it has endured and its integrity remains unimpaired, and this success can be in a large measure attributed to the National Fund.

I cannot hope—nor pretend—to solve all of the complex riddles of the Middle East. But I would like to suggest some perspectives which might help to clarify our thinking about that area and to indicate what lines our longer-range efforts might take. To do this requires, first of all, that we dispel a prevalent myth about the Middle East.

This myth—with which you are all too familiar—is the assertion that it is Zionism which has been the unsettling and fevered infection in the Middle East, the belief that without Israel there would somehow be a natural harmony throughout the Middle East and Arab world. Quite apart from the values and hopes which the State of Israel enshrines—and the past injuries which it redeems—it twists reality to suggest that it is the democratic tendency of Israel which has injected discord and dissension into the Near East. Even by the coldest calculations, the removal of Israel would not alter the basic crisis in the area. For, if there is any lesson which the melancholy events of the last two years and more taught us, it is that, though Arab states are generally united in opposition to Israel, their political unities do not rise above this negative position. The basic rivalries within the Arab world, the quarrels over boundaries, the tensions involved in lifting their economies from stagnation, the cross pressures of nationalism—all of these factors would still be there, even if there were no Israel.

The Middle East illustrates the twin heritage of modern nationalism. In one of its aspects it reflects a positive search for political freedom and self-development; in another, it is the residue of disintegration and the destruction of old moorings. The Arab states, though some have had significantly varying lines of development, have all too often used Israel as a scapegoat and anti-Zionism as a policy to divert attention away from the hard tasks of national and regional development, and from special area problems.

One of these problems, that of the Arab refugees, which has lain like a naked sword between Israel and the Arab states, is a matter on which the books cannot be closed and which must be further resolved through negotiation, resettlement, and outside international assistance. But to recognize the problem is quite different from saying that the problem is insoluble short of the destruction of Israel, or only by the unilateral repudiation of the 1949 borders, or must be solved by Israel alone. Israel today stands as an example for all the Middle East, in spotlighting how economic modernization may be spurred and accelerated against high odds, great physical barriers, and constantly growing populations, as well as against all Communist blandishments. The growing influence of the Soviet Union in the Middle East and the further diminution of direct Western influence in that area as a whole, we shall in all likelihood have to face as realities. And it is sheer delusion to underestimate the cutting force of Arab nationalism or hope to create puppet regimes or pocket Western kingdoms in that area. This would only intensify anti-Western feeling in the Middle East and imperil Western relations with all uncommitted states.

Israel, on the other hand, embodying all the characteristics of a Western democracy and having long passed the threshold of economic development, shares with the West a tradition of civil liberties, of cultural freedom, of parliamentary democracy, of social mobility. It has been almost untouched by Soviet penetration. Some of the leadership groups in the Arab states also draw inspiration and training from Western sources. But too often in these nations the leadership class is small, its popular roots tenuous, its problems staggering. In too many of the countries of the Middle East the Soviet model holds special attraction, the more so since the United States and its Western allies have not been able to develop more than tentative and often only expedient policies which hardly come to grips with the root causes of political disintegration and economic backwardness. To countries with relatively primitive or top-heavy economies and low industrial capacity, the Russian and even the Chinese passage to modernity in a generation's time inspires confidence and imitation— even as does Egypt's move in less than ten years from a seemingly subjugated state to at least a strategic power. We now know that Soviet attraction is not grounded on threat or bluster alone, and that there are tensions and a critical restlessness which would exist even if there were not a Communist threat. Communism presents to many in that area the glamour of novelty, the breaking of fresh ground, of seeming to offer a disciplined, coherent, and irresistible answer to the overwhelming problems of economic management and progress.

In this light a simple military response is not adequate. For, apart from bequeathing to the United States latent anticolonial resentments, military pacts and arms shipments are themselves new divisive forces in an area shot through with national rivalries, without historic frontiers, without, for the most part, skilled classes and political administrators who can pilot new states through the treacherous tides running through the Middle East.

Military pacts provide no long-term solutions. On the contrary, they tend dangerously to polarize the Middle East, to attach us to specific regimes, to isolate us very often from the significant nationalist movements. Little is accomplished by forcing the uncommitted nations to choose rigidly between alliance with the West or submission to international Communism. Indeed, it is to our self-interest not to force such a choice in many places, especially if it diverts nations from absorbing their energies in programs of real economic improvement and take-off. In the Middle East we are moving perilously close to an arms race which, in the long run, will be of benefit to no one. No other area stands more in need of a real disarmament effort. The real mutual advantages for gradual demilitarization rather than build-up are unequaled. Already we have used the area for a pilot test of the United Nations Emergency Force; and this might well be supplemented by a similar international device to regulate arms traffic.

The contours of the outstanding economic and political issues in the Middle East lend themselves uniquely also to a regional approach. The project-by-project, country-by-country pattern of assistance is particularly ill-adapted in this area. The great river basins of the Middle East are international—the Jordan, the Nile, the Tigris, and the Euphrates. And there are other nations in the West besides the United States which can make important contribution in economic and technical assistance. There has been no lack of pointers toward what a regional policy might include—a multilateral regional development fund for both economic improvement and refugee resettlement, the Jordan River multipurpose scheme, a food pool making imaginative use of our agricultural surpluses, and, as a co-ordinating agency, a Middle East Development Authority to pool capital and technical aid in that area. This would encourage a higher and more diversified level of private investment, and enable Arab leaders to participate in economic planning and administration.

Unfortunately, all these and other plans have so far lacked the active political leadership which can break the paralysis of purpose. Only external Soviet aggression, which is only one danger to the Middle East, has been the subject of high-level policy planning. No greater opportunity exists for the United States than to take the lead in such an effort, which could diminish the internal bickering in that tense and troubled area, and bend new energies to new, more promising, and more constructive ventures.

Needless to say, such proposals and programs should not be used as veiled techniques for placing new economic sanctions and pressures on Israel. Nor should they detract from our support of Israel's immediate needs. There is no reason why the United States should not conclude at once the $75-million loan promised through the Export-Import Bank, and make it clear that we will not sanction any barrier to free shipping on the Gulf of Aqaba, which is an international waterway. The choice today is not between either the Arab states or Israel. Ways must be found of supporting the legitimate aspirations of each. The United States, whose President was first to recognize the new State of Israel, need have no apologies—indeed should pride itself—for the action it took. But neither should we foreclose any effort which promises a regeneration of a much wider segment of the Middle East.

The Jewish state found its fulfillment during a time when it bore witness, to use the words of Markham, to humanity betrayed, "plundered, profaned, and disinherited."

But it is yet possible that history will record this event as only the prelude to the betterment and therapy, not merely of a strip of land, but of a broad expanse of almost continental dimensions. Whether such a challenge will be seized cannot be determined by the United States alone. But as we observe the inspiring experience of Israel, we know that we must make the effort—and that we can once again demonstrate that "Rain follows the plow."

15. Africa South of the Sahara

If we are ready to apply the lessons of the past and to act creatively before other, probably unfriendly, forces take the stage—and leave us no choice but to react to their moves—there is no place so full of opportunity as the Africa north of the troubled Union of South Africa and south of the great Sahara Desert. Studying the problems and possibilities of this continent has been one of my special assignments on the Senate Foreign Relations Committee. As the two statements below indicate, I hope that the Subcommittee on African Affairs, on which I serve as chairman, will be able to contribute to the early adoption of a concrete and constructive American program.

SECOND ANNUAL CONFERENCE OF THE
AMERICAN SOCIETY OF AFRICAN CULTURE
NEW YORK CITY
JUNE 28, 1959

Some 2,500 years ago the Greek historian Herodotus described Africa south of the Sahara as a land of "horned asses, dogged faced creatures, the creatures without heads, whom the Libyans declared to have eyes in their breasts, and many other far less fabulous beasts." Apparently when Herodotus found himself short on facts, he didn't hesitate to use imagination—which may be why he is called the first historian.

But we must not be too critical of Herodotus. Until very recently, for most Americans, Africa was Trader Horn, Tarzan, and tom-tom drums. We are only now beginning to discover that Africa, unlike our comic strip stereotypes, is a land of rich variety—of noble and ancient cultures, some primitive, some highly sophisticated; of vital and gifted people, who are only now crossing the threshold into the modern world.[17]

[17] No development of modern times was more remarkable than the end of colonialism in Africa, and the emergence of states whose people successfully ruled themselves; a development which delighted Senator Kennedy as it did many others. That Morocco and Tunisia, with their old Moslem civilization, should hold independent status did not seem remarkable. In 1956 they took their place alongside Egypt, Libya, Ethiopia, and Liberia. It was the emergence of Ghana which most dramatically advertised the opening of a new era. When Senator Kennedy delivered this

It is a land of enormous natural riches, side by side with stark poverty and cruel disease. And, as events are beginning to reveal, it is a land of immense importance to the world—and to the United States. Some may look at it from the viewpoint of the vital natural resources and strategic materials. Some may be interested in military bases or new allies against Communism. Some may feel a responsibility in Africa because the West thrust itself upon the area and cannot be indifferent to the consequences. Some may have a real concern for Africa and her people. But whatever one's point of view, one fact cannot be denied—the future of Africa will seriously affect, for better or worse, the future of the United States.

And so, with the help of such organizations as yours, we are beginning to look at Africa with new eyes. In 1835 de Tocqueville said that "in America I saw more than America; I saw there the image of democracy itself. . . ." Today we can say that in Africa we see more than Africa. We see there a continent so long "behind God's back" coming into its own. We see 200 million human beings awakening from centuries of sleep. We see the ideas of freedom being reborn. We see the birth pangs of independence being suffered anew. We see the problems of national development, of modern civilization, weighing down the shoulders of a new generation. We see, above all, the image of modern man being created in a vast new land under new and difficult conditions.

You are aware of the complexities involved. In your panels on the various problems of Africa and American policies, you have been considering the difficulties that Africans and Americans must encounter together in this new era of history. And when we consider all these difficulties, we realize that we in the United States had it comparatively easy. After winning our independence, we were given

---

speech, Ghana was more than two years old, for it had taken independence (within the Commonwealth) on March 6, 1957; and under Prime Minister Kwame Nkrumah it had made steady progress, though it could hardly yet be called a democracy. Nigeria, Kenya, Tanganyika, and the Belgian Congo were all moving unevenly toward full self-government.

The colonizing nations had done much for all these countries. "Each," wrote an expert, "has offered them the best of itself: the Belgians their technical training, the French their language and logic, the British their institutions." The United States, as Senator Kennedy says, desires a strong Africa; and if strength is to be achieved, it must do its share for both the material and the political advancement of these lands. Only well-planned Western aid can prevent a wave of racial antagonism to the West from sweeping over Africa.—A.N.

133 years in which to develop in relative peace before the First World War ended our isolation. Africa has no such leeway. The world is in Africa now, and Africa is an integral part of the world community.

But even without the pressures of the Cold War, no leisurely pace of change would be possible for Africa. For the word is out—and spreading like wildfire in nearly a thousand languages and dialects— that it is no longer necessary to remain forever poor or forever in bondage. "From a small spark kindled in America, a flame has arisen not to be extinguished," wrote Tom Paine during the American Revolution. And that very flame is today lighting what was once called "the Dark Continent."

It would be a mistake, of course, to apply any sweeping conclusions to all of Africa, or even all of Africa south of the Sahara. For perhaps the greatest challenge about Africa today is its variety. As Ernest Dunbar noted recently in Look Magazine, "A trip through Africa is like a quick tour through the history of mankind." In almost every category the whole range of human possibilities, new and old, good and bad, exist on this continent, often side by side. Uranium production is going on in the midst of primitive agriculture. Automation is being introduced not far from ancient village handicraft. Monarchy, dictatorship, tribal rule, colonial rule, white-settler rule, and republics, and varying mixtures of these are all to be found. In some areas there are only a handful of white people. In others the ratio of white settlers—who also have a real stake in the land—is very large, reaching nearly 25 per cent of the total population in the Union of South Africa.

But racial divisions, ethnic, cultural, and geographic ties, are not reflected in Africa's national boundaries, reflecting instead the trades and deals of the former imperialist powers. I doubt that any ambassador anywhere in the world has a more difficult task than the British County Councilor in Uganda, whose one-thousand-square-mile county includes five separate tribes speaking four languages and representing three distinct racial types. At one and the same time, in the words of The Economist, Africa is "undergoing an agricultural, industrial, technological, urban, social and political revolution. It is passing from a feudal—in some places still prehistoric—stage into the atomic age in a matter of decades. It is recapitulating the history of the last five centuries of European society in 50 years."

In the light of such fantastic variety and revolutionary progress, it is a mistake for the United States to fix its image of Africa in any single mold. We can no longer think of Africa in terms of Europe.

We dare not think of Africa in terms of our own self-interests or even our own ideologies. But neither should we shrink from the tremendous problems Africa presents, with an excess of caution, conservatism, or pessimism. For they are the problems of the greatest triumph modern man might ever know. They are the problems attendant upon newly won, or nearly won, freedom. They are the problems of a continent with an unlimited future—not a poor continent, let me stress in that regard, not even a poor continent today—but a rich continent filled with millions of poor people.

For today, years after the white man supposedly took up Kipling's predestined burden, most of the exploited natives live a life that holds no greater meaning for them than the unending search for enough food for themselves and their children. While non-African nations fattened and prospered materially from African natural resources, the tribes remained destitute. Per capita income—amidst acres of diamonds, lush pastures, and now uranium itself—is generally below $50 a year.

In tropical Africa seven out of ten babies born will not live until their first birthday. Average life expectancy in America today is seventy years—in some areas of Africa it is twenty-eight.

In spite of splendid missionary efforts—many of them American— the pathetic shortage of medical care accounts for the deaths of legions of natives—deaths that could be prevented—from malaria, trachoma, worm infections, and leprosy. Because of the absence of the barest educational facilities, the prevalence of illiteracy has denied to history the body of literature any culture needs to record and perpetuate itself.

But our purpose is not merely to criticize the past or deplore the present. We want to help the states of Negro Africa. We have already given some help. It was not enough. We are giving some help today. It is not enough.

Our goal, for the good of Africa, for the good of the West, is a strong Africa. A strong Africa can only result from a strong people. And no people can become strong in a climate of servitude and social indignity. What can the United States do?

Through our Mutual Security Program, economic aid to Africa has been increased from $10 million in 1956 to $100 million this year. But this is still less than 3 per cent of our total foreign aid budget— less than 3 per cent for the most underdeveloped continent of them all, covering one-fifth of the earth's inhabited surface. Even this represents a substantial increase—between 1945 and 1955, Africa received less than one-sixth of one per cent of American foreign aid, and most of this went to South Africa and the Rhodesias.

It is in this area of economic development that a new American policy toward Africa must begin. Our leaders may talk of "winning the battle for men's minds," which the Vice President stressed upon his return from that continent. There may be importance attached to the prompt recognition of new states, improved diplomatic relations, and membership in international organizations. But the people of Africa are more interested in development than they are in doctrine. They are more interested in achieving a decent standard of living than in following the standards of either East or West.

For the present, this cannot be the development of large industry. These are still, for the most part, primitive economies. There is an acute shortage of technical, managerial, and skilled labor. Our aid now should be concentrated not on large-scale monuments to American engineering but on the village and the farm—on increasing agricultural productivity and diversifying one-crop economies.

And that is why it is not enough to say that private capital should take the lead in Africa. Private overseas investment in Africa has been concentrated largely in the few metropolitan areas—in the cities and districts dominated by whites—on mining gold, diamonds, copper, and uranium. It avoids the jungle village in need of light industry, the farm in need of modern equipment, the hungry and illiterate people in need of a better way of life. I do not overlook all that private capital from America and Europe has done for the African Continent—but it cannot do the job alone. It will not be attracted to nonprofit schools, hospitals, and social services, or even to the necessary network of communication and transportation.

To meet this shortage of development capital in the underdeveloped areas of the world, the Congress has in recent years established the Development Loan Fund. That fund is our best tool for African economic policy today. Unfortunately, only a negligible amount of an already inadequate appropriation has been used for Africa to date. It is essential that this Congress strengthen the Development Loan Fund this year—and thus strengthen Africa's participation in it.

At the same time, far more must be done by way of technical assistance, under the so-called Point Four Program. With more than 80 per cent of the population struggling to get by on a meager subsistence, we have made available to the entire continent in the current budget only $14 million for the promotion of education, technical training, and public health. A 50 per cent increase has been proposed for 1960—but a 500 per cent increase would hardly begin to do the job.

Let me stress, however, that economic progress in Africa is not the responsibility of this nation alone. It is primarily the responsibility of the Africans. It is also the responsibility of those European nations who have for centuries extracted the wealth of that continent. Perhaps the most effective way to provide financial help for investment, development, and personnel might be through multilateral co-operation with African, European, American, and other countries in an African regional economic plan. Such a program should properly be initiated by the African independent states, and be sufficiently elastic to negotiate and co-ordinate bilateral and multilateral arrangements. The African states would participate on a basis of complete equality —as givers as well as receivers.

Such an organization would spread the economic load, substitute co-operation for competition and decrease the sense of dependence of one nation toward another which is certain to lead to resentment. Such a regional organization, moreover, would be more likely to base its decision on proposed projects on objective, rather than political, standards. But whatever final method is used, sound, orderly economic development for Africa should be on the priority agenda of the 86th Congress in Washington.

Tied in closely with Africa's problems of economic development are her problems of education. Illiteracy is prevalent—schools are inadequate—teachers are in short supply—and the problems of language, diversity, and change all pose an unprecedented challenge to educators. It is not enough to tell them how we did it here. Their conditions, their needs, their circumstances are different—and they cannot wait for a century of educational evolution. An African educational development fund—with particular emphasis on the exchange of students, teachers, and trained personnel—making available our technicians and specialists in a whole variety of fields, while at the same time opening our universities and college doors to several times as many African students as now come over—this would be an investment which would be repaid to this country many times over in increased good will, trade, and national security.

But while the benefits to our national security from a new approach to Africa cannot be overlooked, I have not stressed here the economic and educational activities now being carried on in Africa by the Soviet Union. We know such activities exist. We know they are a threat. But let us never assist Africa merely because we are afraid of

Russian assistance in Africa. Let us never convince the people of that continent that we are interested in them only as pawns in the Cold War. Nor do we want them to regard us only as a military guardian, a giver of goods, or a lender of cash.

For Africa and America, with common ties and common concerns, are—and should so consider each other—partners in the world community. We must seek to understand their needs and aspirations—and ask them to understand our problems—to understand in particular, I might add, that racial segregation and violence, which badly distort our image abroad while weakening us here at home, constitute only a small part of the American scene.

This organization and these conferences can play a tremendous role in furthering that mutual understanding. Our many Government agencies and programs can do likewise. And because of my interest in improving those programs, and to increase my own understanding as chairman of the African Subcommittee, it is my intention to visit that continent as soon as possible—to talk with its people—to observe firsthand its problems—and to assess the effect of our programs. I know that I shall return recalling the words of George Washington—ordinarily a calm and solid figure—who declared he felt "irresistibly excited whenever in any country I see an oppressed people unfurl the banner of freedom."

WESLEYAN UNIVERSITY
LINCOLN, NEBRASKA
OCTOBER 13, 1959

Regardless of what Africa has been in truth or in myth, she will be that no longer. Call it nationalism, call it anticolonialism, call it what you will, Africa is going through a revolution.

Africans want a higher standard of living. Seventy-five per cent of the population now lives by subsistence agriculture. They want opportunity to manage and benefit directly from the resources in, on, and under their land. They want to govern their own affairs believing that political freedom is the precondition to economic and social development. Most of all, they want education—for education is in their eyes the backbone to gaining and maintaining the political institutions they want. Education is the means to personal and national prestige. Education is, in truth, the only key to genuine African independence and progress.

I believe that most Americans are sympathetic to these desires of the African people. After all, it was in our schools that some of the most renowned African leaders learned about the dignity and equality of men, and saw in practice the virtues of representative government, widespread education, and economic opportunity. These are the ideas and ideals that have caused a revolution—a largely bloodless revolution, but no less far-reaching for that.

But having been the catalyst to many of these changes, do we see the implications to ourselves? We cannot simply sit by and watch on the sidelines. There are no sidelines. Under the laws of physics, in order to maintain the same relative position to a moving body, one cannot stand still. As others change, so must we, if we wish to maintain our relative political or economic position.

The African peoples believe that the science, technology, and education available in the modern world can overcome their struggle for existence. They believe that their poverty, squalor, ignorance, and disease can be conquered. This is their quest and their faith. To us the challenge is not one of preserving our wealth and our civilization —it is one of extension. Actually, they are the same challenge. To preserve, we must extend. And if the scientific, technical, and educational benefits of the West cannot be extended to all the world, our status will be preserved only with great difficulty—for the balance of power is shifting, shifting into the hands of the two-thirds of the world's people who want to share what the one-third has already taken for granted. Within ten years, for example, African nations alone may control 25 per cent of all United Nations votes.

To thus extend ourselves will require a political decision. But such a decision will take economic and educational forms. For what Africa needs and wants first is education, to know how to develop the resources and run the industries and administer the government; and second, capital, for without the initial capital—to develop the resources and spur the trade—they will never generate sufficient capital themselves to provide for expanding services and development. An initial injection of capital, personnel to train others, and scholarship opportunities is necessary to start this spiral on its way.

As chairman of the Senate Foreign Relations Subcommittee on Africa, I have proposed that we in the United States establish an Educational Development Fund for Africa, and that, in co-operation with many nations, there should be established a multinational Economic Development Fund for Africa. These, or better proposals to accomplish the same purposes, must be carried through while the initiative for constructive and peaceful action is still open to us.

If African progress falters because of lack of capital and education, if these new states and emerging peoples turn bitter in their taste of independence, then the reason will be that the Western powers, by indifference or lack of imagination, have failed to see that it is their own future that is also at stake. As economist Barbara Ward stated it, "The profoundest matter at stake in Africa is the quality and capacity of Western society itself." Will we accept this challenge— or will it be that some future historian will say of us, as of previous civilizations, that "where there is no vision the people perish"?

16. Latin America

The wild, angry, passionate course of the revolution in Cuba demonstrates that the shores of the American Hemisphere and the Caribbean islands are not immune to the ideas and forces causing similar storms on other continents. Just as we must recall our own revolutionary past in order to understand the spirit and the significance of the anticolonial uprisings in Asia and Africa, we should now reread the life of Simón Bolívar, the great "Liberator" and sometime "Dictator" of South America, in order to comprehend the new contagion for liberty and reform now spreading south of our borders. On an earlier trip throughout Latin America, I became familiar with the hopes and burdens which characterize this tide of Latin nationalism.

Fidel Castro is part of the legacy of Bolívar, who led his men over the Andes Mountains, vowing "war to the death" against Spanish rule, saying, "Where a goat can pass, so can an army."[18] Castro is

[18] As the new year 1959 came in, the Cuban dictator Fulgencio Batista went out, ignominiously fleeing from Havana to the Dominican Republic. His place was taken by a comparatively young attorney, Fidel Castro, who two years earlier had landed with only ninety followers at the eastern tip of the island. The regime of Batista and his army had been highly repressive; it had arrested many thousands of people, jailed them, tortured and executed them. Since he had ousted President Carlos Prio Socarras in 1952, civil liberty had been without a home in Cuba. Though Castro's personality and aims were an enigma, his advent was therefore hailed with relief; he could hardly be anything but an improvement on his predecessor. In the worst days of the Batista regime the Assistant Secretary of State for Inter-American Affairs in Washington, Mr. Roy Rubottom, had loudly

also part of the frustration of that earlier revolution which won its war against Spain but left largely untouched the indigenous feudal order. "To serve a revolution is to plow the sea," Bolívar said in despair as he lived to see the failure of his efforts at social reform.

Whether Castro would have taken a more rational course after his victory had the United States Government not backed the dictator Batista so long and so uncritically, and had it given the fiery young rebel a warmer welcome in his hour of triumph, especially on his trip to this country, we cannot be sure.

But Cuba is not an isolated case. We can still show our concern for liberty and our opposition to the *status quo* in our relations with the other Latin-American dictators who now, or in the future, try to suppress their people's aspirations. And we can take the long-delayed positive measures that are required to enable the revolutionary wave sweeping Latin America to move through relatively peaceful channels and to be harnessed to the great constructive tasks at hand.

---

protested that the United States never interfered overtly or covertly with Cuban affairs, and one American ambassador was strongly suspected of giving the regime more support than was seemly. Castro became less of an enigma when he ruthlessly executed many of his enemies, publicly asserted that Cuba would not align itself with the West in the Cold War, and placed Communists in some key posts of government. Still the United States did nothing visible to support the cause of true democracy in the island—though in a note delivered on January 11, 1960, it protested vigorously against the confiscation of American property with an estimated value of five millions.

Senator Kennedy here places himself on record as demanding a more enlightened and vigorous policy in Latin-American affairs. One main indictment of the Republican Administration has been its tendency to equate dictatorial and democratic governments; to treat a tyrant like Perez Jiminez in Venezuela just like the enlightened leader Romulo Betancourt who became President at the end of 1958, and who launched promising experiments in social reform and economic democracy on a basis of political democracy. Another indictment concerns the Administration's failure to take due measures to help Latin Americans out of the poverty and economic backwardness that make democratic government difficult. Our interest has been too much in oil, coffee, sugar, and the sale of our manufactured goods at high prices; it has been too little manifested in a desire to aid the continent. Out of low total income, unemployment —700,000 unemployed in Cuba alone when Castro took power—and the concentration of wealth and power in privileged groups spring left-wing political movements, and the hostility toward America expressed in the demonstrations against Vice President Nixon. We should do a great deal more, declares Senator Kennedy, than merely declare that we will cling to the good neighbor policy.—A.N.

Unfortunately, in no other area has the work of anti-American agitators been made more easy by inconsistent, inconsiderate, and inadequate U.S. economic and diplomatic policies. As a member of the Senate Foreign Relations Committee's Special Subcommittee on Latin American Affairs, I have studied our recent sorry performance firsthand. The Inter-American Capital Development Bank that I urged in the 1958 talk below has come into existence, but this is only one of many steps necessary.

Fortunately, the Commonwealth of Puerto Rico, an island that is in full association with us, and that has taken an enlightened course of democratic economic development, is available to help us bridge the gap between North America and the revolutionary Latin South. The following statement on a new attitude for the Americas was made from that hopeful perspective.

AT A DEMOCRATIC DINNER
SAN JUAN, PUERTO RICO
DECEMBER 15, 1958

We in New England have faced many of the same problems which face Latin America today—the problems of inadequate fuel, water, and power resources—the need for improved and economical transportation facilities—and particularly the need to modernize, stabilize, and diversify our industrial base. Our one-industry towns in Massachusetts, which faced a chronic depression when the textile industry declined, can appreciate the problems facing the one-crop and one-commodity nations of Latin America.

But the needs of most Latin-American nations go far beyond this. Astounding population increases—four times faster than the rate of population increase of Northwestern Europe—have far outpaced increases in national savings, living standards, and food supply. This population explosion has resulted in large measure from a phenomenal reduction of the death rate, from the control of infectious diseases, sanitation improvement, and medical progress. The gap between North America and Latin America in terms of living standards, in terms of wealth versus poverty, grows greater instead of smaller; the gap in terms of economic power, in terms of domination versus independence, grows even greater.

The so-called underdeveloped nations of Latin America need investment capital—not only in oil and mining, where many private investors are willing to risk such capital, but in the development of their transportation, power, and other basic needs. These nations also lack foreign exchange resources—a shortage which makes it impossible for them to buy our goods when they need them—and a shortage which has not been solved by the huge growth in world trade over the last ten years. For unfortunately, much of that growth has been kept within the industrial countries instead of expanding trade between the industrial and the nonindustrial. Finally, our neighbors to the south need know-how—the administrative, technical, and managerial skills required to improve their economies and government, and the educational facilities in which to develop those skills.

What must be done to meet these problems?

1. First, an inter-American agreement for stabilizing commodity prices and markets.

2. Pursuing the same objective, a re-evaluation of our tariff duties and quotas, of our programs for stockpiling strategic and nonperishable commodities, and of the possibilities for inter-American common markets and currency convertibility agreements.

3. An inter-American capital development bank, to which all Western Hemisphere nations contribute and in which they all participate, with a majority of the capital being supplied by American dollars.

4. Concurrent with such a bank, the allocation to Latin-American projects of a larger proportion and total of the capital funds available from the Development Loan Fund.

5. The negotiation of individual tax treaties which would encourage the flow of private investment to underdeveloped lands whose tax forgiveness programs are now without effect in our own tax structure.

6. An increase in technical assistance programs of mutual co-operation between the United States and Latin America.

7. An increase in the exchange of students, and inclusion of undergraduates as well as graduates—not only to raise the educational standards and technical training in these nations, but also to foster the spread of good will and a better understanding of both continents —in both continents.

8. A series of inter-American fellowships in medicine and public health, supported by all members of the Pan American Sanitary Bureau, offering opportunities to study medicine and public health in the United States and elsewhere—including the excellent schools of medicine and public health which have raised the standards so greatly here in Puerto Rico.

9. The judicious use of our agricultural surpluses to relieve critical food shortages without displacing the markets of other Latin-American nations.

10. Tenth, and finally, a new program of loans to encourage the establishment within other countries of a program similar to our own Farmers Home Administration, which through loans and guarantees enables small tenant farmers to buy their own farms.

For the most part, this is not a new program. Many of these ideas have been advanced before. The difficulty is not in giving voice to them but in carrying them out. And perhaps even more important than the contents of such a program is the attitude with which it is devised and carried out—the attitude with which we in the United States regard our neighbors to the south. In the final analysis, I think this question of attitudes will prove to be more important in improving or worsening relations between the United States and Latin America than dollars, tariffs, and treaties of friendship. Unless we in the United States re-examine our attitude toward Latin America, there is little value in re-examining our policies and programs.

If we take our Western Hemisphere friends for granted—if we regard them as worthy of little attention, except in an emergency—if, in patronizingly referring to them as our own "back yard," we persist in a "Papa knows best" attitude, throwing a wet blanket on all of their proposals for economic co-operation and dispatching Marines at the first hint of trouble—then the day may not be far off when our security will be far more endangered in this area than it is in the more distant corners of the earth to which we have given our attention. If we persist in believing that all Latin-American agitation is Communist inspired—that every anti-American voice is the voice of Moscow—and that most citizens of Latin America share our dedication to an anti-Communist crusade to save what we call free enterprise for the Free World—then the time may come when we will learn to our dismay that *our* enemies are not necessarily *their* enemies, and that our concepts of progress are not yet meaningful in their own terms. And finally, if even those who seek to improve these relations talk in terms of *our* promoting a new program for Latin America, instead of working out separate policies and programs for each nation with the spokesmen for that nation—then we may learn too late that there are differences within Central and South America as wide as those that separate North Africa and South Africa.

Permit me to mention in detail three sets of attitudes which are particularly troublesome: our attitude on political relations, espe-

cially in connection with the so-called dictators; our attitude in
diplomatic relations; and our attitude concerning economic relations.

*First, what should our attitude be toward Latin-American politics
in general and dictators in particular?* I realize that it will always be
a cardinal tenet of American foreign policy not to intervene in the
internal affairs of other nations—and that this is particularly true
in Latin America. I realize that we cannot force out any duly constituted government, however repugnant its methods or views may
be—particularly when we have no guarantee that its successors in the
long run will be a real improvement. Imported democracy is never
as meaningful or viable as the domestic brand.

But an announced policy of nonintervention becomes a sham
when it is turned off and on to suit our own purposes. It should apply
to businessmen as well as diplomats, to economic as well as political
revolutions. And how can we call it nonintervention when we are
more willing to offer economic assistance to those who join our battle
against the Soviet Union than to those who do not—or when we
turn loan applications down for reasons of corruption, inefficiency,
and inflation, but not because freedom is suppressed—or when our
aid policies are conditioned upon the role which private enterprise
will play within the recipient country.

It seems to me, moreover, that a policy of nonintervention does
not tie our hands completely with respect to dictatorships in Latin
America or anywhere else in the world. We should not attempt to
influence voters in their choice of governments—but we should always indicate our hope that they will always have an opportunity
to make such a choice—that we are not indifferent to human rights
—and that we look with favor upon the emergence and continuance
of free governments. It is no answer to say, as Mr. Dulles has said,
that there are various degrees of democracy in every government.
For there are also degrees of regard and respect which should govern
our attitude toward these governments—differences of degree which
should be borne in mind when we give a dictator praise, or medals,
or military assistance which will only be used to tighten his hold.
For there is little question that should any Latin country be driven
by repression into the arms of the Communists, our attitude on nonintervention would change overnight.

*Secondly, we need to change our attitude concerning diplomatic
relations with the nations of Latin America.* In recent years, Latin
America has been the stepchild in the Department of State, the
responsibility of lesser officials and too often the haven for ambas-

sadors of less than top-flight quality. Many top embassy posts have been left vacant for undue periods of time—in others, the top officials have been moved in and out too swiftly, with changeovers occurring all at once in the same post. Too often, the job has been selected for the man—rather than the man for the job. We have attempted to measure our interest by the quantity of American personnel in a given nation, rather than the quality. And too many of our emissaries in this area have associated only with the elite and the Americanized, with all too little contact with the leaders of the future, labor, students, small businessmen, and the growing middle class. For we have not always recognized that the ideal contact is between peoples, rather than governments—governments come and go, while lasting personal friendships and impressions remain.

Equally serious, we have permitted the OAS—the Organization of American States—to wither in a back-seat role, concerned much of the time with unimportant policies and briefings rather than real consultations. If we could utilize the potential prestige of this organization, to make it as meaningful as the Buenos Aires Conference of 1936 and the Lima Conference of 1938—if we could use its consultative machinery on major world issues rather than routine intra-hemisphere matters only—then it would be a force for unity far more valuable than any good-will tour or "good neighbor" speech. As President Kubitschek wrote to President Eisenhower in July: "This substantial part of our continent must be freed from the featureless rear guard position which it has held heretofore in the international scene, and . . . its voice heeded wherever the destinies of the peoples are at stake."

It is not enough to say that we will go back to the good neighbor policy of a generation ago. Such a policy governed our relations with an area dependent almost entirely upon agricultural and raw commodities—a diplomatic preserve of the United States which required doing business with only a handful of leaders. Our most important common purpose was our continental coastal defense—the defense of isolationist North America with a relatively small and unimportant Latin America. Most of the Latin-American states were in equal stages of development, and treated equally and identically in Washington.

Now, of course, all this has changed. Although the development of the intercontinental ballistic missile may again elevate the importance of continental defense, the United States has different responsibilities and a different outlook as the leader of the Free

World. Our Latin-American neighbors have developed in different ways and at different rates of speed. They constitute an important group of votes within the United Nations, and a vital force in world economic and diplomatic affairs. Nothing in the Monroe Doctrine or good neighbor policy covered the problem posed by a Soviet economic offensive, which seeks to turn the eyes and ears of Latin America toward the Kremlin. And thus I say that a new, hard look at our attitude on diplomatic relations with Latin America is long overdue.

Third and finally, what changes do we need in our attitude on economic relations? The problem is not so much the proportion of our Mutual Security aid which has gone to Latin America; for those funds have, for the most part, been expended not as a measure of our friendship and regard, but to meet specific crises—whether they be in Greece and Turkey, or Formosa and South Korea. But Latin Americans do want to use American capital within their own political and economic framework. They resent our insisting upon a larger role for their private enterprise, which cannot cope with many of their problems, or a larger role for our private investors, who have limited their interests almost entirely to extractive industries and to only five countries (Brazil, Cuba, Mexico, Venezuela, and Chile).

Nevertheless, we know—or surely ought to know—that Latin America is certainly as essential to our security as Southeast Asia—that Latin America is also plagued by poverty, instability, and Communist political and economic warfare—and that neutralism and anti-Americanism are as strong there as in other parts of the world. Yet our twenty Latin-American neighbors have consistently received less than 3 to 5 per cent of our foreign aid budget.

And far too much of this has been in military assistance—desirable perhaps if it assists in our continental defense, with radar and missile bases and troop patrols to guard our sea lanes in case of war—but undesirable when it tightens the grip of dictatorial governments, makes friends with those in power today at the expense of those who may be in power tomorrow, and emphasizes the role of the military in states that want to be peace-loving. The objective of our aid program in Latin America should not be to purchase allies—but to consolidate a free and democratic Western Hemisphere, alleviating those conditions which might foster opportunities for Communist infiltration, and uniting our peoples on the basis of mutual confidence, stability, and constantly increasing living standards.

But while I may be critical of our attitudes and policies in these respects, I do not think we should be unmindful of the good already accomplished by the United States, of the burdens already borne by our taxpayers and of the problems which certain Latin-American attitudes pose for us. For the development of harmonious relations is, like trade, a two-way street. The deterioration of relations in this hemisphere cannot be blamed entirely upon the United States or cured entirely by the United States. Latin-American nations have complained about our tariff barriers when embarked upon protectionist policies of their own. They have blamed our Government for not making more loans available—and resented us as creditors when they came. They have complained about the selfish nationalism of our agricultural and mineral policies—but have exhibited the same tendencies in their own official programs. They dislike too much foreign capital—yet they ask for more foreign capital. They oppose American intervention in their internal affairs—but think we should have intervened more to help their economies or to oppose certain dictators. They want to be regarded as members of the American family—but they also want to be dealt with as a separate force that cannot be taken for granted.

In short, this problem of attitudes is a mutual problem. It requires mutual understanding, mutual patience, and better communication between both sides. The basic issue is whether we are going to approach the future together or separately. It is just that simple and clear-cut—yet we have not made our answer equally clear. There was a great deal of talk at the time of the demonstrations against Vice President Nixon—a great many promises and assurances—but now, as the crisis seems to pass from the headlines, the assurances are being neglected, the promises delayed and even the talk is dying down.

I am sure that all of us here would agree that the answer to this question—whether we are to face the future separately or together—ought to be crystal-clear. What unites the nations of this hemisphere is far greater than what divides us. We are dependent upon each other economically, militarily, and diplomatically. We are united by our love for peace and liberty, by strong cultural ties, and by the strength of an ancient friendship.

It is not a matter of cost to the United States. A small sum spent now may save us billions later. Investment in a growing area, rich in resource potential—an area which asks not for a charity handout but for financial arrangements in which its members are willing to participate—is not throwing money down the drain. On the contrary, our dollars spent in Latin America return to pay for our goods and services. Ninety-eight cents of every American dollar spent to purchase sugar from Cuba, for example, is spent by the Cubans to buy American exports. And we can be certain that any vacuum we leave through the instability of our own foreign trade policies will be swiftly filled by the Soviet Union.

In short, while I would hope that we would continue to regard ourselves as members of the same family, I would also hope that Uncle Sam—like any political leader—would not neglect his family responsibilities in order to attend to his broader community responsibilities—or that he would confuse the two sets of issues. For inspiration and guidance as to what we can expect from our change in attitude and policies, we need look no further than right here in Puerto Rico. Under the tireless and inspired leadership of Governor Muñoz Marín, this island has become an ideal testing ground for inter-American relations and a pioneer in inter-American development. Despite tremendous handicaps and problems not easily tackled and not yet done away with, you have achieved both political and economic independence accompanied by both political and economic stability. Taking an attitude of neither servile submission nor intransigent nationalism, you have co-operated with the mainland and the Federal Government to the mutual benefit of us all. Rising wages, rising productivity, a stronger industrial base, a responsible labor movement, increased land ownership, and stable political parties have made this island a showcase of economic and political democracy, where the Communists will never gain a real foothold.

These problems which we have discussed are essentially problems of leadership—leadership such as that which you have achieved here in Puerto Rico—leadership which our nation needs today in both domestic and foreign affairs.

17. India and China

The following talks consider our stake in the contest between the two greatest poles of power in Asia—India, the most populous democracy in the world, whose 400 million people comprise some 40 per cent of the population of the uncommitted world; and China, whose 650 million people account for nearly one-fourth of the human race. The 1958 address to the Senate suggests in some detail the measures called for by the critical situation in India. These, or better proposals on the same scale, are still urgently required.

RIVERSIDE, CALIFORNIA
NOVEMBER 1, 1959

Whatever battles may be in the headlines, no struggle in the world deserves more time and attention from this Administration—and the next—than that which now grips the attention of all Asia: the battle between India and China. The real battle is not the recent flare-up over Chinese troop movements around disputed boundaries. Nor is it the war of words over China's annihilation of Tibet. The real India-China struggle is equally fierce but less obvious—less in the headlines but far more significant in the long run.

And that is the struggle between India and China for the economic and political leadership of the East, for the respect of all Asia, for the opportunity to demonstrate whose way of life is the better.

For it is these two countries that have the greatest magnetic attraction to the uncommitted and underdeveloped world. It is these two countries which offer a potential route of transition from economic stagnation to economic growth. India follows a route in keeping with human dignity and individual freedom. Red China represents the route of regimented controls and ruthless denial of human rights.

It should be obvious that the outcome of this competition will vitally affect the future of all Asia—the comparative strength of Red and free nations—and inevitably the security and standing of our own country. India's population is larger than the total populations of the continents of Africa and South America combined. Unless India can compete equally with China, unless she can show that her way works as well as or better than dictatorship, unless she can make the transition from economic stagnation to economic growth, so that it can get ahead of its exploding population, the entire Free World will suffer a serious reverse. India herself will be gripped by frustration and political instability, its role as a counter to the Red Chinese in Asia will be lost, and Communism will have won its greatest bloodless victory.

But do we realize how this contest is coming out? The harsh facts are that in the last decade China has surged ahead of India economically. In steel production, China has moved from a position of inferiority to marked superiority. In terms of industrial capacity, education, and even household consumption, China has slowly pulled up and now moved ahead.

But the struggle is not over—and the potentialities for gain in India are still great. But if these opportunities are lost now, they may never come again.

It is not enough that we participate on a crash basis, for temporary relief. We must be willing to join with other Western nations in a serious long-range program of long-term loans, backed up by technical and agricultural assistance—designed to enable India to overtake the challenge of Communist China. The tool for this program can well be the Development Loan Fund; and the basis for a joint effort by several Western nations is contained in a resolution sponsored by Senator Cooper of Kentucky and myself, and by Representative Chester Bowles in the House. This kind of careful, co-ordinated, long-range aid could make the difference.

But it is not enough merely to provide sufficient money. Equally important are our attitude and our understanding. For if we undertake this effort in the wrong spirit, or for the wrong reasons, or in the wrong way, then any and all financial measures will be in vain.

We want India to win that race with Red China. We want India to be a free and thriving leader of a free and thriving Asia. But if our interest appears to be purely selfish, anti-Communist, and part of the Cold War—if it appears to the Indian people that our motives are purely political—then we shall play into the hands of Communist and neutralist propagandists, cruelly distort America's image abroad, and undo much of the psychological effect that we expect from our generosity.

Instead we must return to the generous spirit in which the original Point Four Program was conceived, stress our positive interest in, and moral responsibility for, relieving misery and poverty; and acknowledge to ourselves and the world that, Communism or no Communism, we cannot be an island unto ourselves.

IN THE SENATE
MARCH 25, 1958

Mr. President, there are clearly certain fixed facts in the world power balance which the Western alliance can influence only slowly or slightly—and then only after hard work, patience, and sacrifice. But there are—especially in the underdeveloped world—opportunities for intelligent and creative action.

This is particularly true of India, where so far democracy has prevailed in the face of heavy obstacles. Two national elections have been held on the basis of universal suffrage. The parliamentary framework is no mirage. It is sustained by capable political leadership and a first-rate civil service.

The granting of independence to India preceded by only a short time the coming to power in China of the Communist regime. These have been the two cardinal events in postwar Asia. China and India both began their first Five-Year Plans at roughly the same time. Each country began with an economy in which almost 85 per cent of the population was rural. Each country possesses a high resource potential and a relatively low ratio of agricultural cultivation per acre. Each system was actually in danger of running critically close to the minimum level of human well-being; in 1950 the per capita income in each country was below $50—lower than twenty years before. India had an advantage in having a larger pool of trained and skilled persons, a somewhat better transportation network, and a better ability to mobilize internal investment. But like China she had not developed extractive processes for her rich resources. She needed to import much of her machinery and she suffered from poor food yields as well. And India after 1948 had massive problems of population redistribution and economic dislocations as a result of the partition.

Yet India was able to create an environment for economic development. Without imposing the totalitarian direction that China required, India was able to take real strides forward, economically and politically.

India's Second Five-Year Plan is now near the end of its second year. In contrast to the First Plan it stands in great peril. It may even collapse. India has just experienced a very poor rice and grain harvest.

In part this deepening crisis is the handmaiden of success—the fact that the Indian economy is expanding, that the government has sought not to impose a rigid series of controls, that it has permitted a considerable sector of private enterprise. This plan, moreover, is ambitious—almost two and a half times as large as the first plan. It hopes to carry India across the most difficult threshold of economic growth—the establishment of capital-generative basic industries such as steel. It seeks to raise national income by about 5 per cent annually or 3 per cent on a per capita basis. This could serve to accelerate development at a rate permitting India to double national income in real terms in the next twelve years. If successful, it could vigorously mobilize India's rich resources in hydropower, iron ore, manganese, coal, bauxite.

The essential features of the Plan include four steel mills—one of which is well advanced—which absorb a large fraction of investment and which would expand crude steel output to 4.5 million tons; railway and transport improvements costing over $2.5 billion, machine molding shops and a step-up in hydroelectric and coal output, as well as critical but less expensive plans for agriculture, irrigation, service industries, housing, and education.

Clearly the plan developing at a time of poor harvests and growing unemployment—which depends so vitally upon the importation of machinery from abroad—is contingent upon international credit. Yet this is not a time when there is much international venture capital, private or public, and the price of such funds is high. The World Bank's interest rate is 5.5 per cent. The interest rate announced by the International Development Fund is almost equally high, while some short-term capital rates have run as high as 13 per cent.

It is easy to dismiss India's needs with the assertion that she has launched a pretentious and impossibly large scheme calling for a scale of effort and cumulative capital infusion wholly beyond her capacity. Yet is this so? Hardly, when we consider that the plan has a level of investment of less than $7 per year per head and when we lay it beside the contemporary effort at totalitarian planning being made by China. If the plan succeeds, India's rate of investment and savings will still be less than 10 per cent of national income, compared with 20 per cent in Russia, 15 per cent in prewar Japan and 12 per cent in China. India, a country with a population twice that of all Western Europe will still only have an investment capacity equal to that of Sweden with its population of seven million. The Second Plan investment per year is only equal to the total absorbed last year by the American Telephone & Telegraph Company.

India, moreover, has taken stern measures of economic self-discipline. The current economic program of the Indian Government can properly be characterized as austere. The level of taxes is high, especially after the recent addition of wealth and expenditure taxes; stiff import controls and licensing have been imposed to ease the drain on India's foreign exchange reserves. Foreign travel has been almost prohibited. Though few persons have an income level that contributes much taxation in a nation whose per capita income is under $60, persons of measurable income are taxed about as heavily as anywhere else in the world. In fact, the real question is whether these austerity measures may not soon reach the point of becoming self-defeating—by drying up too much private capital, debilitating the previously buoyant private sector by the rigidity of import controls, or sapping the incentives on which much of the plan was predicated.

Unfortunately, a serious foreign exchange crisis has forced India to pare its plan to the core. Her foreign reserves have been more than halved in the past year. Import restrictions on consumer goods have been tightened and many expenditures under the plan curtailed, extended in time, or canceled. Office and industrial buildings, communications facilities, housing and health centers have been the victims of the cutback. But these measures only begin to close the gap. The heavy expenditures lie in the heart of the plan—steel, transport, irrigation, power, tool plants.

Can the Indian Government cut more deeply into the plan without deflating all its vital energies and breaking the springs of its momentum? Informed judgment tells us that it cannot, for a genuine program of economic development is a seamless web which cannot be pulled apart or rewoven from cheaper materials. The Indian economy has reached a level of complexity and maturity in which the various elements of the plan are intermeshed. Steel and coal and transport and machinery are part of a single complex and all must grow together. Extractive industries cannot grow unless the resources are accessible; almost all industries depend on an economical energy and machine base; education and housing are the muscle for a developmental effort. Without them there will be a husk without a kernel.

In short, further serious cuts or extended stretch-outs in the plan would not save money. They would only veil and compound even greater costs in the future—or decree the eventual death sentence of the plan and India's democratic experiment in Asia.

This is not to say that there are not some possible cuts and postponements, some frills, but it is equally possible that for the maximum effect there should be a somewhat greater infusion of investment into the private and overhead sector of the plan and into rural development, which tend to create the sort of enterprises which are especially useful in yielding high employment and in breaking down the barriers between the rural and urban economies.

If the Second Plan collapses, so may democratic India and the democratic hope in all of Asia setting in motion forces which would erode the broad security interests of the United States and its allies.

However sharply one may reject the concept of American ideals impelling us to help others in need, however blind one may be to the dependence of our own economic well-being upon our closing the enormous prosperity gap between ourselves and have-not nations, no thoughtful citizen can fail to see our stake in the survival of free government in India.

It is absolutely imperative that the Western nations and India keep their gaze on and summon their efforts to the achievement of the broad goals and the type of over-all scheme envisaged originally in the Second Plan. Continued slippage and a mood of "let drift" will only leave India with a dismal economic performance and a climate of blighted expectations, the outcome of which has perhaps already been foreshadowed in the Indian State of Kerala, where educated but despairing citizens freely elected a Communist government.

Is it not time that India and its foreign friends reach an understanding about the real scope of its need? If we cannot take this central problem from under the shroud of uncertainty, there is a great danger that reliance will be placed on purely stopgap, patchwork remedies.

The situation in India has many marked parallels with the problems of European recovery ten years ago. Like that of postwar Europe, the Indian economy has reached a crucial and precarious point of success or failure. Secretary Marshall in 1947 urged the European countries to make a reckoning of their primary requirements. This was done through the OEEC and confirmed by such studies as the Harriman Report and the surveys of the Herter Committee. After such a review and candid presentation of needs, it was possible for Congress to commit itself to the Marshall program of European recovery.

At the present time the United States is furnishing India about $70 million in hard currency assistance, most of it on a loan basis. About $60 million is for economic development purposes—such as machinery and steel plates—and the remainder in technical assistance. India is also receiving $360 million worth of surplus agricultural commodities—largely grain—over a three-year period, with a portion of the local currencies resulting from the sale of these commodities loaned back to India for economic development purposes. Most of the deliveries under this agreement have already arrived. Although the total is thus already larger than we were providing under the First Plan, it falls short of her requirements—even after the assistance likely to come from other nations and the World Bank.

In looking to the success of India's economic plan, I would suggest a three-pronged series of actions:

I. IMMEDIATE LEGISLATION AND ADMINISTRATIVE ACTION

Our starting point must be the immediate and emergency needs of the Indian Government and the proposals being made by the administration this year.[19] In my judgment they provide a useful—but in themselves inadequate—first step. I recognize that their inadequacy stems in part from a Congressional failure to activate the International Development Fund in the manner conceived by its sponsors last year and by the unresponsiveness shown by Congress to the foreign aid program last year. But this Congressional numbness was caused in its turn by cumulative evidence that our foreign assistance

[19] India was indeed, when Senator Kennedy spoke, at a critical point in her career. Informed leaders of the country had been shocked in 1958 to learn that food production had actually fallen. The inexorable growth of Indian population, though birth control measures have been officially encouraged, makes more food year by year imperative. After large expenditures on dams, irrigation systems, fertilizer factories, and agricultural education, an upturn was expected which did not come. Leaders of the Congress party meeting in Hyderabad in 1958 passed a resolution asking that the next Five-Year Plan should aim at a doubling of food supplies. It is agreed that the improvements just mentioned, along with better tillage, better implements, more insecticides, and a more rational system of land tenure, could work wonders. But large-scale foreign aid would be a necessity.

To assist in India's First Five-Year Plan, ending in 1956, the United States contributed $330 million. The most important parts of this went to the betterment of agriculture and transportation. This assistance was of vital importance. In carrying on her Second Five-Year Plan, which emphasizes the development of heavy industry, India has again needed Western help. Partly because of exchange difficulties, she had to ask a $500-million loan from the United States. Senator Kennedy's demands for a more generous attitude could not have been more timely. Russia has been building a large steel plant for India with a long-term grant of credits, and has undertaken the construction of other important plants on the same basis. Various Asiatic leaders have proposed a new Marshall Plan for their continent.

Senator Kennedy was joined by Senator Cooper of Kentucky and Representatives Bowles of Connecticut and Merrow of New Hampshire in proposing a joint study of necessary aid to India by allied democratic nations. The survey is being initiated under the auspices of the World Bank and the State Department as this book goes to press.—A.N.

programs were losing direction, were oscillating between several guideposts, were not reaching visible goals and measurable results.

I would suggest therefore that we explore first the ways in which the agreements already concluded by the Administration can be reinforced.

First, there is no reason why the balance of the 1951 wheat loan, about $170 million, cannot be converted so that it is repayable in local currency, in line with the provisions later made under Public Law 480. This would help to improve India's credit position.

Second, the loan of $125 million which has been negotiated through the Export-Import Bank could be supplemented. But for underdeveloped countries the Export-Import Bank policy is restrictive and rigid.

A difficulty in Export-Import loans is that it generally requires twelve to fifteen months to set them fully in motion and specifically to commit the money. It would be a great help to India if this time interval could be shortened so that the effects of the loan could be felt by the summer of this year.

Third, it is unfortunate that the first year's appropriation gave the International Development Fund a capital base of only $300 million. This low figure makes it necessary to consider so many other expedients for countries with legitimate needs. I would hope that Congress at the very least would respond to the request which the President has made for a further appropriation to the revolving fund of $625 million. This is the very minimum figure which will make this fund a flexible and effective tool. It also gives us and recipient nations strong incentive for better planning and for a more rational evaluation of the political and psychological effects of aid. It may discourage the year-by-year, project-by-project appropriations which cannot be spent effectively. In my estimation the interest rates established for the fund are needlessly high and could be somewhat reduced to ease the servicing and cost of these loans. Moreover, we must make sure that the funds loaned are not tied only to direct dollar purchases. If Congress can carry out—or improve—the President's recommendations for the loan fund, we shall be much better equipped to serve the developmental needs of India as well as those of other nations.

Fourth, there is a special need of increasing and making as flexible as possible the loans and grants for agricultural goods and foodstuffs.

Certainly the greatest possible emphasis on long-term loans rather than short-term credit is desirable in this area. Since Public Law 480 allows some local currency loans, it would be worth while also to explore again the possibility of the United States using such currency receipts for the purchase of goods in third countries under aid programs to the latter. We have learned that Public Law 480 can produce working capital and that perhaps 25 per cent of developmental assistance in some countries can take this form.

The agricultural crisis in India is paramount. Not only did India suffer a grain harvest debacle in the monsoons of this past fall, a loss almost equivalent to the total United States program newly devised for India. But the elimination of the food crisis is also essential to the control of price inflation, to the development of an agricultural tax base in India, to allowing the Indians to resolve their fundamental economic problems of resource exploitation, employment, and capital mobilization. This is peculiarly an area where the United States can help imaginatively and effectively, if we carry the potential inherent in Public Law 480 into fuller execution. We can further convert our great economic dilemma of agricultural surpluses and waste into a capital asset for the poorer nations.

Fifth, the United States should make every effort to satisfy the joint Indian-Japanese request for about $50 million to develop Indian iron ore supplies for the Japanese steel industry. Whether this sum is drawn from the President's special fund or some other source, it would be a most promising investment in Asian development. It would diffuse benefits and further improve the growingly cordial relationships between India and Japan. Japan, the other great free nation of Asia, is slowly establishing real trade possibilities with several countries in Southeast Asia, and it can help India in its Five-Year Plan in a number of significant ways.

II. AMERICAN ACTION OVER THE LIFE OF THE PLAN

It is important that the United States view the Indian Five-Year Plan in its totality and in its true time dimensions. Our assistance, as I have suggested, should be geared to the fulfillment of the large goals, not the patching of holes and filling of small gaps. We must stress the continuities, the full cycle, the whole operations. This is in our own self-interest by reducing the final cost, by defining the destination, by giving us a standard for measuring performance. It is to India's interest, by allowing her to gather momentum to maintain good morale, to set the example of achievement to other nations, to relieve the perpetual suspense created by annual reappraisals and short-term solutions.

In the fall of 1947 the Congress passed an emergency-type program

for the start of the Marshall Plan. We shall have to do the same for
India this year. But simultaneously in 1947 the Congress set to work
on considering and passing an expression of commitment to a European recovery program and providing a distinguished select committee
which could study intensively the needs of the several European
countries. We should again follow the example. Either Congress can
again authorize a select committee or it can send subcommittees of
the Foreign Relations and Appropriations Committees to India. At
the same time the Congress should act upon a resolution expressing
American interest in the success of the Five-Year Plan and a willingness to commit itself to aiding its achievement.

III. MULTILATERAL ACTION IN SUPPORT OF INDIAN ECONOMIC DEVELOPMENT

Though the United States must make the largest contribution in
leadership and in direct assistance, the Indian Five-Year Plan can, in
closing a payments gap over the life of the Plan of as much as $3
billion, find support in many other countries.

I have already mentioned the case of Japan in connection with the
joint India-Japan request, and there are further opportunities in con-
verting the Indian advantage in coking coal into a pig-iron advantage
for Japan. But there is an even greater reservoir of interest and support within the Atlantic Community. Germany has just recently made
a new contribution of $140 million toward one of the steel mills and
is contemplating more forms of assistance which are well within its
capacities. France has extended a small line of credit despite its own
economic difficulties. It is possible that the Italians may build a rail
spur and some port facilities in return for a supply of coal. Canada, a
country which enjoys great respect and confidence among the Indian
people, is considering further agricultural surplus assistance and some
other proposals beyond about $50 million already arranged. Great
Britain, despite its payments difficulties, has already committed $45
million, while many other NATO countries are actively considering
ways and means of helping.

There have also been a number of important private investments
which contribute toward the plan. With American leadership it is
certain that many other countries, as well as the International Bank,
which is already underwriting some of the cost of the private steel
mill and of rail expansion, will materially bolster their economic
effort.

The will to help is evident; it exists within the Atlantic Community, within the Colombo Plan membership, in Japan, and among several smaller free nations of the world. How can we best prod and join these disparate intentions and programs so that they mutually reinforce each other and produce the impact required in the common interest?

Many of us have long urged multilateral assistance and joint effort, but we have had difficulty in finding the proper framework and cause. At the recent meetings of the Atlantic Alliance this issue barely reached the surface of discussion, yet all countries present revealed a receptivity to such a notion. Governor Stevenson, in particular, during his consultant period and since, has underscored the desirability of setting in motion such a joint effort. Here, it seems to me, the opportunity has arrived and the situation is ripe for such a step.

I would urge that a subcommittee of the OEEC be at once designated to go to India and to recommend plans by which long-term assistance could be given by all member nations through an international consortium. Not only will this permit the various nations better to mesh their programs; but it will also make easier a proper merger and balance between foreign government and private investment in India.

Such an OEEC body could draw on the best business and economic minds of the Atlantic world and could inspire the latent will to action which exists in countries such as Sweden, the Netherlands, Italy, Canada, Germany, and elsewhere. It could do much to change the whole psychological relationship between India and the Western partners. We know that there exists in India a real fund of friendship for the West and an absorbing interest in our techniques. From our own country almost all official and private visitors have experienced an intense and friendly reception, even when they have spoken frankly with their hosts. Great Britain is still—or more than ever—a country with whom the Indians feel a close affinity, as Prime Minister Macmillan has recently observed personally. The work of our private foundations and scholars in India has won wide respect in India. An OEEC committee, if it could include among its members persons of broad experience such as John McCloy of the United States, Sir Oliver Franks of Great Britain, Professor Tinbergen of Holland, Albert Kervin of Belgium, or Erland Waldenstorm of Sweden, could give a powerful impetus to such an international consortium.

By its example, such a committee could furnish a model for other later efforts—perhaps in Pakistan—and it could consider improvements in foreign assistance such as simplification in the handling of counterpart funds and local currencies which would have broader application. It could perform a most valuable service in recommending ways in which other countries and the United States could in combination turn their food surpluses to productive use. This is especially important for the United States and Canada, both of which could well integrate their efforts outside of existing trade markets. The export of surplus crops has been a very damaging factor in United States-Canadian relations, yet there are clearly joint alternatives which allow agricultural shipments for constructive purposes which carry neither the evils of dumping nor the hardships of sale.

I feel confident, Mr. President, that if the United States raises its sights in this year's program for India and acts as the catalyst for a multilateral approach to India over the longer cycle, then most foreign creditors will double their contributions, while some other countries will do something where they are now doing nothing.

Mr. President, I offer these suggestions in the hope that they may furnish some guides by which we can break the paralysis of which I spoke, by which we can give confidence among both parties and to the public at large that there are constructive alternatives in American foreign policy, that we are not chained in futility.

Let us consider the various objections raised against such a program.

First. Private investment: The first view is that India's economic future must rest with private investment—that this is the only durable basis of economic growth. Certainly, India can expect and is receiving a good measure of private investment. The World Bank has repeatedly shown confidence in the private sector of the Indian economy. The Standard Oil Company has built a refinery; Krupp of Germany was instrumental in beginning the construction of the Rourkela steel mill; and private investment has financed the Tata steel plan. And there is little question that dollar-for-dollar private capital is both the most durable and resilient form of assistance. Through our own action in improving the international investment guaranty program, in providing tax incentives, and in negotiating tax conventions, we would spur international private investment somewhat. And the Indian Government could also take some measures which would build up private investment.

But, even under the best conditions, private investment cannot cover the gap. The fact of private-capital depletion and starvation remains, and there is an overabundance of private-capital outlets. The United States channeled over $3 billion into private foreign investment last year, but less than 10 per cent of this flowed into under-developed states. Well over three-fourths is attributable to investment in Canada, in Latin America, and Middle East oil.

There is every reason to believe that future private investment in India will expand with the rise of Government assistance and that Government assistance now will expand rather than confine such private opportunities.

There are certain types of investment in underdeveloped countries —education, health, transport, fuel, and power—which private capital cannot underwrite. Yet they are essential to the creation of a setting in which efficient and profitable private operations can grow. What is certain, however, is that in future years there can be an increase in joint public-private capital ventures and in partnerships between local and foreign private capital.

Second. Pakistan: A second objection which deserves serious attention and frank comment is that our special and valued treaty relationships and military pacts with Pakistan do not make possible such an international effort for India. I myself have for some time investigated the possibility of devising a program which would jointly serve the needs of India and Pakistan.

I have regretfully concluded that the current political cleavages between India and Pakistan do not allow such a program. My hope is that the kind of program I have suggested may help to create the climate in which, for example, the staff work already done by Indian and Pakistani engineers on the Indus River could be brought to fruition. At the moment Pakistan is more nearly receiving the amount of aid which she can effectively absorb. Needless to say, we look forward to the time that her plans and economic momentum allow her to use even more. The choice is not one between India and Pakistan. Our responsibility is to aid each in its basic development programs. I hope the time is not far off when these types of multilateral efforts can be adopted to aid the economic growth of Pakistan.

Third. The budget and the recession: It may be argued that any proposal of this nature faces an impossible hurdle as a result of this year's budget, and the economic recession. The impression has been conveyed to some people that foreign aid can only be viewed as an alternative to programs of housing, education, urban redevelopment, and irrigation. It has been urged, for example, that we should stop building irrigation projects abroad and shift to building them at home.

The truth is that we can more easily afford an expanded foreign aid program this year than in the past few years. And our national interest, especially in the light of the shrinking markets in the United States for foreign goods and materials, requires it even more. A vigorous design of national recovery, if launched without delay, should include expanded programs for missiles, school building and education, urban redevelopment, conservation, and foreign aid.

Unemployment is an agonizing waste of resources. Looked at in another way, this tragic waste provides an opportunity to get things done that have to be done. There is no need to make work in this recession; there is more than enough to be done in the public interest. Our economy affords no excuse for a series of second-best years. There is no conflict between domestic needs and foreign security needs. And at no time would cuts in foreign aid—conceived as economies at home —mean such a drastic loss of ground abroad.

It is often the very people who minimize the damage done by weaknesses in our domestic economy who are also minimizing the capacity for growth which our economy possesses.

At the moment there are approximately five million unemployed and several million more underemployed. Each full-time worker in our economy produces about $6,000 toward the national gross product. If three million of the currently unemployed could go back to work in the next year—and they certainly should—they will add about $18 billion to the gross national product per year. But there is greater potential than that. We have been leveling off in our economy for over a year. If we were back on the normal growth curve, we would be producing about $25 billion more than we are now. A year from now, due to the rise in the working force and productivity increases, we could be $12 billion higher than that. There is more than adequate margin in our economy, plenty of capacity to grow, and abundant opportunity to make the kind of foreign assistance effort which the times demand. This is possible if we recover our balance in both domestic and foreign policy.

Mr. President, we must remember that foreign aid serves to invigorate our international trade relations. There is no question but that foreign assistance now will mean trade later. There are in our nation innumerable industries which are the healthier for having expanded export markets. A very large portion of the money we loan abroad finds its way directly or indirectly to American industries. This is not a foreign giveaway. The Indian loan opportunity is one which has a high return to India and its creditors alike.

Fourth. Soviet assistance to India: The final matter that deserves comment is the range of Soviet assistance in India. We now all know that economic warfare and ruble diplomacy are the distinctive tools-in-trade of the Khrushchev regime. The U.S.S.R. made no contributions toward the First Indian Five-Year Plan, nor did it provide wheat during the crisis of 1951. Beginning in 1953, however, Russia began to send specialists and technicians to India and negotiated the agreement for the Bhilai steel mill, toward which it gave a twelve-year loan at 2 per cent, worth $140 million; recently another low-interest loan of $126 million was added. The other big projects which are Soviet-financed are a steel machinery plant with $56 million credit, a large thermal power plant of $32 million, the development of the Korba coal field of $16 million, and an optical glass factory. Various forms of technical assistance and expert studies are also being provided by the Russians, the most important being a large group of 175 seismic and gravity-cum-magnetic experts and another group which is developing a pharmaceutical industry using Indian raw materials. There is also a growing flow of Indians to Russia for technical training and education. This illustrates dramatically that one of Russia's most powerful new weapons is its ability to export that precious commodity—knowledge.

But these developments must be seen in their proper light. Western assistance and trade are much more widely diffused; they are much more likely to reach and touch the lives of ordinary Indians—especially through food and agricultural assistance. In fact, Soviet assistance is largely confined to inflexible prestige projects which contribute far less directly to the human condition of Indians. The Russians cannot parallel the contribution being made or likely to be made by Western countries. Of course, the Russian programs have useful lessons for us: the danger of neglecting technical assistance and cultural and educational exchange—no substitute for development assistance but a psychologically and practically powerful form of help; and the need for the United States to identify itself as closely as possible with Indian economic goals.

India, in fact, seems to offer us an extraordinary opportunity to match systems with the Soviet Union on favorable terms, to show our true concern for economic development, and to push India well ahead in its competition with the Chinese economy, which is also experiencing serious trouble, especially in the agricultural sector of its Second Plan.

Nor let us, Mr. President, become confused by all the talk about competition with the Russians in foreign assistance. Our policies cannot be merely a series of reflex actions dictated by Russian moves and offers. To make foreign aid the vehicle of a popularity contest or a cut-price proposition is senselessly self-defeating. The fact is that we cannot compete with the Russians in barter arrangements, interest rates, and the like.

It is on the ultimate frustration of underdeveloped nations that the Russians count for their success, and nothing would serve their interests better than to draw us into a trade race and numbers game. We must continue to concentrate on projects and programs which can succeed. That is our big asset: that we want recipient countries to succeed while the Russians do not. We have no other grounds for acting. We might recall the words of Richard Cobden, spoken over a century ago: "I need not tell you that the only way in which the soul of a great nation can be stirred is by appealing to its sympathies with a true principle in its unalloyed simplicity."

Mr. President, let us recall again the profile of the Asian Continent. India, with its nearly 400 million souls, and China, a country in the neighborhood of 600 million. Let us not be confused by talk of Indian neutrality. Let us remember that our nation also during the period of its formative growth adopted a policy of noninvolvement in the great international controversies of the nineteenth century. Nothing serves the ultimate interests of all of the West better than the opportunity for the emergent uncommitted nations of the world to absorb their primary energies now in programs of real economic improvement.

This is the only basis on which Asian and African nations can find the political balance and social stability which provide the true defense against Communist penetration. Our friendships should not be equated with military alliances or "voting the Western ticket." To do so only drives these countries closer to totalitarianism or polarizes the world in such a way as to increase rather than diminish the chances for local war.

In considering the economic future of India we shall do well to recall that India has passed the point of economic take-off and is launched upon an effort which will by the end of the century make her one of the big powers of the world, with a population of just under one billion and capable of harnessing all the resources of modern science, technology, and destruction. No greater challenge exists in the future than the peaceful organization of a world society which includes not only the wealthy industrial states of America, Western Europe, and Russia, but also powerful new industrial states in Asia, Latin America, Africa, and the Middle East. How these states emerge from their period of economic transition will not only color but quite likely cast the historic setting of the next generation. This question was recently set in these words by Professor W. W. Rostow before the Senate Foreign Relations Committee:

> Shall these new powerful states emerge to maturity from a totalitarian setting, their outlook dominated by bitter memories of colonialism and by memories of painful transition made without help, while the rich West stands by, concerned only with the problems of defense? Or shall these states emerge from a democratic setting, built on human values, shared with the West, and on memories of shared adventure in the decisive periods of transition?

The answer to this question will not be long in the making if we do not act now and over the next few years, for India, the most important of all the uncommitted states, has entered its formative period. A successful Indian program is important at least as much for the example it can set for the economic future of other underdeveloped countries as for its own sake. The United States, Western Europe, and Japan have it in their power to make a demonstration that the democratic process is a persuasive method of creation, not frustration.

There is no visible political glory for either party in coming to the aid of India, particularly at a time of high taxes and pressing defense needs. The task of "selling" such a program to the American people is far more difficult than that of a decade ago, for we were more familiar with the people and problems of Europe, our ties were closer, their economies were more directly aligned with our own and held more certain promise of success. But the need—and the danger— are as great now as then. India today represents as great a hope, as commanding a challenge, as Western Europe did in 1947—and our people are still, I am confident, equal to the effort.

I realize that it is difficult to give resonance to such words and proposals in the mood which has governed the approach to foreign aid and economic policy in both parties during the past sessions of Congress. But this mood has, in part, been induced by the persistent counsels of caution, by the lack of vision, the purposefulness with which we have approached the problems of the underdeveloped world. If we are to break the aimless drifts and deadlocks in policy, if we are to regain the initiative in world affairs, if we are to arouse the decent emotions of Americans, it is time again that we seek projects with the power of stirring and rallying our hopes and energies. Once again our national interest and creative magnanimity can merge in the service of freedom.

IV
AMERICA'S
READINESS
FOR
WORLD
RESPONSIBILITY

In the eighteenth and nineteenth centuries, we could concentrate now on foreign problems, now on domestic problems. If we erred in one place it seemed not to affect our power of action in a second place. But the line dividing domestic and foreign affairs has become as indistinct as a line drawn in water. All that happens to us here at home has a direct and intimate bearing on what we can or must do abroad. All that happens to us abroad has a direct and intimate bearing on what we can or must do at home. If we err in one place, we err in both. If we succeed in one place, we have a chance to succeed in both. For, in a real sense, all of us, as individuals and as public officials, now belong simultaneously to a national and international constituency.

A recession in our economy can mean an economic crisis in most of the non-Communist world; a world-wide economic crisis can cause a depression for us at home. For a healthy, prosperous domestic economy we need a healthy, developing world economy, and vice versa. This same two-way relationship applies to every one of our major domestic problems.

As Henry L. Stimson wrote in 1947: "No private program and no public policy, in any section of our national life, can now escape from the compelling fact that if it is not framed with reference to the world, it is framed with perfect futility."

In the following discussions of what were once considered only domestic problems I have tried to think anew about them, in their world perspectives, and to propose policies that meet our world responsibilities.

18. Civil Liberties and Our Need for New Ideas

NATIONAL CIVIL LIBERTIES
CLEARING HOUSE ANNUAL CONFERENCE
WASHINGTON, D. C.
APRIL 16, 1959

Faced with the severest test this nation has ever known, the test of survival itself, it is high time we examine the role of civil liberties in helping us meet this test.

The fundamental truths upon which our constitutional structure of civil liberties is based are not very complicated or very subtle. On the contrary, our Founding Fathers held "these truths to be self-evident, that all men are created equal, that they are endowed by their Creator with certain unalienable Rights, that among these are Life, Liberty and the pursuit of Happiness. That to secure these rights, Governments are instituted among Men, deriving their just powers from the consent of the governed."

In short, although our civil liberties also serve important private purposes—above all they were considered essential to the republican form of government. Such a government required that the consent of the governed be given freely, thoughtfully, and intelligently. Without freedom of speech, freedom of assembly, freedom of religion, freedom of the press, equal protection of the laws, and other unalienable rights, men could not govern themselves intelligently.[20]

The authors of the Constitution made clear their own belief that self-government on the one hand, and the truth on the other hand

[20] Civil rights won a resounding victory when the 85th Congress in its first session passed a measure (approved September 9, 1958) establishing a bipartisan commission in the field with power to investigate any denial of voting rights, or any refusal of equal protection of the laws because of race, color, religion, or national origin. It provided also for an additional Assistant Attorney General to carry on legal proceedings to uphold equal rights, and it strengthened the punitive provisions of the law. Senator Kennedy labored vigorously for the measure, which passed the Senate 72 to 18. Dean Acheson hailed it as the greatest achievement in the field since the Thirteenth Amendment. But civil liberties—a term embracing wider and higher privileges and safeties than those implied by civil rights—still needed the most vigilant protection, and at some points an aggressive championship. Mr. Kennedy seized a fitting opportunity to plead for their defense.—A.N.

that all men are created equal and endowed by their Creator with certain unalienable rights are in fact two sides of the same coin. It is up to the American people, said Hamilton in the first *Federalist Paper*, "by their conduct and example, to decide the important question, whether societies of men are really capable or not of establishing good government from reflection and choice. . . ."

The basic question confronting us today is whether these fundamentals still hold true, whether we really believe in this idea of a republic, whether today the American people would ratify the Constitution and adopt the Bill of Rights—or whether the dangers of external attack and internal subversion, promoted by a foe more sinister and more powerful than any our Founding Fathers knew, have so altered our world and our beliefs as to make these fundamental truths no longer applicable. The Constitution, of course, is still in force—but it is a solemn contract made in the name of "We the People"—and it is an agreement that should be renewed by each generation.

All of us in this room have in recent years expressed our concern over this problem. We are concerned about those who dismiss the safeguards of the Bill of Rights as legal technicalities which should not be available in times of danger. We are concerned about those who regard the promise of equal protection of the laws—and the goal of full, first-class citizenship for all Americans—as expendable. We are concerned about the erosion of our rights in times of clear and present danger. We insist—or, at least some insist—that individual rights must come before national security.

It seems to me, when we go back to the fundamentals, that this is a mistake—that the case for civil liberties will always be a losing one as long as it is couched in these terms. I am willing to predict bluntly that so long as the Bill of Rights is weighed in a scale against the interests of national security, most of the people and their representatives will choose national security, the Supreme Court to the contrary notwithstanding. As Hamilton observed in the eighth *Federalist Paper*, "Safety from external danger is the most powerful director of national conduct. Even the ardent love of liberty will after a time give way to its dictates."

What we should be saying, it seems to me, is that there is no such conflict and no such choice to make. Freedom and security are but opposite sides of the same coin—and the free expression of ideas is not more expendable but far more essential in a period of challenge and crisis. I am not so much concerned with the right of everyone to say anything he pleases as I am about our need as a self-governing people to hear everything relevant. If our people are to choose between political parties, between a balanced budget and a progressive America, between more bombs or fewer tests—if we are to know how we really stand in the eyes of the world—then we need to know all the available facts.

We need to receive reports from all parts of the world; and to know the facts in all agencies of the Government. We need to be able to go everywhere we can get in, to see things for ourselves. We need to keep our doors open to visitors from around the world. Above all, we must keep our minds open to criticism and to new ideas—to dissent and alternatives—to reconsideration and reflection.

Only in this way can we as a self-governing people choose wisely and thoughtfully in our task of self-government. And it is only in this way that we can demonstrate once again that freedom is the handmaiden of security—and that the truth will make us free.

The Communists, on the other hand, have no such inner strength —and this is one of our advantages and the seed of their destruction.

It disturbs me when I read that during the winter season here in Washington the grass is dyed bright green where President Eisenhower participates in a public function. I hope this simulated cheerfulness is not symbolic of the kind of information we are given about the state of the world. For it is essential when conditions are bleak in our world relations that they not be painted in false colors. Let us not, like the Russian Czar, be fooled by a Potemkin world. The best insurance against this is the full practice of civil liberties.

I want to make sure we know all the facts and hear all the alternatives and listen to all the criticisms. For the Bill of Rights is the guardian of our security as well as our liberty. Let us not be afraid of debate or dissent—let us encourage it. For if we should ever abandon these basic American traditions in the name of fighting Communism, what would it profit us to win the whole world when we would have lost our own soul?

But to keep that faith alive—to keep that message meaningful at a time of doubt and despair and disunity—will require more thought and more effort on our part than ever before. It will require leadership better equipped than any since Lincoln's day to make clear to our people the vast spectrum of our challenges.

For the Russian peasant has looked up from his hoe to fling Sputnik into outer space—opening not a new frontier of hope for all mankind, but a new and somber frontier of fear. We cannot hope to escape a prolonged and powerful competition with Soviet power—a competition which demands that we act from enlightened impulses but never act impulsively.

The hard, tough question for the next decade, for this or any other group of Americans, is whether any free society—with its freedom of choice, its breadth of opportunity, its range of alternatives—can meet the single-minded advance of the Communist system.

Can a nation organized and governed such as ours endure? That is the real question. Have we the nerve and the will? Can we carry through in an age where we will witness not only new break-throughs in weapons of destruction—but also a race for mastery of the sky and the rain, the ocean and the tides, the far side of space and the inside of men's minds? We and the Russians now have the power to destroy with one blow one-quarter of the earth's population—a feat not accomplished since Cain slew Abel.

Can we meet this test of survival and still maintain our tradition of individual liberties and dissent? I think we can. It is the enduring faith of the American tradition that there is no real conflict between freedom and security—between liberty and abundance. Through centuries of crises the American tradition has demonstrated, on the contrary, that freedom is the ally of security—and that liberty is the architect of abundance.

So let the debate go on—and may the best ideas prevail.

For, as Walter Lippmann wrote: "The freedom to speak can never be maintained merely by objecting to interference with the liberty of the press, of printing, of broadcasting, of the screen. It can be maintained only by promoting debate."

For what we need now in this nation, more than atomic power, or airpower, or financial, industrial, or even manpower, is brain power. The dinosaur was bigger and stronger than anyone else—he may even have been more pious—but he was also dumber. And look what happened to him.

I do not confuse brain power with word power. No age has ever been more prolific in words. But words are not enough. Missiles are not enough. Atoms are not enough. All of these may help us gain time to find a solution—but they are not a solution themselves.

What we need most of all is a constant flow of new ideas—a government and a nation and a press and a public opinion which respect new ideas and respect the people who have them. Our country has surmounted great crises in the past, not because of our wealth, not because of our rhetoric, not because we had longer cars and whiter iceboxes and bigger television screens than anyone else, but because our ideas were more compelling and more penetrating and wiser and more enduring. And perhaps more important, we encouraged all ideas—the unorthodox as well as the conventional, the radical as well as the traditional.

I do not say that we have lost ground in the battle for civil liberties. On the contrary, during the lifetime of this organization—a comparatively brief period in the lifetime of our nation—tremendous strides ahead have been taken, but much more needs to be done. We must vote in the Senate during the coming week on whether to retain the present unworkable non-Communist affidavit requirements of the Taft-Hartley Act—or whether to achieve a balance of ridicule by applying it to employers as well as union officials. Still later this month we shall hold hearings on the bill which I have introduced with Senator Clark to repeal the loyalty oath provision contained in last year's National Defense Education Act. Such an oath has no place in a program designed to encourage education. It is at variance with the declared purpose of the Act in which it appears; it acts as a barrier to prospective students; and it is distasteful, humiliating, and unworkable to those who must administer it.

I doubt if many of our high school graduates are members of the Communist party. If they are, at the tender age of seventeen, perhaps a college education will free them. To make all students sign, however, represents a significant victory for those who believe that only by imitating the totalitarians can we remain free and secure. I do not agree.

To cite still another example, I am hopeful that in the near future the Congress will act upon the immigration measures which Senator Humphrey and I have proposed—in order to eliminate the discriminatory features that damage our image in the rest of the world —to keep alive this important part of the traditional American dream —and to encourage the reduction of barriers that hamper our information and understanding concerning the rest of the world.

There is much, much more to be done. There are still violent attacks upon the Supreme Court, the citadel of our liberties. We face new inroads on the public's right to know, new sacrifices to the twin fetishes of secrecy and security, new expansions instead of limitations on wiretapping. A man can still be deported, denied a passport, or fired from the Government without elementary due process. Churches, schools, and synagogues are still being bombed, though I have worked closely with your chairman on legislation to end this problem; and the ideals of equal opportunity and equal education are yet to be realized. This is not only a problem in those areas where defiance of court orders and denials of equal rights are most blatant—it deserves attention as well in our own cities and in our own lives, where more subtle pressures operate—in our neighborhoods and churches—in our newspapers and clubs—and in our own attitudes.

Moreover, there is much we must do to reshape our economic life, if the achievement of equal education and equal opportunities is to mean anything. For even under fair employment practices, Negroes in a recession are likely to be the first fired and the last rehired—and the unemployment compensation they receive during the interval is beneath the standards of decent subsistence. Equal housing opportunities are of little avail if only slums are available—as they are to some fifteen million Americans today. Improved education is of little value for a Negro working in a job not covered by our minimum wage laws, and earning—as a field hand or service employee—considerably less than one dollar an hour. Action must be taken on all of these fronts—and I know that the members of your constituent organizations will be working with us on them.

A tired nation, said David Lloyd George, is always a Tory nation. And the United States today cannot afford to be either tired or Tory. For however difficult, however discouraging, however sensitive these issues must be—they must be faced.

In the words of Woodrow Wilson: "We must neither run with the crowd nor deride it—but seek sober counsel for it—and for ourselves."

19. The Soviet Challenge to American Education

SOCIAL SCIENCE FOUNDATION
DENVER UNIVERSITY
FEBRUARY 24, 1958

We are in a crisis. The Russian Sputniks did not begin it. The American Explorer did not end it. For our crisis is not a military crisis alone —our greatest threat is not one of nuclear attack. The hard truth of the matter is that we stand in greater danger of losing out in our titanic competition with the Russians without a single missile ever being fired.

A year ago, a discussion on foreign affairs would probably not have mentioned education. Today we cannot avoid it. I do not know whether the Battle of Waterloo was actually won on the playing fields of Eton. But it is no exaggeration to say that the struggle in which we are now engaged may well be won or lost in the classrooms of America.

The development and maintenance of a modern defensive force is directly related to the scientific talent available. We already know of our lag in satellites, missiles, jet engines, and rocket fuels. An estimated 9 per cent of our tactical bombers have been kept out of service for lack of sufficient technical personnel. Others lag on the assembly line—for production of a jet airplane requires an estimated eighty times the engineering manpower required for a fighter plane in 1940. According to AEC Commissioner Libby, our greatest single deterrent to nuclear progress is a shortage of trained technicians.

But our lag in education achievements is even more costly in the competition for international prestige and good will. Alexander Nesmeyanov, Chairman of the Soviet Academy of Science, has promised "great efforts . . . to beat the United States on all scientific fronts." While we rush to devote our efforts to matching their space satellites, they may go on to score other spectacular break-throughs. We may see a Soviet cyclotron bigger than any in the Free World. We may see a Communist atomic-powered merchant vessel or airplane. We may even be surpassed in such American specialties as electronic computers and automation. Or the Soviets may next gain world-wide prestige through some stunning success in biology, meteorology, or oceanography.

More important, while we in the United States are unable to produce enough engineers and scientists to meet our own needs, more than two thousand Communist technicians are working today in nineteen underdeveloped countries. Increased *millions* of these skilled technicians, Premier Bulganin told the Communist Party Congress, are Russia's "gold reserve."

In Burma, Khrushchev and Bulganin offered to build and staff a technological institute in Rangoon "as a gift to the people of Burma from the people of the Soviet Union." In both India and Russia, four thousand Indian nationals are receiving training from the Soviets in connection with the Soviet-sponsored Bhilai steel mill.

There can be no doubt, then, that we must prepare not only American missiles for the current struggle—but American minds as well. There is no "crash" program that can do the job. The structure of American education must be painstakingly rebuilt from the bottom up—with more and better schools, more and better teachers from the primary grades on.

It will take time. If we begin now, we may regain our pre-eminent position in science and scholarship by the 1980's or even the 1970's. But the early 1960's are already lost.

The Russians, after all, have spent at least two and one-half times as much of their national income on education. Within five years, it is estimated, they will have three times as many scientists and engineers as we do.

Nor are other subjects unimportant—for example, foreign languages.

Up to one million scientific articles are published every year in languages other than English. Recently, several of our industrial laboratories spent five years and over $200,000 conducting studies of the design of electrical circuits. When they finished, they discovered that this very work had already been done and described in a Soviet journal before their own studies had even started.

In Russia, on the other hand, about 90 per cent of all serious scientific books in any language are purchased and studied. There are more than 41,000 teachers of English in Russia today. How many of us understand Russian? The Soviet ten-year school curriculum includes for every student six compulsory years of foreign language, from the fifth grade on—and English is the most popular choice.

All these facts call for careful thought and action. It is within your power to see that your local schools no longer produce mathematical illiterates—or students who can identify all the wives of Henry the Eighth, but not the countries bordering Afghanistan—or scholars whose education has been so specialized as to exclude them from participation in current events—men like Lord John Russell, of whom Queen Victoria once remarked that he would be a better man if he knew a third subject, but he was interested in nothing but the Constitution of 1688 and himself. Civilization, according to the old saying, "is a race between education and catastrophe." It is up to you to determine the winner.

LOYOLA COLLEGE ALUMNI ASSOCIATION BANQUET
BALTIMORE, MARYLAND
FEBRUARY 18, 1958

We have been assuming that our superior wealth would obtain a superior education for our children. But we have failed to devote more than a tiny fraction—at most 3 per cent—of our national income for this purpose, as contrasted to the Soviets' 10 per cent. We have taken pride in our American inventive genius, but we have too often applied it to gadgets and luxuries, while the Soviets intensified their basic research. We now realize that their traditions of scientific genius are as fully developed as our own. We have comfortably assumed that Marxist dogma and totalitarian repression would produce only stultified minds and ridiculous theories (such as Lysenko's genetics). But tonight we are not laughing at the Sputniks.

There are still others who are convinced that every Russian achievement is simply a crude imitation of our own. But the truth of the matter is that in many areas we are seeking to imitate the Russians. A year ago an American firm asked the Soviets for the right to manufacture a Russian-developed turbodrill. It could dig oil wells through hard rock ten times as fast as any American drill. Our scientists admire the Soviet Sputniks. Our aeronautical engineers envy their intercontinental jet bombers. Our atomic physicists were impressed by their atomic reactors which produce 5,000 kilowatts of commercial electric power and were in operation nearly four years ago.

In short, we have badly deceived ourselves about Russian intellectual achievements. We have been complacent about our own supposed monopoly of know-how. We have been mistaken about their supposed ignorance, and we have completely failed to understand the crucial importance of intellectual achievements in the race for security and survival.

Our lack of educational achievement is not only costly in terms of scientific weapons. The millions of uncommitted people who hold the key to the future live in the so-called underdeveloped areas. Their greatest need is not arms or propaganda or treaties. They need technicians and technical assistance. They want "know-how" and they want results. "We shall see," Mr. Khrushchev told Southeast Asia during his 1956 tour, "who has more engineers, the United States or the Soviet Union."

Students from all of these areas are thronging to the University of

Moscow and other excellent Russian institutions. We can hardly expect them to return home as dedicated missionaries for Western ideals. And Russian science may score an even more spectacular success if it devises and exports new ways of irrigating the desert, of exploiting the ocean bed, harnessing jungle rivers, changing the weather, or conquering the plagues afflicting these peoples for centuries.

Who has the best system of education today—the U.S. or the U.S.S.R.? Direct comparisons are difficult and in many ways meaningless. But let us at least be aware of what we are facing.

American students who finish high school complete twelve years of instruction; comparable Russian students receive only ten years. But in those ten years they receive more hours of instruction than American students do in twelve. They attend classes six days a week, ten months a year. They do not enjoy the long summer vacations originated in our system in response to the needs of an agricultural community.

They have approximately seventeen pupils per teacher, we have twenty-seven. Aside from some choice in the selection of foreign languages, they have no elective subjects. The ten-year curriculum includes, on a compulsory basis, five years of physics, five years of biology, four years of chemistry, one year of astronomy and ten years of mathematics up to trigonometry and elementary calculus. Few, if any, twelve-year curricula in America cover as much.

Atomic Energy Chairman Strauss has stated: "I can learn of no public high school in our country where a student obtains so thorough a preparation in science and mathematics, even if he seeks it—even if he should be a potential Einstein, Edison, Fermi or Bell." Only a small fraction of our high school graduates have had even one year of chemistry. An ever smaller proportion have had one year of physics. In fact, more than half of our high schools do not teach any physics at all. In the last year for which statistics are available, we produced only 125 new physics teachers—although we have at least 28,000 high schools.

Our lag in mathematics is even more shocking. A Russian child learns how to use a slide-rule in the fifth grade. Their schools last year produced roughly 1.5 million graduates with a thorough training in arithmetic, algebra, geometry, astronomy, trigonometry, and elementary calculus. But we graduated less than 100,000 students with any background in advanced mathematics at all! One reason, perhaps, was revealed by the Educational Testing Service. A survey of 211 prospective elementary school teachers found that 150 of them had always hated arithmetic. A large proportion of our high schools offer no classes in advanced mathematics or even geometry at all. In the words of Admiral Rickover: "It is time we face up to the fact that few American students at age twenty-one or twenty-two know as much after a four-year college course as most European secondary school graduates know at age eighteen or nineteen."

What are the facts on the college level? Russian college students receive on the average twice as many instruction hours as Americans. Their students are paid for going to college. Their college education is furnished by the state, and their professors receive pay several times above that awarded most other occupations. As a result, Soviet enrollments in institutions of higher learning already exceed our own; and they are growing faster.

The Russians are graduating ten times as many engineers as they did a generation ago—and at a rate two and one-half times greater than the United States. They have enrolled and are graduating more scientists. In addition, their technical institutions turn out tremendous numbers of engineering technicians. Though not full-fledged engineers, these technicians are invaluable in both the Soviet defense effort and foreign aid program.

What do we do to begin now? We can sit back and wait for the Russian system to collapse. We can hope that education will prove to be their undoing. We can believe that our system will prevail in the long run because our side is right, or because we have more money, or because we have more brains.

On the other hand, we could compete with the Russians by imitating them. We could force students to go into science and engineering whether they wish it or not. We could draft scientists for governmental research. We could arbitrarily restrict the production of consumer goods while we develop new scientific weapons. We could pour unlimited money into special projects without regard to other needs. We could reserve our universities for only those whose talents we seek. We could impose upon our students a workload injurious to their health and personality. We could remove all elements of choice in our high schools and colleges, all influence of public opinion, all vestiges of academic freedom.

I do not say that either of these courses would be doomed to failure. We have followed the course of complacency up to now—and have survived. The Communists have followed the course of control—and they have done well. But I cannot believe that anyone of us believes either course should be followed.

The answer lies rather with those qualities to which we pay tribute here. Consequently, we must look to citizens such as you for leadership in today's educational crisis. We must encourage other institutions to follow the example of Loyola, which has been reorienting its program to meet the needs of this modern age.

The Federal Government must be willing to put into the construction of new schools each year for the next several years at least as much as the cost of one aircraft carrier. But emphasis must not be on quantity alone. Nor must we correct our deficiencies only in the areas of mathematics and science. We are colossally ignorant today about other countries, other languages, other cultures and religions. This is especially true of the Middle East, Africa, Asia and Ceylon and Russia.

We must reverse those trends that see only four out of five of our top students finishing high school—and only two out of the five going on to college. We cannot continue to pay our college faculties and schoolteachers less for improving the minds of our children than we pay plumbers and steam fitters for improving our homes.

Much of the responsibility rests with the Federal Government: for the construction of new facilities on the school and college level, for the financing of new scholarships, teaching materials, and the rest. But the basic responsibility rests with you as parents of our future leaders and as citizens of a democracy under fire. If you prefer more effective detergents or longer tail fins over sending technicians to Latin America, our scientists will be meeting your requests. If you agree with our former Secretary of Defense that in pure research "you don't know what you are doing," then our scientists will emphasize more practical gadgets. If you scoff at intellectuals, harass scientists, and reward only athletic achievements, then the future is very dark indeed.

But if, on the other hand, you and I and all of us demand a better education for all, the politicians as well as scientists, for diplomats as well as engineers, for all citizens in all occupations, then we may face the future with hope and with confidence. Let us not despair but act.

Let us not seek the Republican answer or the Democratic answer but the right answer. Let us not seek to fix the blame for the past. Let us accept our own responsibility for the future.

20. *A New Horizon for Negro Education*

CONVOCATION OF UNITED NEGRO COLLEGE FUND
INDIANAPOLIS, INDIANA
APRIL 12, 1959

Developing through higher education the full potential of so many millions of our young citizens whose skills might otherwise be lost to our nation by the irrationality of racial discrimination is not only an essential act of justice—in this world of crisis it is also an urgent requirement of national security.

To place the importance of education and of Negro education in particular in proper perspective we must view it against the background of our troubled world. For it is only from the perspective of our international responsibilities and opportunities that your work assumes its full dimensions.

The graduates of all American colleges today will play a preeminent role in shaping the course of that world. They cannot escape the responsibilities of leadership. As Prince Bismarck once put it: "One-third of all the students in German universities break down from overwork—one-third break down from dissipation—but the other third rule Germany." (I leave it to you to decide which category predominates in your own school.) I want to make sure that these future leaders—facing the most critical, complex world and most urgent peril history has ever known—are prepared to deal with these problems.

It is necessary, therefore, that we discuss our educational problems in the context of the demands for American leadership in world affairs, for American contributions to peace, for American assistance to the undeveloped nations of the world, and for American strength in the face of harsh threats around the world.

When written in Chinese, the word "crisis" is composed of two characters—one represents danger and one represents opportunity. The danger signs are all around us. With less than half our productive capacity the Soviet Union has at least equaled us in several crucial areas of military science and technology.

Soviet economic growth continues to progress at a faster pace than ours. In addition, 650 million people in China are being harnessed to the industrialization of that other Communist colossus. Our danger is not merely that the balance of power may shift in favor of the Soviet-Chinese coalition—it is not that this combination, representing 30 per cent of the people in the world, will overtake us in industrial production. Rather the greatest danger lies in the possibility that we will become increasingly estranged from our allies and friends and the uncommitted people of the world. The vast majority of these people are colored, poor, and in need of economic development—and so far we have been failing them.

Along with danger, crisis is represented by opportunity. The space age offers the opportunity for new voyages of discovery. Atomic energy and automation can mean the opportunity for unprecedented abundance. Modern science and technology make it possible for poverty to be abolished everywhere in the world. New developments in means of transportation and communication offer the opportunity to extend the principles on which we based our republic to all mankind.

As Lincoln said, the Declaration of Independence "gave liberty not alone to the people of this country, but hope to all the world." It "gave promise that in due time the weights would be lifted from the shoulders of all men, and that all should have an equal chance." Never before have we had so excellent an opportunity to fulfill that promise of an equal chance.

The awakening nations of Africa, the restless people of South America, the suffering millions in Asia are all looking for leadership. They need our aid, our strength, our skills, our sympathy, and—above all—our understanding. It is not enough to talk grimly of agonizing reappraisals and massive retaliation—we must participate in the advancement of democratic ideals and the economic development of this rising tide of national liberation. It is up to you in the colleges you represent to recognize these challenges and to take advantage of these opportunities on behalf of the Free World.

Some of our education for world responsibility comes from the harsh logic of events. Some can only come through the experience of actually engaging in world-wide activities—for we still learn by doing. But much of our education will have to be grasped in our colleges and universities.

Here, it seems to me, you can play an increasingly important part. For Negro colleges and universities share the general crisis of American education at the same time they face a special crisis of their own. The unanimous decision of the Supreme Court five years ago tolled the end of the era of segregated facilities.

In the transition period to an integrated society, you will, of course, have to play an increasingly important role in remedying the results of inferior education at the lower levels due to continued segregation. This will be an era of ordeal. In some states you will have to continue to carry the main burden of Negro education for some years. With the rise in school population which is already bursting existing facilities, your great responsibility will grow greater.

I should like to suggest an added dimension to that task. One way to speed the transition and make it more successful will be to raise the sights of everyone—students, teachers and parents, Negroes and whites, the society at large—let them raise their sights beyond the difficulties of racial integration at home to see the challenges of our contracting universe. Integration is itself a world-wide process—in India it means Brahmans and untouchables, Hindus and Moslems. In the Middle East it is Arabs and Jews. In Africa it is colonials and natives. The closing of the gaps caused by segregation policies here in America is part of a world problem.

It is my hope, therefore, that at least some of our Negro colleges and universities, perhaps because the crisis for them is greater and sharper than that facing American education generally, will adapt their curriculum with this in mind. The new curriculum would be designed to fit Americans for the rigors facing them on the new frontiers of the world.[21]

In the nineteenth century successive waves of immigrants, speaking foreign languages and with foreign customs, came to our shores. They were crowded into city tenements and subjected to humiliating discriminations by the already established Americans. The Irish in Boston knew something of this discrimination. But education was available to these immigrant groups or their children. In addition, they had a westward-moving frontier to which they could go and embark on a new life.

For Negroes the pattern has been far more difficult and there is no American frontier. But there is an unlimited and unexplored region beyond the frontier of knowledge and experience. And there is plenty of room for expansion in the social, political, professional, and industrial work involved in world development. Here old prejudices are not entrenched—race is not important—talent is all that counts.

Pericles told ancient Athens that it should be the school of all

[21] The response of some Negro educators to Senator Kennedy's appeal was enthusiastic. One Negro leader, Ralph Bunche, a graduate of the University of California (Los Angeles), had already won a Nobel prize for his work in composing racial frictions in the Near East. An impressive number of Negro men and women had received Fulbright grants for educational work abroad. The curricula of various Negro colleges and universities, which in increasing numbers are open also to whites, give ample attention to international affairs.—A.N.

Greece. America today can be the school of all the world. But American educators must act with the necessary vision. If Negro colleges and universities will assume leadership—in training students for their global responsibilities—they will contribute mightily to the strength of America, help destroy the forces of poverty, and turn the battle for men's minds in favor of freedom.

In our nation's quest for new talent, new ideas, new brain power, new manpower, no college can escape its responsibility—and no qualified young man or woman can be denied. Irrational barriers and ancient prejudices fall quickly when the question of survival itself is at stake.

The demand for teachers, doctors, lawyers, and businessmen will continue to grow. But there will be new and unprecedented demands upon your colleges for community leaders skilled in the arts of persuasion and conciliation—social workers and psychologists, capable of handling the explosive problems of a transitional age—scientists and engineers, qualified to fill the critical gap in our defenses and new industries that care nothing about a man's color and everything about his brain power—and, to use one final example which to me is pressing, we will need from your colleges men and women trained for our nation's foreign service, demonstrating by their work abroad that this is the land of the free, as well as the home of the brave.

21. For the Repeal of the Loyalty Oath

IN THE SENATE
JANUARY 30, 1959

I am introducing today a bill to eliminate the loyalty oath provision of the National Defense Education Act of 1958.

This provision, Subsection (F) of Section 1001, presently requires those scholars, scientists, teachers, mathematicians, and other students who apply for a loan or grant under this program to sign an oath of loyalty with an affidavit declaring that they do not believe in, belong to, or support any subversive organization. This subsection received very little attention when the bill passed the Congress last year—it should receive more attention now.

No thought was given, to my knowledge, to the question of how this section would be enforced—who would investigate the veracity of these affidavits—who would determine whether students who did not belong to any subversive organization might have said something indicating "support"—or where the Department of Health, Education and Welfare was going to find the money to police this provision.

Nor was there any discussion as to what danger to the nation was being avoided by this requirement—or why Congress was singling out recipients of Federal scholarships and student loans and not those who receive old age benefits, crop loans, or other unrelated payments.

Card-carrying members of the Communist party, of course, have no hesitancy about perjuring themselves in such an affidavit. This provision will not keep them out of the program. But it may well keep out those who resent such a requirement, those who find it distasteful or humiliating, those who are overapprehensive in their interpretation or who fear unnecessarily the Government's interpretation of their views, or those who are conscientiously opposed to test oaths. To be sure, most of those thus excluded by this provision might be said to be nonconformists and dissenters—but surely, in our efforts to attract into scientific pursuits the best talents, the most inquiring minds of our nation, we do not wish to exclude the nonconformists and the dissenters. Those who are willing to sign such an affidavit are not always by that act necessarily proven to be either more loyal or more talented than those who do not sign.

The Secretary of Health, Education and Welfare is understandably concerned about how this provision is to be implemented and its implementation financed. The presidents of our leading universities—including most recently the presidents of Yale, Harvard, and Princeton—are understandably concerned about the effect of this provision on the program, on the students, and on the academic freedom of their institutions—institutions which, in the words Jefferson prescribed for the University of Virginia, should be "based on the illimitable freedom of the human mind."

And we in the Congress should be concerned, Mr. President, as to whether this unnecessary, futile gesture toward the memory of an earlier age will not defeat the very purposes of last year's bill. For, unlike the Soviets, we cannot take steps to keep our brightest minds *in* scientific careers—but we can take steps that keep them *out*. That is the great danger of this provision—and I hope this Congress will strike it.

IN THE SENATE
JUNE 29, 1959

Mr. President, I am gratified by the action of the Senate Committee on Labor and Public Welfare in reporting out my bill to
eliminate from the National Defense Education Act the section
which would require any scholar, scientist, teacher, or other student
who applies for a loan or grant under that act to sign an oath and to
execute an affidavit declaring that he does not believe in, belong to,
or support any organization which believes in or teaches the overthrow of the U.S. Government by force or by any illegal method.

No one can quarrel with the principle that all Americans should
be loyal citizens and should be willing to swear allegiance. But this
is quite different from a doctrine which singles out students, who
seek only to borrow money to complete their education—in our
interest as well as theirs— as a group which must sign a rather vague
affidavit as to their beliefs as well as their acts.

The hearings which my cosponsor, Senator Joseph S. Clark of
Pennsylvania, and I have conducted on our bill make it abundantly
clear that this provision hinders the objectives of the National Defense Education Act—seriously handicaps our colleges and universities—and unnecessarily slanders the students who apply for loans so
that they can complete their education.

Such an affidavit is superfluous at best and discriminatory and subversive of the purposes of the Act at worst. The Act announces in
the very first section that there is a need for cultivating and protecting
our resources of human skills and brains. It points out:

> The present emergency demands that additional and ade-
> quate educational opportunities be made available. The defense
> of this Nation depends upon the mastery of modern technology
> developed from complex scientific principles. We must increase
> our efforts to identify and educate more of the talent of our
> Nation. This requires programs that will give assurances that no
> student of ability will be denied an opportunity for higher edu-
> cation because of financial need.

Yet the affidavit requirements of the act have caused at least nine
of our colleges to refuse all participation under it. Many others are
reluctant to participate. Representatives of virtually all our colleges
have testified that the section is offensive and should be repealed.
More than just the right of the Government to demand an oath

of allegiance as a condition to a loan is involved. If we are to be faithful to our basic principles of freedom of thought, if we are to encourage the restless minds in our universities to go beyond the frontiers of knowledge, if we are to remove the inhibitions that might foreclose inquiry, we must resist any attempt to force our students into a preconceived mold.

It is not enough to say that we will undoubtedly have enough college students to fill our colleges regardless of the ultimate fate of this provision. We need to develop the best talent in the nation; and, in the words of the Act, "No student of ability will be denied an opportunity for higher education because of financial need."

The loyalty oath is a direct descendant of the religious test of the Middle Ages. These oaths were so repugnant to our Founding Fathers that our Constitution has a specific provision prohibiting them.

Those who framed the Constitution knew, as men of good will have always known, that no one can be forced to be devout by being forced to swear that he does not believe in the locally unpopular religion.

Moreover, the imposition of this condition to a loan of funds for educational purposes is an insupportable invasion of educational autonomy, which has grave implications for the integrity of our educational system.

Finally, and entirely apart from these policy considerations, this requirement is technically defective for the following reasons:

First, it raises serious constitutional questions in seeming to approve the concept that "belief" as opposed to overt action may be a basis for sanctions.

Second, it imposes an impossible burden upon our educational institutions who interpret the section, for each school may have a different concept for what is necessary to prove a belief in an organization which believes in the overthrow of the U.S. Government by unconstitutional methods.

Third, as the Secretary of the Department of Health, Education and Welfare pointed out in his testimony, the inclusion of the oath and affidavit requirement in the National Defense Education Act will make it necessary for educators and students to go through a meaningless, unenforcible procedure that adds greatly to the cost of administering the program without making any real contribution to national security.

Mr. President, the oath and affidavit requirements of the National

Defense Education Act are repugnant to our history, our traditions, our law, and our basic philosophy. They have interfered with our efforts to improve our educational opportunities without benefiting us in any way. Rather, they represent a serious new danger to the freedom of thought and inquiry that we as a nation are committed to support.

22. Seven Peaceful Revolutions of Our Time

SEATTLE, WASHINGTON
JUNE 20, 1959

Today at least seven peaceful revolutions are rocking our nation and our world.

These seven peaceful revolutions, each of them startling to behold and fantastic in its impact, constitute the basic agenda of our time—our unfinished business—the real issues of the 1960 campaign.

1. *First is the revolution in population.* The year 1960 will conclude the largest ten-year growth in the history of our country—a growth which equals the entire population of Poland or Spain—and a growth which has been concentrated largely in our metropolitan areas. At this rate, we will double our population by the end of the century, only forty-one years away. Most of the world is also going through such a burst of population.

But this population explosion—largely in our metropolitan areas—has not been matched in public plans and programs. Fifteen million American families live in substandard housing, says the Bureau of Census—nearly five million of our urban homes still lack plumbing of any kind—nearly seven million urban homes need to be totally replaced—and still our crowded cities grow. And yet urban redevelopment projects initiated as far back as 1950 are still incomplete. Our inadequate streets and highways are clogged. Public transportation has broken down. Most airports are not ready for the jet age. Our older cities are decaying at the core—and now we are witnessing a new and disturbing phenomenon: suburban slums.

Along with more people have come more children. Between 1946 and 1958, nearly 51 million children were born in this country—a number greater than the entire population of 1880—and, as a result, we face the most critical classroom shortage in our history. Hundreds of thousands of boys and girls must go to school part time. Millions more must go to school in classes of forty or more.

We have not been prepared for this crisis. The Republicans have defeated every effort to obtain Federal assistance for new school construction.

But while we have more and more young Americans, we also have more and more older Americans. Soon 10 per cent of our population will be over the age of sixty-five. But their social security checks have been eaten away by inflation—their chronic illnesses are not covered by group insurance. Their housing needs are unmet. Those still able to work are the first to be fired and the last to be rehired. They are, in the words of the song, "too old to work and too young to die."

These problems of population pressure will continue. They exist on a world as well as national level. They cannot be ignored, they cannot be halfheartedly met, they cannot be vetoed out of existence.

2. *Second is the revolution on the farm.* In 1958, on the smallest acreage in forty years, with a farm population of five million below that of the previous decade, our farms nevertheless produced the largest crop—and the largest surplus—in our history.

But under our present farm program, our abundance is a curse and not a blessing—for the family farmer, for the nation, and for the hungry world. A Democratic farm program would express the nation's conscience by sharing the nation's abundance—with the needy of other nations and with our own needy here at home. This revolution in American agriculture, extended wisely to the world, can mean the end of hunger everywhere.

3. *Third is the revolution of technology and energy—the wonders of automation and atomization.* Mechanical computers can now conduct centuries of calculation in a few hours. In every kind of endeavor, machine is replacing man—and man is looking for work. In the midst of prosperity and high employment, we still have over 3.5 million unemployed—a third of them out of work for more than four months—and a long list of distressed areas with chronic labor surpluses.

We rejoice in the wonders of automation. But we cannot forget our unemployed workers and our depressed cities. We must gear our technological progress to the needs of a developing world. There is no excuse for continuing unemployment in the light of these great world-wide needs.

We must also recognize, and be prepared for, the new demands this age will place upon our sources of energy—electrical energy, atomic energy, and every other kind. Every American uses every year an amount of energy which would require nine tons of coal or its equivalent—180 times as much as the average Asian—and yet our demands are still growing, as are those of the rest of the world.

This requires that we make the maximum use of our natural resources—that we harness our rivers for the public good—and that we begin now a program of civilian atomic reactors that will give us the energy we need.

4. *Fourth is the revolution in the standard of living.* As a people, we Americans enjoy the highest per capita income the world has ever known. For most Americans, poverty, famine, and pestilence are words from the ancient past. Moreover, the means for raising the standard of living of all the people of the world to a level of decency now exist.

But the harsh facts of the matter are that this revolution of living standards is not even shared by all Americans, not to mention most of the world's people. Millions of workers have no Federal protection against substandard wages, particularly women in our retail stores and service establishments. Millions of others are receiving little more than the one-dollar minimum. Increasing and extending our minimum wage laws—so that all Americans can share this revolutionary standard of living—is an essential national program. This must go hand in hand with our world program of technical and economic assistance to the less developed nations.

5. *Fifth in the field of national security is the revolution in weapons development.* In terms of military proximity and warning, we are closer to the Soviet Union today than France was to Germany in 1939. Devastation is literally minutes away.

This challenge cannot be met by men who have delivered us into our present position of unpreparedness—by those who fix weapons policies as a part of our budgetary policies. We must refuse to accept a cheap, second-best defense—and see that we mobilize the money and brain power to do the necessary job.

6. *Sixth is the revolution in the underdeveloped nations of the world.* The astounding explosive growth of the world's population, which will also double in this century, is centered largely on those nations of the Middle East, Asia, Africa, and Latin America least able to support it.

The world may be enjoying more prosperity than ever before—

but, strange as it may seem, it has never seen so much poverty in all its history. If these nations—including such key nations as India, engaged in a fierce economic competition with Red China that will determine the future of all Asia—are to get ahead of their population increases, they must step up the expansion of their economies, they must increase their capital development, and this means they must obtain development capital from the wealthy nations of the West. Our best tool to help the underdeveloped world is the Development Loan Fund. The Republicans have starved this fund— they have stunted its growth. We must fill the gap.

7. *Seventh is the revolution of nationalism.* In Asia, Latin America, and particularly in Africa, man's eternal desire to be free is rising to the fore.

But the principles of self-determination are still being contested in some parts of the globe. Too often it is a struggle between a white minority and a colored majority, with dangerous implications for our future. This requires that we in this nation make completely clear our strong, unequivocal stand on civil rights—not only to help us abroad but to strengthen us here at home.

We cannot doubt that these peoples eventually will, and ought to be, free and equal. The only question is one of timing—and whether, once that freedom is achieved, they will regard the United States as friend or foe. This nation, the home of the Declaration of Independence, should have led this nationalist revolution instead of helping to throttle it—and I am hopeful that, if it is not too late, a new Administration can still fulfill that role.

23. *Conventional Forces in the Atomic Age*

LAKE CHARLES, LOUISIANA
OCTOBER 16, 1959

No problem is of greater importance to every American than our national security and defense. And no aspect of our defense capabilities under this Administration should be cause for greater concern than our lag in conventional weapons and ground forces.

We must be prepared in this nation to fight an all-out nuclear war—or else we cannot deter an all-out nuclear attack upon us. We must have more and better missiles, more and better warning systems and—until we do—a stronger Strategic Air Force. A capacity for massive retaliation is the only answer to the threat of massive attack. But it is not the only answer to all threats of Communist aggression. No civilized, peace-loving nation is enthusiastic about initiating a nuclear holocaust—an Armageddon which would unleash on both sides enough destructive power to devastate the world many times over. Nor is there any certainty that our allies would be willing to support such a move, except where the stakes were very high.

So in practice our nuclear retaliatory power is not enough. It cannot deter Communist aggression which is too limited to justify atomic war. It cannot protect uncommitted nations against a Communist takeover using local or guerrilla forces. It cannot be used in so-called "brush-fire" peripheral wars. It was not used in Korea, Indochina, Hungary, Suez, Lebanon, Quemoy, Tibet, or Laos. In short, it cannot prevent the Communists from gradually nibbling away at the fringe of the Free World's territory and strength, until our security has been steadily eroded in piecemeal fashion—each Red advance being too small to justify massive retaliation with all its risks. And history demonstrates that this is the greater threat—not an all-out nuclear attack.

But unfortunately our defense priorities ignore this history. Under every military budget submitted by this Administration, we have been preparing primarily to fight the one kind of war we least want to fight and are least likely to fight. We have been driving ourselves into a corner where the only choice is all or nothing at all, world devastation or submission—a choice that necessarily causes us to hesitate on the brink and leaves the initiative in the hands of our enemies.

We have steadily cut the numbers and strength of our ground forces—our Army and Marines. We have steadily failed to provide our conventional forces with modern conventional weapons, with effective versatile firepower. And we have particularly failed to provide the airlift and sealift capacity necessary to give those forces the swift mobility they need to protect our commitments around the world. Do you realize that some of our units entering the Lebanon "pipeline," so to speak, at the time of the Iraqi revolt, emerged at the other end only to find that by then the dust had settled—we had already recognized the new regime—and it was time to be evacuated?

Back in 1954, when these manpower cuts began, I offered an

amendment to prevent a cut in Army divisions from nineteen to seventeen. Senators Gore, Mansfield, Symington, Humphrey, Monroney, and Lehman joined in sponsoring the amendment, and a majority of Democratic Senators supported it. But the amendment lost—and so did the cause of our ability to fulfill far-flung commitments in Berlin, the Middle East, the Far East, and throughout the world. And we lost, General Gavin told us once he left the Army, because "Congress was assured that our combat strength was not being reduced. We were simply cutting the fat. . . . [But] the contrary was the case."

The Administration's answer to all of this—other than to boast of its massive retaliatory power, which is no answer at all in a local limited war—has always been to stress its reliance on so-called tactical atomic weapons and on "clean" bombs. They say their plan is to use these smaller nuclear armaments as conventional weapons in a limited war—and that their effectiveness is so great that any enemy will be deterred from an attack by a smaller ground force possessing these weapons. In this way, says the Administration, we can save men and money—and our defense policies must save money.

But small atomic weapons suffer from much the same handicaps as large atomic weapons. If we use them, the Russians use them. And even the smallest atomic weapon—a shell with a one-kiloton warhead, for example—would unleash one hundred times the destructive power of World War II's largest conventional bombs—and they were considered long-range strategic instruments of total war, not for tactical objectives. And even the smallest atomic weapon today produces fission—and thus fall-out—and thus can reduce the area in which it is used (a friendly area presumably, in these local wars) to a complete shambles. And as the enemy's losses increase, so will its temptation to raise the ante to all-out nuclear warfare.

Inevitably, the use of small nuclear armaments will lead to larger and larger nuclear armaments on both sides, until the world-wide holocaust has begun.

In short, their use—like that of our massive retaliatory capacity—will still involve great risks. They will still be of limited value against guerrilla-type action. They will still cause such destruction as to make "liberation" through that route meaningless. They will still be employed only with the greatest hesitation, for fear that they will turn a limited war into a world-wide atomic nightmare.

We need tactical atomic weapons—to deter their use by the Russians, to serve as a shield for our conventional forces on the battlefront. But we still need those conventional forces on that front. We still need the air and sea transport necessary to get them there. Throughout military history, any enemy has been less likely to use the kind of forces he knows we possess—but he will not hesitate to use those forces he knows we do not possess. And the Russians and the Red Chinese, aware of our weaknesses, and using satellites or guerrillas where possible, will continue to nibble away at our periphery.

But we can still reverse this trend. We can increase our manpower, modernize our conventional arms, reorganize our personnel policies, and provide the necessary air and sea transport. And we can stop advising our allies that they no longer need to bear the cost of conventional forces in this nuclear age. We need not match the Russians and Chinese man for man. We cannot hope to do so. But we can build, alongside of our atomic might, conventional forces and weapons that will prevent any quick Communist takeovers on the ground—enough to let them know that they will be in for a long, costly struggle if they pursue this means of attaining their objectives. That we can do—that we must do before it becomes too late.

24. Citizens of the World: The Duty of the Scholar

UNIVERSITY OF WISCONSIN
MADISON, WISCONSIN
JUNE 16, 1958

Every American is now involved in the world. "The tragic events of . . . turmoil through which we have just passed have made us citizens of the world," said Woodrow Wilson. For a time we tried to dodge this new responsibility, but the world depression, World War II, and the Cold War have finally conveyed his message: "There can be no turning back. Our own fortunes as a nation are involved—whether we would have it so or not."

The emphasis in recent months, as our educational crisis becomes clearer, has been on educating more scientists and engineers, to develop better weapons, to fight bigger wars. We are concerned, too, about language training for our diplomats, about future military leaders, about competing with the Russians in physics and oceanography and a host of similar vital subjects. All this is important. But arms and science alone will not save us.

In our concern for the future of America, we dare not neglect the education of its politicians.

I realize that most Americans are not concerned about the education of politicians. No education is considered necessary for political success, except how to find your way around a smoke-filled room. Those of you who are graduating this spring are urged to follow any number of other careers. But few, if any, will urge you to become politicians. Mothers may still want their sons to grow up to be President, but, according to a famous Gallup poll of some years ago, some 73 per cent do not want them to become politicians in the process.

Successful politicians, according to Walter Lippmann, are "insecure and intimidated men," who "advance politically only as they placate, appease, bribe, seduce, bamboozle, or otherwise manage to manipulate" the views and votes of the people who elect them. Years ago the humorist Artemus Ward declared: "I am not a politician, and my other habits are good also."

Politics, in short, has become one of our most neglected, our most abused, and our most ignored professions. Unfortunately, this disdain for the political profession is not only shared but intensified in our academic institutions. For both teachers and students find it difficult to accept the differences between the laboratory and the legislature. In the former, the goal is truth, pure and simple, without regard to changing currents of public opinion; in the latter, compromises and majorities and procedural customs and rights affect the ultimate decision as to what is right or just or good.

And when they realize the difference, most intellectuals consider their chief function to be that of the critic—and politicians are sensitive to critics (possibly because we have so many of them).

Of course, the intellectual's attitude is partly defensive—for he has been regarded with so much suspicion and hostility by political figures and their constituents that a recent survey of American intellectuals by a national magazine elicited from one of our foremost literary figures the guarded response, "I ain't no intellectual."

And so the worlds of practical politics and academic scholarship have drifted apart. "Don't teach my boy poetry," a mother recently wrote the headmaster of Eton; "don't teach my boy poetry, he's going to stand for Parliament."

But this mutual suspicion was not always the case—and I would ask those of you who look with disdain and disfavor upon the possibilities of a political career to remember that our nation's first great politicians were traditionally our ablest, most respected, most talented leaders, men who moved from one field to another with amazing versatility and vitality. A contemporary described Thomas Jefferson as "a gentleman of 32, who could calculate an eclipse, survey an estate, tie an artery, plan an edifice, try a cause, break a horse, dance a minuet, and play the violin."

John Quincy Adams, after being summarily dismissed from the Senate for a notable display of independence, could become Boylston Professor of Rhetoric and Oratory at Harvard and then become a great Secretary of State. (Those were the happy days when Harvard professors had no difficulty getting Senate confirmation.) Daniel Webster could throw thunderbolts at Hayne on the Senate floor and then stroll a few steps down the corridor and dominate the Supreme Court as the foremost lawyer of his time.

This link between American scholarship and the American politician remained for more than a century. A little more than one hundred years ago, in the Presidential campaign of 1856, the Republicans sent three brilliant orators around the campaign circuit: William Cullen Bryant, Henry Wadsworth Longfellow, and Ralph Waldo Emerson. (In those times, apparently, the "eggheads" were all Republicans.)

It is clear, in any event, that these were men of talent—that in former times our foremost scholars were interested in becoming our foremost politicians.

I would urge therefore that each of you, regardless of your chosen occupation, consider entering the field of politics at some stage in your career. It is not necessary that you be famous, that you effect radical changes in the government or that you are acclaimed by the public for your efforts. It is not even necessary that you be successful.

I ask only that you offer to the political arena, and to the critical problems of our society which are decided therein, the benefit of the talents which society has helped to develop in you. I ask you to decide, as Goethe put it, whether you will be an anvil—or a hammer. The formal phases of the "anvil" stage are now completed for many of you, though hopefully you will continue to absorb still more in the years ahead. The question now is whether you are to be a hammer—whether you are to give to the world in which you were reared and educated the broadest benefits of that education.

It is not enough to lend your talents to merely discussing the issues and deploring their solutions. But "Would you have counted him a friend of Ancient Greece," as George William Curtis asked a century ago during the Kansas-Nebraska Controversy, "who quietly discussed the theory of patriotism on that Greek summer day through whose hopeless and immortal hours Leonidas and his three hundred stood at Thermopylae for liberty? Was John Milton to conjugate Greek verbs in his library, or talk of the liberty of the ancient Shunammites, when the liberty of Englishmen was imperilled?" No, the duty of the scholar—particularly in a republic such as ours—is to contribute his objective views and his sense of liberty to the affairs of his state and nation.

If you are to be among the rulers of our land, from precinct captain to President, if you are willing to enter the abused and neglected profession of politics, then let me tell you that we stand in serious need of the fruits of your education. We do not need political scholars whose education has been so specialized as to exclude them from participation in current events. What we need are men who can ride easily over broad fields of knowledge and recognize the mutual dependence of the two worlds of politics and scholarship.

We want from you not the sneers of the cynics nor the despair of the fainthearted. We ask of you enlightenment, vision, illumination.

25. A Farm Program to Promote World Peace

MIDWEST FARM CONFERENCE
SPRINGFIELD, ILLINOIS
OCTOBER 24, 1959

The time to repair the roof is when the sun is shining—and the time to build a sound, long-range farm program is now.

I do not pretend to say that a Democratic Congress or Administration will have all the answers to all the problems. I do not agree with those who think that all we have to do is dismiss Mr. Benson and get a new Secretary of Agriculture. This problem is bigger and deeper than one man or even one Administration. There are no quick, easy, painless remedies. On the contrary, I think the farmers themselves are getting tired of hearing from politicians in either camp about some new short-term expedient, a wonder drug aimed at treating some current symptom, instead of getting at the real problem. I do not intend to fill your ear with such promises today.

But, without attempting to speak for all Democrats, without attempting to write a farm bill here and now, and forgetting for the moment about parity indexes, acreage allotments, production payments, and all other techniques, let me say that I believe any Democratic farm program must be based on the following six fundamental principles:

1. *First,* farm abundance should be treated as a blessing and not as a curse. There are still more than 1 billion 800 million people in other lands trying to get by on less than a subsistence diet. There are still tremendous possibilities for using food as a means of capital investment in underdeveloped countries, even in those that have no food shortages. There are still markets in Europe and elsewhere buying less of our foodstuffs today than they did twenty years ago. There are still seventeen million Americans going to bed each night suffering from malnutrition. This country still stands thirteenth in terms of milk and dairy product consumption, and fifth in terms of meat consumption per person. And above all, there is still a fantastic population growth in this country. Next year's census-takers, going from door to door, will find that we have become a nation of 180 million people. We will by the end of this century have doubled our population. And every year, as our population grows larger, we are losing some 400,000 acres of cropland by erosion and another one million acres to our growing cities, airports, reservoirs, highways, and military reservations.

At the same time, the population of the world is multiplying faster than the world's capacity to produce food. Even if our entire food surplus this year were distributed around the world to all the hungry and all the needy, it would mean only the equivalent of approximately two teacups full of rice every seventeen days for each hungry person.

In short, what Mr. Benson now complains about in terms of a food surplus could soon turn into a permanent food shortage. We dare not continue a course designed to abandon our soil, waste our water, and cut back our cropland if we are to assure every American a minimum standard of nutrition for all time to come.

If we can but look at our farm abundance in this light, we see it as a national asset, not a liability—an asset which the Communists do not have and cannot obtain—a weapon more powerful for preserving the Free World than any in our arsenal of armaments.

Two specific programs are needed. We need a "food for peace" program that has real imagination and drive—that can use our surpluses as a powerful instrument for aiding economic development, strengthening alliances, and helping less fortunate people in all parts of the globe. But we also need to do more for the needy and hungry here at home. And I hope that the Congress next year will take action on the bill which I have introduced directing a full-scale attack upon this problem—taking the job out of the hands of Mr. Benson, who has shown little interest in it, and giving it to the department responsible for those on pensions or public assistance.

2. *Secondly*, any national farm program should be based primarily on the promotion and preservation of the family farm. That is the basic unit here in Illinois—that is the way it must continue to be. We have no wish to become a nation of giant commercial corporation farms and absentee landlords. Our whole vitality as a nation depends on a contrary course. So let us beware of programs that aid most those who need it least.

3. *Third*, any future farm program should be run for farmers by farmers. Basic administration on the local level should be in the hands of farmer committees elected by farmers themselves. No bureaucrat, no economist or scientist, knows the needs and trends and variations of the local farm picture as well as the local farmers. On the national level, we need a Federal Farm Board comprised of leaders from the key commodity groups—a board which can explain the farmer's needs to the Administration and the Administration's hopes to the farmer. This would be a board made up of real farmers —and by farmers, I do not mean some of those whom Mr. Benson has appointed to high offices—so-called "farmers" who own one cow and ten banks. I mean those who contributed so much to the local administration of our farm programs in the past—and who can and should do so in the future.

4. *Fourth*, any Democratic farm program should encourage, not retard the growth of the co-operative movement. Co-operatives can help the farmer escape some of the cost-price squeeze. They can give him some stability and bargaining power which he otherwise could not have. They can help both the farmer and the consumer by cutting this growing spread between the price at the farm and the price at the store. In those Scandinavian countries which have nationwide co-operatives marketing arrangements, I am told the dairy farmer gets approximately seventy cents of every dollar spent by the consumer. Here it is forty-five cents—or only a little more than half that figure.

The Federal Government could aid these co-ops, and enable them to pool their financial resources for mutual benefits, in the same way that it has helped REA co-ops. It can offer technical assistance, financial credit, and legal authority.

5. *Fifth,* any future farm program must concentrate on cutting the farmer's costs. The high interest rate policy of this Administration has hurt the farmer looking for credit more than anyone else—and it has held him back even further by making it more difficult for him to buy more efficient machinery on the installment plan. The REA program of this Administration has not been one of promoting lower electric rates for our farm homes. It has done little or nothing about the families that still lack electricity—and little or nothing about the 40 per cent of our farm families in this great electronic age who have no telephone service whatsoever.

6. *Sixth and finally,* any future farm program should assure our nation's farms of a fair share of the national net income. This does not mean that farm prices must always rise—but they should not be the only ones to fall. The farmer does not want to ration poverty —he wants to share abundance. He has made a tremendous capital investment in his farm—and he wants a comparable return on that investment. He puts in a long, hard work-week all year around—he wants comparable wages for his labor. Economists predict that during the next two years wages will go up—business income will go up—our standard of living will go up. We cannot let the farmer down.

A program based upon these six fundamental principles would, I am convinced, restore common sense and common justice to our farm policy. Only then will it be possible to gear national production to international need—to grow food for stomachs and not for storage—to support the farmer's prices and income at a level which will cover his costs and a reasonable profit, and at the same time substantially reduce the cost of this program to the American taxpayer.

26. The Years the Locusts Have Eaten

KEYNOTE ADDRESS, ANNUAL CONVENTION
DEMOCRATIC PARTY OF WISCONSIN
MILWAUKEE, WISCONSIN
NOVEMBER 13, 1959

Twenty-three years ago, in a bitter debate in the House of Commons, Winston Churchill charged the British Government with acute blindness to the menace of Nazi Germany, with gross negligence in the maintenance of the island's defenses, and with indifferent, indecisive leadership of British foreign policy and British public opinion. The preceding years of drift and impotency, he said, were "the years the locusts have eaten."

Since January, 1953, this nation has passed through a similar period. When we should have been decisive we, too, were in doubt. When we should have sailed hard into the wind, we, too, drifted. When we should have planned anew, sacrificed, and marched ahead, we, too, stood still, sought the easy way, and looked to the past.

And these, too, were precious years, vital years, to the greatness of our nation, as the thirties were to Great Britain. For on the other side of the globe another great power was not standing still and she was not looking back and she was not drifting in doubt. The Soviet Union needed these years to catch up with us, to surpass us, to take away from us our prestige and our influence and even our power in the world community. They want to "bury" us, as Mr. Khrushchev says, not necessarily by war but by possessing the most powerful military establishment, by boasting the most impressive scientific achievements, by dominating the most markets and trade routes, by influencing the most needy or neutral nations through aid and trade and diplomatic penetration. That is how they hope to "bury" us—to extend their sphere of influence, to build respect for the Communist system, and to prove to the underdeveloped countries that their route, the Communist route, is the better route to industrial development.

And that is what the Soviets have been working on these last seven years of American drift—"the years the locusts have eaten."

I do not say that all was perfection in 1952, under the last Democratic Administration. But we *were* in 1952 the unchallenged leaders of the world in every sphere—militarily, economically, and all the rest. We were building strength and friendships around the world. We were successfully containing the spread of Communist imperialism. And we *were* the leaders of a Free World community that was united, dynamic, and growing stronger every day.

And now it is 1959. The Russians beat us into outer space. They beat us around the sun. They beat us to the moon. Half of Indochina has disappeared behind the Iron Curtain. Tibet and Hungary have been crushed. For the first time in history, Russia has its long-sought political foothold in the Middle East—and even an economic foothold in Latin America. And meanwhile we have been forced to abandon the Baghdad Pact, to send Marines to Lebanon and our fleet to Formosa, to endure our Vice President being spat upon by our former "Good Neighbors," and to forget our plans for a meaningful NATO.

But all these more dramatic, more publicized events only symbolize what has happened. The seven-year record of Russian gains and American gaps is not a pleasant one. But let us total up the balance sheet. Let us face the facts.

1. *Militarily.* I would not say that the Russians possess an over-all superiority. But we have fallen behind the Soviet Union in the development and production of ballistic missiles—both intercontinental and those of intermediate range. They have surpassed us in the thrust of rocket engines, jet engines, and new types of fuel. They now have more long-range, modernized submarines than we do— more, in fact, than Nazi Germany had entering World War II—and they may well be pulling ahead of us in numbers of long-range jet bombers with a nuclear bomb capacity. Their continental air defense is thought to be superior—their installations better dispersed, better concealed, and better protected.

There is no doubt, of course, of their superiority in numbers of military manpower, both mechanized and otherwise. All of NATO possesses 21 divisions; the Soviet Union has 175 divisions—2.5 million men. They develop new weapons, General Gavin estimates, twice as fast. They devote twice as much of their resources to military efforts as we do—even though we are twice as rich. They have passed us in the production of military end items, and caught up with us in total military expenditures. They make decisions faster. They seem to utilize their military intelligence better. And they have the largest espionage network in the world's history.

All this they have done—while we, for seven years, have cut our forces, reduced our budgets, held back our missile programs, wasted our money and time and scientific talent, and all the while assuring the American people that we could never be second-best. Democrats in the Congress tried to fight these trends. But we did not control the Defense Department, or the Budget Bureau, or the White House.

2. *In education, science and research,* the story under this Administration has been the same. We harassed our scientists. We overcrowded our schools. We cut back our research. We underpaid our teachers. We let brilliant students drop out after high school. The President would not support an adequate program to construct desperately needed classrooms, at either the public school or college level.

But meanwhile, in the Soviet Union, the Russians were putting twice as much of their resources into education. Their teachers commanded top salaries. Their classrooms contained fewer pupils per teacher. Their curricula were stronger in terms of science, mathematics, physics, and languages. Their most talented students were kept in school. The new Soviet budget puts its biggest increases in science and education.

And as a result, it is estimated that they will soon have three times as many scientists, technicians, and engineers as we do. They are already graduating more. And their brilliant scientific achievements are not only aimed at capturing headlines—they are aimed at capturing the hearts and minds of men. The Philippine Ambassador to the U.N., Carlos Romulo, stated the blunt truth in these words: "The masses of Asia and Africa have remained quiet for several generations [believing] . . . that the West was invincible. [But] this belief has been shattered. . . . The Soviets sent a satellite into orbit around the earth, another around the sun, and then landed a space rocket on the moon. To underdeveloped countries these achievements, plus Soviet advances in technology, education, economic and military power, have been little short of miraculous."

I am convinced that American education and American science, given the necessary funds and effort and leadership, can also work miracles—miracles that could well surpass any the Russians have ever envisioned. But it will take a new Administration to do the job.

3. The third vital area of competition is *in economic power.*

"Development of Soviet economic might," said Mr. Khrushchev to the Twenty-first Communist Party Conference, "will give Communism the decisive edge in the international balance of power." No area of competition is more vital to our leadership and prestige. But for seven years we have kept our sights low, fluctuating between inflation and recession, handicapped by serious pockets of high unemployment, low purchasing power, and declining farm income, hamstrung by high interest rates and tight money. While our annual average rate of growth was thus roughly 3 per cent, the Russians were up to 6 per cent, twice as high. Their industrial capacity is expanding nearly three times as fast as ours, at an annual rate of 9.5 per cent. To be sure, they started a lot further back and they still have a long way to go—but thirty years ago this was a relatively backward nation! If these trends continue, they could increase their defense budget by over 50 per cent in the next seven years with no new strain.

Today, despite our greater wealth, they roughly match our contribution for defense, foreign aid, industrial investment and research and development—and their new 1960 budget, a peacetime record, continues this emphasis. In 1958, for example, Russia produced four times as many machine tools as the United States; but we produced fifty times as many automobiles. We were way ahead in washing machines, refrigerators, freezers, and TV sets.

Much of our steel output—which has been declining—goes into these autos and appliances, into our homes, office buildings, and shopping centers. But practically all of Russia's growing steel capacity —expanding 9 per cent every year—goes into heavy steel shapes and plates—for missiles, planes, and satellites, for submarines and guns, for machinery and tools to expand their own industry at home and those of hopeful nations abroad. Unlike our own, their steel output since 1951 has nearly doubled—and another 50 per cent increase is expected by 1965.

Similar statistics could be cited for Soviet coal, oil, and lumber— three American industries with chronic problems that have been badly neglected or postponed under this Administration. Similar data could be cited for Soviet fuel and energy output, and their use of commercial atomic power—and yet we in this country continue to waste great hydroelectric dam sites and delay an already dawdling atomic power program. By 1965 they aim to outproduce us in cement. Already their transportation system is growing faster than ours. They are investing more in their railroads. Soviet jet transports were in operation three years before our Boeing jets began their first commercial service—and Moscow, controlling as it does so many of the best air routes, is rapidly becoming one of the air capitals of the world.

4. *In agriculture,* while we are weakening our farm economy and penalizing our farmers for their increased efficiency and productivity, the Russians—as Mr. Khrushchev made clear—are determined to pass us. Already their agricultural production is expanding faster than their population. Their grain production is up an estimated 30 per cent. Their production of fertilizer has expanded, on the average, some 11 per cent every year since 1951. And now they are out to match us in meat, butter, and milk. If our agricultural economy collapses, if our so-called surpluses remain a liability to the taxpayers instead of a blessing to a hungry world, then they, not we, may become the world's greatest arsenal of food. But this need not happen—and I am hopeful that a new Administration, and a new Secretary of Agriculture, would see that it does not happen.

5. Finally, look at the contrasting changes *in aid and trade abroad.* When we abruptly abandoned the Aswan Dam in Egypt as economically unfeasible, the Russians went ahead to finance it. When we refuse Latin-American countries loans for their oil development programs, because we think it should be left up to private enterprise, the Russians move in and make the loan. While we starve the Development Loan Fund—our best tool to help the underdeveloped world get on its own feet—the Sino-Soviet bloc has already actually passed us in economic assistance to selected key areas, the potential trouble spots of the world: Indonesia, Ceylon, the United Arab Republic States of Egypt and Syria, Afghanistan, Yemen—and, more recently—Iraq, Nepal, and Ethiopia.

The number of Red technicians in other countries has increased at twice the rate of our own. The loans available to underdeveloped nations are at an interest rate below that of any Western source. They sell machinery below cost—they buy strategic commodities above the world price. With less expenditure but more direction, their economic offensive continues to score.

Their *cultural* program is a part of this. They have spent more than one-half billion dollars over the past few years to send their artists, dancers, and other entertainers all over the world—we have allotted $2 to $3 million a year for this purpose. They spent $50 million on their exhibit at the Brussels World's Fair—we spent $14 million.

This is what has been going on—for seven long years . . . and that is why I say they are "years the locusts have eaten." I do not say the picture is all bad. I do not say that the other side of the ledger is all blank. But neither can we afford to ignore these facts and their implication any longer.

I do not think the American people have been made aware of these facts. We have been complacent, self-contented, easygoing. It brings to mind the words of Franklin Roosevelt in 1928, after two terms of Harding and Coolidge. "The soul of our country," said F. D. R., "lulled by material prosperity, has passed through eight gray years."

"Eight gray years"—"years that the locusts have eaten." Years of drift, of falling behind, of postponing decisions and crises. And, as a result, the burdens that will face the next Administration will be tremendous. The gaps between ourselves and the Soviet Union will be many—and dangerous—and still growing. "If they succeed and we fail," CIA Chief Allen Dulles has warned, "it will only be because of our complacency—and because they have devoted a far greater share of their power, skill, and resources to our *destruction* than we have been willing to dedicate to our own *preservation*."

But it is not too late. For we have in this country all the strength and all the vision and all the will we need—if we will only use them. And perhaps these seven gray years, and these spectacular Russian gains, have awakened us from our sleep. The Russian pennant on the moon has shown us our task. Mr. Khrushchev's confident boasts have outlined our challenge. And I think we can live up to it. I think we can make up for the "years the locusts have eaten." I think we can close the gaps and pull ahead.

But to do this we must put an end to this depression of our national spirit—we must put these dull, gray years behind us and take on the rendezvous with destiny that is assigned us. We must regain the American purpose and promise and become again the creative and purposeful people which, except when we have doped ourselves, we really are. Let us, then, with full production and full employment at home, begin to play our full part in the development of a world of peace and freedom—let us join the human race.

27. Are We Up to the Task?

WASHINGTON, D. C.
JANUARY 1, 1960

Certainly it is time for a change—time for us, in the words of Walter Lippmann, "to come alive and to be alert and to show vigor, and not to keep mouthing the same old slogans, and not to dawdle along in the same old ruts."

But the primary point is that, whether we like it or not, this is a time *of* change. As a people that set out to change the world, I think we should like it, however difficult the challenges. For no nation is at its best except under great challenge. The question for us now is whether in a changing world we will respond in a way befitting "the land of the free and the home of the brave"—whether we will be at our best in these crucial years of our world leadership —whether we will measure up to the task awaiting us.

That task is to do all in our power to see that the changes taking place all around us—in our cities, our countryside, our economy, within the Western world, in the uncommitted world, in the Soviet empire, on all continents—lead to more freedom for more men and to world peace. It is only when the iron is hot that it can be molded. The iron of the new world being forged today is now ready to be molded. Our job is to shape it, so far as we can, into the world we want for ourselves and our children and for all men.

This will require that we recapture our national purpose and redouble our energy. For we seem to have lost both the sense of the promise of America and the will to fulfill it.

Our Declaration of Independence gave hope to all the world because it spoke in terms of liberty for "all men," and not for just the privileged few. And in every succeeding statement of American purpose—the Gettysburg Address, Wilson's "Fourteen Points," the "Four Freedoms," the Preamble to the Marshall Plan legislation, the Preamble to the "Point Four" legislation—that same emphasis on the rights and needs of "all men" has been present. In different contexts we gave these testaments of national faith and purpose a specific meaning which led a grateful humanity everywhere to raise monuments in their hearts where they honored the very word "American." Yet we cannot rest on those monuments today.

The world is now waiting for us to reapply the faith we inherited from our fathers, and to give them a new creative validity in the uncharted world that surrounds us. The road ahead, to be sure, is a hard road, a road that man has never traveled before, a road full of great obstacles. But America has never long faltered in the face of new challenges.

It is true that in the 1920's we retreated into isolation, stagnation, and normalcy, keeping out new immigrants and new ideas, winking at corruption at home and ignoring dictators abroad—and then finally collapsing into a deep economic depression.

But in the first one hundred days of the New Deal this nation recovered faith in itself and its future. "Governments can err," F. D. R. said, "Presidents do make mistakes; but the immortal Dante tells us that divine justice weighs the sins of the cold-blooded and the sins of the warm-hearted in different scales. Better the occasional faults of a Government that lives in a spirit of charity than the consistent omissions of a Government frozen in the ice of its own indifference."

History repeats itself and once again we have lived through a temporary period of national retreat. On too many pressing issues we have had "a Government frozen in the ice of its own indifference." Some of these are old problems which we had no excuse to ignore. For so long as there are slums in which people have to live, so long as there are schools that are overcrowded or antiquated or inadequate, so long as there are men in search of decent jobs and homes, so long as there are sick people in need of medical care, so long as anyone suffers discrimination by reason of color, race, religion, or national origin, the work of America is not done. What makes the neglect of these old domestic problems even more inexcusable are the new problems in the world to meet which a strong, healthy America is so necessary.

"No nation has ever been great that was not called to greatness by its leaders," Edward R. Murrow has remarked. The signs of our lack of national leadership—of our loss of national vision—are all too clear and present. Not having been called to greatness, not having been shown the great goals and the great dangers ahead, we have, as a nation, gone soft—physically, mentally, spiritually soft. With a tough test facing us for a generation or more, we seem to be losing our will to sacrifice and to endure. We are in danger of betraying our traditions. We have altered our national scale of values. The slow corrosion of luxury—the slow erosion of our courage—is beginning to show. Nearly one out of every two young American men is rejected by Selective Service today as mentally, physically, or morally unfit for any kind of military service. Still more are screened out after induction. And those taken have been described by one general as "a disappointing lot" on the whole. The Navy releases statistics showing more men in naval prisons than the entire Norwegian and Danish navies combined—and showing enough men branded deserters to supply a full crew for an aircraft carrier.

What has happened to us as a nation? Profits are up—our standard of living is up—but so is our crime rate. So is the rate of divorce and juvenile delinquency and mental illness. So are the sales of tranquilizers and the number of children dropping out of school.

We are, I am afraid, in danger of losing something solid at the core. We are losing that Pilgrim and pioneer spirit of initiative and independence—that old-fashioned Spartan devotion to "duty, honor, and country." We don't need that spirit now, we think. Now we have cars to drive and buttons to push and TV to watch—and precooked meals and prefab houses. We stick to the orthodox, to the easy way and the organization man. We take for granted our security, our liberty, and our future—when we cannot take any one of them for granted at all. The words of Omar Khayyam have become our slogan: "Take the cash and let the credit go, nor *heed* the rumble of a distant drum."

I do not say that we have all weakened. There was, in Korea, a young prisoner of war who was singled out of the line-up upon capture and asked his opinion of General Marshall. "General George C. Marshall," he replied, "is a great American soldier." Promptly a rifle butt knocked him to the ground. Then he was stood up again to face his captors—and again he was asked: "What do you think of General Marshall?" And again he gave the same steadfast reply—only this time there was no rifle butt, no punishment at all. They had tested his will, his courage to resist, his manhood—and now they knew where to classify him.

Where will we be classified when our own will and spirit are tested? Among the weak or the tough-minded? Among the lovers of comfort or the lovers of liberty? In this next decade there are not going to be any easy answers. There are not going to be any convenient escapes. There are no lazy ways to place the blame and burden on anyone else. It is all up to us—up to each and every one of us.

In the last few years I have been saying all this to many groups of fellow Americans—I have given the talks brought together in this book, and many others—and everywhere I have found people ready to be shown the new dimensions of our problems, ready to face the full facts of this crisis, ready to pay the price of survival. Traveling around the country, I have become convinced that the American people are ready to enter into full partnership with the newly developing free peoples, ready to accept the Soviet challenge to compete peacefully on all levels, ready to resume, on earth and in space, the pioneering that made America great. I believe that we Americans are ready to be called to greatness.

In 1960, as in 1932, the American people can, as I hope they will, turn from the party of memory to the party of hope. But the fundamental call to greatness is coming not from any party or any person but from history and the hard logic of events. From the lessons we have learned in two world wars, one world depression, and the Cold War, as well as from the history of this republic, the American people will now, I trust, be granted the vision of a new America in a new world. This is the vision without which our people will perish.

V
DISCUSSION
WITH
JOHN FISCHER

Believing that the readers of this volume would be interested in an informal discussion of issues raised here, the publishers asked John Fischer, Editor-in-Chief of Harper's Magazine, to meet with Senator Kennedy. The discussion took place in New York City on December 9, 1959. The answers were given extemporaneously.

Discussion with John Fischer

Q: Senator, many people seem to believe that one of the central questions in American foreign policy is how we're going to finance it; how the country can best find the money to cover its essential defense and foreign policy program, including closing the missile gap, building mobile surface forces to cope with situations short of total war, development of anti-missile missiles, space research, aid to underdeveloped countries. How can we do all this in addition to our domestic welfare programs? Do we have to pay higher taxes? Or do you see some chance for drastic savings in such items as farm subsidies and veterans' benefits? Or do you think some combination of both will give us the financial leeway to finance everything?

SENATOR KENNEDY: I think we will have to begin by deciding what is essential for the security of this country, and then determine in what way we're going to finance that agenda. These decisions will require sacrifices from us. Make no mistake about it. Security is never sold on the bargain counter. But the sacrifices will be reduced if we show high intelligence and courage in the defense of our public interests. I would certainly include on our list of essentials national defense, with an invulnerable nuclear retaliatory force plus sufficient conventional forces to limit the development of brush-fire war (which is really the most likely kind of military struggle we'll face in the next decade); and assistance to those nations—enough to make an economic break-through—who are newly emerging. I would say those are things that must be done.

Now, the question is, how much of it can be financed out of an increase in the gross national product, how much must be financed by new money, and how much must be financed through a deficit?

I would say that we could first do a great deal more, probably, in these areas than we think we can do. I remember Louis Johnson's view, at the end of the forties, that a $15 billion military budget was the maximum this country could sustain—and now we're up to $41, $42 billion. Quite obviously we can afford to do it, if the Soviet Union, which still has an industrial productivity little more than a third of ours, is able to devote as large an amount to military purposes as we are—quite obviously you can't say that the capitalist system cannot afford it and their system can afford it.

Now, if we had a sufficiently stimulated rate of growth, we would get additional tax revenues—normally, without any increase in taxes. We must attempt to avoid the recession which some economists predict will come upon us in 1961 (for you will recall that the recession of '58 cost us $12 billion in tax revenue) by more effective monetary and fiscal policies. Finally, I would say that if unemployment is high—four million and up—then quite obviously it would be the greatest mistake to try to increase taxes, because such a policy might have a deflationary effect. That would be an economic judgment which would have to be made at the time. In other words, would the dangers of an inflationary rise resulting from the deficit be greater than the dangers of a deflationary drop resulting from a tax increase? I would say that we would have to make a cold judgment based on conditions then existing as to which would serve the national economy better.

My judgment after fourteen years in the Congress is that you will not get a reduction in veterans' appropriations in the sixties. I think the problem will be to keep them within appropriate bounds, which I think we must do. What we want to do is make sure that, in these domestic programs which are important but do not involve the survival of the country, we always apply the rule of reason. I think the veterans of the United States, of whom I'm one, take that view too.

I hope there will be a substitute for Mr. Benson's farm program which will provide somewhat less expenditures, but I don't think we can successfully predict that. And there are great national assets in agricultural surpluses, if properly distributed, here and around the world, which must be taken into account.

So in answer to your question: I would have no objection to increasing taxes, if that represented the best economic judgment at the time. We did decrease them in '47; we decreased them in '54. I would have no objection, in fact I would think it would be necessary, if that were the only method by which these essential policies could be implemented. I think the things which *have* to be done *must* be done in the sixties. And I don't think either political party should go to the American people telling them that, if they are successful, in the sixties life is going to be easier and softer.

Q: And providing they are told what sacrifices are necessary and why.

KENNEDY: That's quite correct. I think the threat of inflation has really been somewhat limited in the last two years, and in the prospect of the next years—but under the present Administration it has been regarded as the supreme threat. I would consider there were other threats—in space, in the southern half of the globe, in the tremendously increasing military superiority in decisive weapons of the Soviet Union. These are all threats. Inflation is a threat. Deflation is a threat. So we have to make the best judgment between alternative forces. But I'm confident that, if the Soviet Union, under its system, can do what it is doing, under our system we can do more.

Q: Since you don't see much hope for major economies in domestic programs, do you think we might get some help by plugging some of the wider and more flagrant tax loopholes?

KENNEDY: Yes, I do. Of course, sometimes we put too much weight on that as a device. It makes it sound easier: we can carry out these increased programs; all we have to do is plug the tax loopholes. I think that's a trap which is easy to fall into. I think you could get more revenue by plugging some of the loopholes; but I think that we also have to be able to face up to the fact that we may not get enough revenue. It is true, of course, that our tax revenues, our present tax level, is going to bring in the sixties a greatly increased national revenue.

Q: To pass on to another subject, Senator. Do you believe that a real unification of the armed forces is becoming necessary, and if so, along what lines?

KENNEDY: Probably real unification—meaning a common uniform and integrated forces in the field—in other words, Army, Navy and Air being dominated by a single command and being a single service—that's still some years away. There's a good chance that it may come perhaps by the mid-sixties, but I don't think it will come until missiles become the dominant element in the American military arsenal. Quite obviously, when that day comes, when the Army needs missiles for its control of the battlefield, as well as for long-range strategic forces, and when the Navy has more complete dependence on the missile field—then quite obviously the pressure of this common weapon, and the dependence on it of all of our military elements, would increase the prospects of the kind of unification that General Gavin and others have talked about. I would say, in short, that it's still too early to attempt to crowd into one package these three units, but that weapon development would make it necessary, I would think, sometime within—or toward the end of, rather—the next five years.

Q: Before that time, do you think that something can be done to eliminate the fratricidal rivalry between the services that has been so expensive, for example, in missile development?

KENNEDY: I do, to a degree, though I'm not sufficiently expert to know whether some of that really represents an inability to make a precise judgment on which missile and which system would turn out to be the better, rather than being the result of service rivalry. But I do agree that these rivalries should be reduced.

Now, I would think that one of the problems really is to make sure that our money is being spent in the wisest possible way. For example, are the Joint Chiefs making an objective judgment in dividing up the budget, or is each service fighting for its own, fighting with the other two to decide how much it will get out of the budget? In addition, after that apportionment has been made, there appears to be a struggle going on within the various pressure groups inside each service. Then there is the problem of which service should get the new weapons. Should we now be talking about building a nuclear aircraft carrier, or should we really be going ahead more vigorously with the Polaris submarine? I would say the latter. But the appropriations for the next aircraft carrier, which would not go into service for the next two or three years or even four years, seem to me to be perhaps the result of the tremendous vested interest in air power held by the Navy.

I would think—though it may not be possible to cut all ties with the past—that by freeing the Joint Chiefs of Staff from their immediate command positions within the services and really making them almost civilian—military heads still, but with no direct command responsibilities—might then make it possible for them to speak for the total service, rather than for their own. Now, that's asking quite a good deal from all of us, to break that kind of a tie with the past, but I would think you'd get a better objective military judgment than you're getting today.

Q: Transform them from commanders into military advisers?

KENNEDY: That's right. Now, if you still have a Navy and Army and Air Force man doing this, and a Marine, by how much can you break that service commitment? I think that there's every evidence, though, that some have done that, even under the present system, to some degree. We need more of this national commitment instead of a competition between service points of view.

I don't think the President, for example, in all fairness to him, has shown a bias to the Army. There's no real evidence of that. Although there are perhaps other reasons for that in his case, it does show that we can rise above our past.

Q: Which leads naturally to the structure of the National Security Council. There seems to be a widespread feeling in Washington that this has not in fact served its original purpose as an effective instrument for making and carrying out a unified military and diplomatic policy. Do you think that it needs some drastic changes to make it more effective?

KENNEDY: Well, I would think really that this is a judgment which the next President could reach better than members of the Senate or even potential or actual Presidential candidates. Every President operates differently. What the Security Council, of course, is attempting to do is to take these extremely complicated and far-reaching matters and present them to the President in a way that will enable him to make some reasonable judgment on them. So quite obviously the Council is needed. The questions basically are whether the staff at the lower levels really develop the position papers which bring relative unanimity at the Council, and whether, for example, the Secretary of the Treasury has too dominant a voice, and whether a new President might insist on other groups participating which do not have the departmental background, perhaps setting up almost a small inner cabinet with a special relationship to the Security Council.

I believe every head of a department is overburdened. My judgment would be that they delegate and rely on subordinates, so that instead of really getting the best minds in the country to study a problem without prior commitment to an agency, you're really getting a staff operation, which gives the President a pre-compromised final solution without revealing to him the alternatives that might have been open. That appears to be the way President Eisenhower prefers to work. I'm hopeful it isn't the way a future President will work because I am convinced that discussion and differences and new points of view should be brought to bear on the President.

Looking at the Eisenhower visitors' list every morning in the paper, and looking at the make-up of the Security Council, and looking at those with whom he communicates and those who attend the private dinners, I am not sure that it represents the varied influence that would be useful for the President to have on these great questions.

Q: In other words, you think that a President who would be willing to listen to different alternatives and decide between them might function quite differently from a President who insists on an agreed paper being brought up by all the services?

KENNEDY: That's correct. I think the Security Council and those who constitute its membership would, of course, continue to function under any President. But I would hope that there might be other groups, less committed to represent a particular department, less engaged in the great tasks that press on a Secretary—that they also could bring to bear some views, some independent judgments, on the President, so that constant realistic alternatives, fully developed alternatives, on which he could make a final judgment, could be presented to him rather than merely a consensus rising from the secondary staff level. Under the latter system the President gives an endorsement rather than a judgment.

Q: One other question on the machinery of foreign policy—am I right in thinking that there has been a growing feeling in the Senate that we do not now have a real bipartisanship in foreign policy—the kind of partisanship that, in Senator Vandenberg's phrase, would "bring the opposition party in on the take-off as well as the crash landings."

KENNEDY: That phrase is always used by whoever is in the minority party to justify greater participation. But looking at it pragmatically, is the Congress really equipped to participate in the take-off? I'm not so sure. Merely bringing three or four prominent Democrats in, if there's a Republican Administration, and three or four Republicans if it's a Democratic Administration, gives the appearance of bipartisanship but doesn't really achieve bipartisanship in policy. Secondly, the President, constitutionally and practically, is the man who must make these judgments.

For example, in the Lebanon case, on the question of American troops for Lebanon, as you will recall: he called in the heads of the appropriate committees, the Speaker of the House and the leaders of the Senate, and informed them of the problem. It would have been almost impossible for them at this stage, except perhaps to raise questions of doubt, to have brought very much influence to bear.

The President, speaking as the President, as the Commander in Chief, says, "This is what I believe to be in the national interest." In those cases, it is almost inevitable, unless he's suffering from a mental aberration, that his judgment will be sustained.

I do agree, in the case of Indochina, that the conference which took place between the Secretary of State and the leaders of the Congress did, I think, influence Mr. Dulles to take a less vigorous line, and Admiral Radford to take a less vigorous line, on American intervention at the time of Dienbienphu. I would say this is almost the only time that I can recall, in the fifties, or really since the late forties, that the members of the opposite party have had a real influence on the major foreign policy decisions. They certainly didn't on the Eisenhower Doctrine in the Middle East and policy in the Far East, nor did the Republicans on the Korean intervention.

Bipartisanship is an overworked word in foreign policy. What I consider to be real bipartisanship in foreign policy is not to exploit an international problem for the benefit of a political party at home. It does not mean, in fact it would be a great mistake if it did mean, that criticism, discussion, presentation of alternatives were prohibited in the foreign policy field and could only be developed in the domestic field. That would really be a terribly serious misreading of the concept of bipartisanship. The nation's interest must come first, in foreign policy; and as part of that, it seems to me, it's up to the minority party to present realistic and constructive alternatives when they believe it in the national interest.

Mr. Vandenberg's phrase is neat; and he played a great role in a great bipartisan operation. But, in that operation, the consent of the Congress was necessary—in that major treaties were being submitted to the Congress. Now we do not have the kind of struggle we had over NATO and over the UN when Congressional approval was required—so that the position of the Congress is a somewhat secondary one. Of course, the President did send the Formosa and Middle East resolutions to us. In those cases, however, he had announced them in advance. It would have been a great rejection of him if we had turned them down, even though in both cases there was a good deal about them that was unwise.

Q: But you had no alternative?

KENNEDY: That's right. You have to sustain the hand of the President. In the struggles, the treaty struggles, of the forties, it was possible for Senator Vandenberg, as leader of the minority, to play a very constructive role. It was a role of supporting the administration of the opposite party. That opportunity hasn't been given in the fifties, not because of Democratic refusal, but just because events have dictated an increasing control by the President and a lessening of the power of Congress in foreign policy.

Q: Let us go into some specific questions about foreign policy. Do you at the moment see any hope of a satisfactory accommodation with the Soviet Union on Berlin? If so, along what lines?

KENNEDY: I would say the chances are rather dim for a permanent solution of Berlin. But I do think it may be possible for us to reach a *modus vivendi* with them, particularly if they feel that any real attack on our position in Berlin would bring war. I would think that both sides might reach a precarious balance, which might later be affected by international events on any occasion. Berlin and the problems suggested by Berlin are going to be with us for many years. I think, hopefully, we would like to get a commitment, perhaps guaranteed by the United Nations, to reaffirm the concept of a corridor into Berlin and therefore free access to it, which would be controlled either by the United Nations or by the West Germans and the Berliners or by England, France and the United States. In return for that, we might agree to some thinning out of troops in Berlin, but that would be rather meaningless because there are not many there now anyway. We might agree to cease propaganda activities. German reunification, which represents the long-range goal, is certainly not in the cards for many years. These are matters which could be discussed at the summit. But whether the Russians would ever agree to a firm commitment in regard to an entrance, which is a prerequisite to stability there, I don't know.

Q: You don't feel that the equation of power between us and the Russians gives ground for much hope, I take it?

KENNEDY: Well, I think the importance of Berlin—the peculiar geographic location of Berlin—the necessity for the East German government to have increased status—the importance of East Germany to the Soviet economy and its political system—its relations with Poland: all those mean that this is really a great area for a power struggle. The difficulties we have in Germany, in Berlin, are there because of the importance of Germany, and the importance of West Germany to us, to the defense of Western Europe, to the security of

Western Europe. All these mean that great pressure will be brought to bear over the question of Berlin.

Q: I have heard a number of responsible West German statesmen state, in the last six months, that they had real doubts about whether the United States would be willing to go to war over Berlin—or indeed over Germany as a whole. They can't quite believe that we would risk having New York, Washington, and half a dozen other American cities wiped out overnight simply to maintain our position in West Germany. Do you think this is a justified doubt in their minds?

KENNEDY: Well, if that view became generalized—if the Soviet Union began to hold that view—I think that would be a great disaster for them and for us. West Germany has been a primary goal of Russia's policies since 1945. If they endangered our position there, I should think it could very well lead to military action, because I think we would fight. I think you must demonstrate your determination to fight. Otherwise you're holding a very tenuous position in Berlin. They could cut us off too easily. If we took the view which some Englishmen took, that Prague or the Sudetendeutsch were not worth a war in '38—if we took that view about Berlin, my judgment is that the West Berliners would pass into the Communist orbit, and our position in West Germany and our relations with West Germany would receive a fatal blow. With West Germany neutralized, all Western Europe would soon be neutralized, and it would be a decisive victory for the Soviet Union. For us to think that what the central struggle is about is just Berlin would be a great mistake. They're fighting for New York and Paris when they struggle over Berlin. Therefore, I think we have to make it cold—and mean it— that we would fight.

Q: Are we in a position, however, to fight anything except an all-out nuclear war?

KENNEDY: No. Quite obviously we have limited ground forces there —even though we have contributed the major portion of the active troops to the defense of NATO—but I don't think that the European powers themselves have met their obligations in regard to NATO; and I think we could do more ourselves. You recall that when the NATO agreement was signed the presumption was that NATO would have a good many more active divisions on the line

than they do today. The French have theirs in Algeria. Other countries have been unwilling, particularly as they think a war unlikely
in Western Europe, to make their comparative contributions. Some
countries seem anxious to put more of their resources into the development of an atomic capacity. They are less anxious to maintain
their more conventional forces, when actually what's needed in
Western Europe are traditional forces.

But I think that the Soviet Union would realize that a blatant
invasion of Western Europe would be a signal for an all-out war.
The real problem is the more subtle struggle for Berlin, where they
try to choke us off, where they try to end it not with a bang but with
a whimper, which never seems quite worth a war, because they
choke us off step by step. That's going to be the real struggle. It's
going to be a test of nerve and will.

Q: And you think that the Western Alliance can muster the unity
and the nerve and the will to resist this?

KENNEDY: I think they must. I think there is perhaps an area where
we could both make some agreement which would respect the relative
position of both of us in that section of Europe, and still permit
Berlin to live easier. But you cannot possibly get an agreement there
unless they think that we mean what we say; that if they attempt to
drive us out, directly or indirectly, it would mean war, which could
spread to the world. If that is clear, then possibly we could.

I think we should discuss it. I don't agree with those who feel that
any discussion is really a concession.

Q: To go a step beyond Berlin, do you see any possibility of some
partial disengagement in Central Europe, along the lines of any of
the plans suggested by George Kennan or Mr. Gaitskell in England
or Rapacki in Poland?

KENNEDY: Well, I thought there was really more chance two or three
years ago than I do today. I think it's rather difficult to extract the
missile capacity now from the West Germans, and to extract Germany from NATO. They may not have the warhead but they have
the missiles. The Russians have made it quite clear that when they
talk about disengagement they mean disengagement from all of
Europe, presumably including even England. They would disengage
only to the Russian frontier. It really would not be necessary for
them to hold troops within, say, Poland or Hungary, to maintain
their position, when the troops are only a hundred or two hundred

miles away and ours are back in the United States. Even though it might be still unlikely that they would begin an overt invasion of Western Europe even if our troops were withdrawn, there is still the fact that the Western Europeans do not have and cannot have the kind of confidence in us they would have if our troops were going to be involved themselves. Therefore, there might be a greater disposition to neutrality if we were out of there. I would say you can't disengage now.

Q: And you think there is no middle ground between standing where we are now, and pulling back to our own shores?

KENNEDY: We would leave Western Germany, which is the key, and they would then withdraw to Poland. Our position in West Germany always is bound up with the feeling of the West German people. What would be the feeling of the West Germans about our withdrawing from their country? The Communist control over East Germany would remain. We have no control over West Germany. Our withdrawal would be followed by a rise in neutralism.

So I would say that today I do not believe that disengagement represents a reasonable alternative to our policy there.

Q: Does that leave any other area for possible fruitful negotiations except disarmament?

KENNEDY: No, I would say disarmament is the key area. And I do think we could perhaps reach, as I said before, some agreement on Berlin that would ease the situation. But disarmament is the key.

Q: You feel that that is where we ought to concentrate our diplomatic efforts?

KENNEDY: Well, I think an agreement on nuclear testing, which is the first step, represents a much better hope than troop withdrawals from Central Europe.

Q: In another part of the world . . .

KENNEDY: May I continue? One of the reasons that some of us are most concerned about the lead that the Soviet Union is developing in long-range missiles is that, even though our intermediate-range missile flying from Western Europe gives us equality with the long-range missile flying from the Soviet Union to the United States, that equality really is based on the willingness of Western European countries to let us fire those missiles, in case of a prospective attack.

Now, if the attack is confined to the United States—or the threatened attack involves interests, for example, in the Far East which may not be vital to those Western European countries—then I would think that, particularly if the Soviet Union should threaten to attack any country from which was fired a missile against the Soviet Union, there might be strong pressures within that country to delay, to refuse to give us automatic permission.

Therefore, in the final analysis, though these missile bases are important in contributing to the sense of security of the countries involved, and though our troops in the shield of Western Europe—the pane of glass, so-called—are also important in indicating our commitment to the defense of Western Europe, in the final analysis the security of the United States and the peace of the world will depend on our ability to fire a missile from the United States, under our control, in case of a threatened attack or if a vital interest of ours was endangered.

I think that's extremely important. Therefore I do not accept with equanimity the argument of those in the administration who say that our intermediate-range missile gives us equality. We won't have security until we have either Polaris submarines widely dispersed and constantly at sea, or fully protected intercontinental ballistic missiles in hardened bases here in the United States, which can be defended. Until we have these, we're not really going to have security against the ultimate weapon.

Q: Doesn't it strike you as peculiar, in view of what you have just said, that we have not yet gone on double shift in manufacturing the Atlas missile, which is our one best bet at the moment?

KENNEDY: I believe a greater effort is most essential. You recall Winston Churchill's speech when the Soviet Union was attempting to get us out of Berlin in 1949, at a time when we had atomic superiority: "If this is what they do in the green wood, what would they do in the dry?" We're now moving into the period of the dry wood as their missile lead increases, and I think we can expect their belligerence to increase also. The next administration will have to deal with the Russians over Berlin, and with the Chinese over Quemoy, with relatively deteriorating military strength—that is what alarms me most.

Q: Do you think this is an argument for speeding up our own missile program beyond its rather stately pace at the moment?

KENNEDY: I would think it would be the first priority. In other words, I'm not that much convinced that the Chinese or the Soviet Union have said a farewell to arms, in spite of Mr. Khrushchev's messages of good will.

Q: To move to another part of the world—it's obvious, I should think, that one of the most difficult areas that the next President will have to deal with is the Middle East. Do you see any way we can reconcile the United States' emotional commitments to Israel with the equally obvious need to encourage Arab economic development and better relations with the Moslem world?

KENNEDY: The tie with Israel goes back before its earliest founding as a state. America has for many years, under different Presidents and different political administrations, supported the goal of a Jewish national homeland in Palestine as being consistent with America's national interests, and it is the national interest of the United States, and our treaty commitments, that should govern our policies toward all countries.

In 1947 the United Nations by a better than two-thirds vote approved the idea of a Jewish state. We have made very clear commitments through the Tripartite Agreement and through the United Nations to protect the integrity of Israel. It is to our own interest to meet those commitments. The goal of American foreign policy in the Middle East, like American policy in other regions, should be the preservation of peace—by promoting the integrity and independence of peace-loving countries in that area and by lending an economic helping hand to those countries which want to help themselves.

If we want peace in that area, we must be extremely interested in the development of Arab economies. I am confident that those who are friends of Israel must be too, because it will bring a greater stability to the area and to their own country. It would bring a greater vested interest in peace. Peace is essential to the survival of Israel and to the survival of the Middle East. The problems in the Middle East are stubborn and deep-seated. But they will not be solved, they will only be aggravated, by appeasing violent emotionalism or aggression. Turmoil in the Middle East is an open invitation to the Soviet Union to exploit discontent and hunger. American foreign policy must persuade the countries of the Middle East that it is in their own best interests to preserve the peace, and that with peace will come the opportunity for raising the sorely depressed living standards in that area. That, of course, is the goal of the enlightened leaders in both Israel and the Arab countries.

I do not see our commitments to Israel and the Arab countries in the Middle East to be in conflict. I think in the best sense of the word they are complementary.

Q: You think that some way could be found to be friends with both Arabs and Israelis?

KENNEDY: I think there must be. I think it would be the greatest mistake to attempt to appease the Arabs by joining the Soviet Union in denunciation of Israel. At the same, no one would do a service to Israel to say that only Israel must stand in the Middle East, and that the rest of the Arab world must sink to an increasingly lower standard of living. That gives no security to the Middle East, no security to the United States, certainly no security to Israel. The Arabs want to be neutral. They want to build the Middle East. I think there's a great Pan-Arab feeling which could be expressed in economic terms. I think that's in the long-range interest of the United States. I would like to see the Arab world strong enough to be independent of either the Russians or the West, and not trying to play one side against the other in order to defend their security. The greater economic unity and political independence those countries have in the Middle East, the more secure is the Middle East.

Q: You are less disturbed than Mr. Dulles was, for example, by countries taking a neutralist foreign policy?

KENNEDY: Oh, I think it's inevitable. That's the great trend. During the immediate years ahead this is likely to be an increasing trend in Africa and probably also in Latin America. In Asia, however, there may be some movement away from a wholly uncommitted neutralism as a result of the growing awareness of the Chinese threat. The desire to be independent and free carries with it the desire not to become engaged as a satellite of the Soviet Union or too closely allied to the United States. We have to live with that, and if neutrality is the result of a concentration on internal problems, raising the standard of living of the people and so on, particularly in the underdeveloped countries, I would accept that. It's part of our own history for over a hundred years. We should look with friendship upon those people who want to beat the problems that almost overwhelm them, and wish to concentrate their energies on doing that, and do not want to become associated as the tail of our kite.

Q: Do you think it was a mistake for us, under Mr. Dulles' administration, to try to force a good many of these underdeveloped countries into military pacts with us?

KENNEDY: I would think that the Middle East and Asia were not the areas that Mr. Dulles was most successful in.

Q: Southeast Asia and Latin America are getting to be somewhat similar?

KENNEDY: Yes, I would say that Mr. Dulles was probably more successful in Germany, really, than he was in some of these other areas. The Aswan Dam refusal, the concept of the Baghdad Pact, which was his, and the Eisenhower Doctrine, which is being rejected really in every country—all these, I would think, are unhappy monuments to Mr. Dulles in the Middle East. Because of what is happening in Iraq, for the first time people in the Middle East have realized that the Communists are also their enemy as well as the enemy of the United States.

In addition, I think that the British and the French have realized that these countries are going to be increasingly independent and will increasingly reject any paternalism that comes from the West. I regard that as a natural evolution. This desire to be independent, from which the movement flows, benefits us in the long run. We have no desire to dominate these countries. They're going to be as opposed to domination from the Soviet Union as they ever were from the West. And as we do not want to participate in that kind of a control ourselves, I would think that it is in the long-range interest of the United States. It's a fact anyway, so we might as well learn to live with it.

Q: Would you feel that the same argument holds in Latin America, where the fact that countries have had long-standing alliances with us or been economically dependent on us seems to have resulted in a good deal of hostility to the United States?

KENNEDY: I would hope that we can maintain our traditional ties with Latin America. But I was interested to note on one of the votes this week in the United Nations—relating to membership on the Security Council—that three of the Latin-American countries voted against the position that we were taking. Representatives of Latin-American countries at the UN and in Washington have constantly charged that the United States has ignored them. Although it is true that the President did not visit South America during his first seven years in office, that's partly an unreasonable position on their part.

But one of the very first responsibilities and tasks of the new Administration, particularly if it's a Democratic Administration, would be to attempt to restore (to the degree possible, and times have changed) some of the good will which existed in the thirties, between the United States and Latin America.

We are the heirs of Franklin Roosevelt and the Good Neighbor Policy. Striking that chord again—making them feel that this is a primary matter of concern in foreign policy and that this accord must be reached, before we attempt to redress balances anywhere else in the world—I would say that that would represent the greatest possible opportunity in long-range good will to the United States. Otherwise, our role will become more difficult in Latin America. It may become more difficult anyway. The sixties aren't going to be the thirties. The Latin Americans were satisfied merely with the hand of friendship in the thirties. Now their needs are much more vigorous and wide-ranged.

I would say there is the great early opportunity for a new Administration in foreign policy.

Q: You're thinking of much heavier capital investment in Latin America?

KENNEDY: Well, the one fact which I think the United States must recognize is that the real struggle in foreign policy is going to take place in these countries, stretching a little to the north of the Equator and all the way south—Latin America, Africa, the Middle East and Asia. Can these countries facing staggering problems make an economic break-through? The United States is going to have to participate in this effort. If anyone says to the American people that the burden is too heavy, that we carried the burden in the forties in Europe and in the world in the fifties, and that someone else should therefore do it now, if anyone says that and the American people believe it—then we might just as well recognize that the struggle is over, that the United States hasn't got enough stamina to sustain the burden of leadership which must be borne if the free world is to be successful. We can rightfully hope that others are going to join us and make a proportionate effort, but the United States is the leader and we have to accept that.

That is why Senator Cooper and I have taken such a vigorous

interest in the establishment of a Free World Mission to India and Pakistan. Though we were disappointed that the mission which was created in December was not broader in membership and outlook, still I hope very much that this mission which was proposed in our resolution will provide fresh leverage and a chance for the Western nations to concentrate on one of its great common tasks. From these discussions in South Asia we may develop informal precedents and models from which we can move on to other economic enterprises which the nations of the West will inevitably face—especially on the continent of Africa.

I'm also delighted that the Administration is finally getting to the concept of the Inter-American Bank; I hope there'll be a greater development of the inter-American commodity agreements. I hope there'll be more ample credit facilities within the countries themselves for domestic use; that they will be more responsible in handling their domestic affairs, particularly financially; and that we will give them some guarantees in regard to the commodities which they're dependent upon, which they export to the United States, in order to survive internally.

The recession of '58 was only a 5 or 6 per cent drop for us, but, as you know, it had an almost catastrophic effect upon Chile and some of the other countries who have to sell us their raw materials. We have to protect them from those whiplashes.

Q: We've not been very successful in protecting markets for our own domestic raw materials, particularly wheat or corn. Do you think we could finance a stockpile program for rubber, cocoa, other primary products in Latin America?

KENNEDY: No, I don't think that we can conduct an international Benson program for commodities. Quite obviously, our resources are not unlimited. But I would think that we could give them greater assurances that in the lean years the effect would not be as large as it has been since World War II.

Q: A commitment to take a given quantity at a given price, one year after another?

KENNEDY: Over at least a two- or three- or four-year period, rather than this 50 per cent drop in the price of raw materials which we had in the case of some South American countries in one year. That they can't, of course, sustain.

Q: How do you think we can best cope with the appeal that Communist China is making to these poverty-ridden people?

KENNEDY: When they talk about the relative rate of growth of the United States and the Soviet Union, it seems to me perhaps that's not the dominant issue. The Soviet Union's comparative rate of growth is cause for concern—but regardless of what might happen in the Soviet Union, I don't think the people of America are going to decide the Communist system is better. The real question is which system travels better—particularly whether the example of Peiping, with its forced drafts on agriculture, education and industrialization in the last decade, will achieve a more impressive record than India, which has a comparable population problem and which started roughly at the same area, and which also has the problem of an over-dependence on agriculture with great unemployment and population increases. That, I think, is the real issue. Which holds up the example over the next ten years, China or India?

Therefore India becomes the key area. It has more than 35 per cent of all the underdeveloped people in the world within its borders. It has excellent economic planning, responsible leadership, democratic government. Its first five-year plan was successful, but its second five-year plan ran into difficulties, and now the third five-year plan is about to be presented.

I don't really think that some of the countries of Western Europe —especially Germany—have borne their proportionate share of the burden of long-term assistance.

I supported the effort of the Senate Foreign Relations Committee two years ago, led by Senator Fulbright, to provide for a billion and a half appropriation annually for five years for the Development Loan Fund. This year we tried again. This year the Committee cut it to a billion, but as you know the Administration did not support even this, and the compromise brought about a limited figure. The Development Loan Fund, if enlarged, could serve as a support for the World Bank, and permit soft loans at low rates of interest, repayable in local currency. Unless we are ready to do that on a scale commensurate with the needs, then China's example rather than India's will serve as a great inspiration. If India fails and China succeeds, I would say that *the* decisive struggle in the cold war in the next ten years will have been lost.

So the agenda is rather long for the United States, and not easy.

Q: Do you think it would be a good idea for us to get over the notion that foreign economic programs are temporary emergency measures? They are a long time continuing—

KENNEDY: Certainly you would have to say that through the next decade the change is going to be continual; there is not going to be an opportunity for reduction. I know a great many people are opposed to foreign aid in the United States, but when they say they are opposed to foreign aid, I hope they mean they are merely opposed to waste. But if we are not going to bear these burdens—and I would include an effective foreign aid program as part of our leadership of a free society—then I would say that we might just as well say it now and be ready to yield the stage.

Q: In these underdeveloped countries, do you think they can ever solve their economic problems as long as their population keeps rising at the rate of about 3 per cent a year, doubling every forty years?

KENNEDY: Well, I would think it was a population increase closer to 2 per cent. But then you have to have an annual rate of increase of at least 6 per cent in your gross national product, so that you have a 2 per cent increase to take care of the population increase, another 2 per cent to provide increased standard of living of the population, and another 2 per cent to provide increased momentum in the years ahead. In terms of food, at least, if you provided for the kind of agricultural production increases necessary, if you provided for the calorie output per acre in India that you have in Japan or even in Western Europe—which is not impossible with new fertilizer, the control of water and education of the farmers—you could increase that production faster than the population. We've had a population increase in the United States which was as great as any place in the world, but our food production increases faster. Those with whom I've talked at the experimental stations of the Department of Agriculture point out what the Dutch and the Japanese produce per acre; and would indicate that increased productivity in the United States, which is really a technological explosion in the United States in food production (which is the heart of our agricultural problem), is going to continue; and that, with a concentrated technological effort, it can be done in other areas of the world also.

I think it's possible to sustain a growth where the resources of the world, if properly managed, could increase faster than the population. I'm not saying it's going to be done, but it can be done, and that must be our goal.

Q: Am I right, however, in thinking that no nation, except possibly Communist Russia and Communist China, has ever achieved annual growth rates of 6 per cent a year for a considerable period? It's much greater than we ever achieved.

KENNEDY: I would think that since the war the countries of Western Europe and Japan, which started at a rather low level—I'd have to recall their exact growth rate, but I would think that their growth rate was in several instances bigger than that. Economists such as Professor Rostow and others believe that the Indians could do it, in their third five-year plan, if they receive sufficient foreign assistance. What is the alternative? I think we must do it. Otherwise you just say you're going to ration poverty among an increased number of people.

Q: Do you see any hope at all of slowing up the rate of population increase?

KENNEDY: You mean through birth control?

Q: By any method whatever.

KENNEDY: Of course, the population increase is a matter of more children surviving and adults living to an older age, which gives us an immediate problem now. I'm not sure that the mathematical predictions of doubling the population every forty years will be fulfilled. Once the average person around the world can hope to reach three score and ten, once nine out of ten children live through the first year rather than two or three out of ten, I don't think you're going to get that arithmetical, geometrical, doubling every forty or fifty years.

Now, on the question of limiting population: as you know the Japanese have been doing it very vigorously, through abortion, which I think would be repugnant to all Americans. Some other countries have instituted programs of birth control, including the Indians. Their success has been rather limited. Most people consider their families to be their families, and that it is other people's families that provide the population explosion. The techniques are rather imperfect, and it should be remembered that in the experience of the countries which have used them, these techniques have not had a significant effect on the population increase expected. As you know, the Chinese were pushing it for a while, but are not now.

Q: They have appeared to abandon it.

KENNEDY: So have the Russians, who believe this policy would indicate the inability of the Communist system to solve its problems. I believe it is a judgment which the countries and the people involved must make as to whether they wish to limit their population. Since it involves so personal a decision I think it would be unwise for the United States to intervene.

Q: You mean that we should not try to influence them either to follow that course or to refrain from that course?

KENNEDY: I think really it is a judgment that they must reach. But perhaps out of this debate there may come a useful effort. I would say to those here in the United States who are strong proponents of birth control, and to those who are strongly opposed to it, that they both should support greater economic assistance to those countries by the United States. The proponents should remember what Mr. Nehru said: "You give us sufficient economic resources and we will deal with that problem ourselves." Many Congressmen from the South are opposed to greater economic aid, a good many conservative Republicans are opposed to it. The fights in the Congress are very close. We've been beaten on the floor of the Senate every time, in our attempt to increase economic aid to where it should be. If we're going to add this issue—I'm not now talking about where equity lies—but if you're going to add this burden onto the bill what you'll end up with is not much foreign aid and no birth control.

Q: It's a matter of policy, rather than morals; you think it is a subject we would be wiser to avoid?

KENNEDY: Well, I'm talking about it now as a matter of public policy. I've been around Congress for fourteen years and I'm a strong supporter of foreign aid. I would just say that if you load this subject onto our somewhat limited foreign aid bill, you might end up with less foreign aid, and therefore make less of a contribution to the solution of the problem of those peoples, thus defeating your own ends.

Now, those people who are opposed to birth control—which includes not only Catholics but members of other faiths—have to understand that the population increase is going to continue and represent a real challenge. By the position they are taking they are morally committed, in my opinion, to sustain a real American effort of assistance in those areas. They can't merely say, "We're against birth control, we're against American funds being used for birth control," and then at the same time say, "We're also not going to support a realistic program of foreign economic assistance."

So perhaps out of this rather acrimonious discussion, you will develop two groups, both of whom, for different reasons, perhaps, will support, for the long-range reason of helping people, a more realistic program.

Q: So you think that some good may come out of this rather artificial controversy after all?

KENNEDY: Well, I think it might be improper to say it's artificial. It's a serious matter to many people.

Q: To sum up, Senator, what would you say are the main points of difference between your views on foreign policy and those of the Eisenhower-Nixon Administration?

KENNEDY: The basic differences are not so much in broad policy objectives as in basic attitudes which affect day-to-day decisions all around the globe—our neglect of Latin America, our vacillation in the Middle East, our timidity in Eastern Europe, our shortsightedness in India, and, tied in with all of these, our emphasis on budgetary considerations over security considerations. This Administration may go out of office on a crest of "peace" popularity—but it will leave on the next Administration's doorstep the most critical problems we have ever faced: the growing missile gap, the rise of Communist China, the despair of the underdeveloped nations, the explosive situations in Berlin and in the Formosa Straits, the deterioration of NATO, the lack of an arms control agreement.

This Administration has not faced up to these and other problems squarely—nor have they been willing to tell the American people the frank truth about them—if they themselves know the truth—what they mean in terms of real danger and what it will take to ease those dangers. And worst of all, they will not leave behind sufficient military power to enable us to deal with these situations—Berlin, Quemoy-Matsu, and all the rest—from a position of strength—not strength for war alone, but for peace. "We should arm to parley," as Churchill said.

You ask about my own position. While the Legislative Branch can only rarely initiate action in foreign affairs, I have tried in these last several years to point up some new approaches—to Algeria and North Africa, on a new economic approach to Poland and Eastern Europe, on a joint mission to frame a new economic aid program to India and the whole underdeveloped world, on new approaches to Africa, Latin America, the Middle East and our defense requirements. These efforts, at least initially, were opposed by the Administration. Reacting instead of acting, they usually found themselves at the mercy of events instead of anticipating the danger and shaping a firm and consistent policy to meet it.

I do not say they have nothing to their credit. But their few achievements in foreign policy have been primarily in those areas where it has been possible to continue Democratic programs and to rely on bipartisan support. They have failed to create a single policy, in all of their long years in office, to match the wisdom of the Marshall Plan or the success of NATO. And yet can there be any serious doubt that there have been tremendous opportunities in these last few years?

I think a new Administration must be willing to tell the people the truth, and place the real dimensions of our crisis before them. It must be willing to bring back to the State Department men of stature, competence and creative imagination within both parties—for it is the men, not merely the stated policies, that determine the effectiveness of American foreign policy. It must be willing to take a much broader view of budgetary and inflationary questions in order to deal effectively with the needs of other nations to achieve an economic break-through.

I have tried to indicate, in some of the speeches reprinted in this book, what else needs to be done specifically—on assistance to underdeveloped areas, on our own defenses and elsewhere. I think a new Administration—a new Democratic Administration—could reverse the present deterioration. But above all I would not conceal the fact that to solve these problems we must accept in our public life what we know is true in our private life—that nothing is achieved without effort and sacrifice. Peace is not a condition that exists as we move into the sixties. Peace is still to be won.

Index

Abbas, Ferhat, 77
Acheson, Dean, xiv, 161 n.
Adams, John Quincy, 188
Adams, Samuel, 10
Aden, 111
Adenauer, Konrad, 11 n., 96-97
Afghanistan, 197
Africa, 5, 6, 7, 124 ff., 174
Agricultural Surplus Disposal Act, 92, 93
agriculture
  in China, 48
  in India, 48, 150
  in Poland, 86, 88-89
  in U.S., x, 181, 189-192, 197
Aiken, George D., 17
Algeria, 65 ff., 111, 214
Altgeld, Gov. John R., ix
Antarctica, 29
Aqaba, 106
Arab League, 78
Arabs, 65, 75, 78, 79, 106-108, 109 ff.,
    120-121, 123
arms race, 12, 22, 26, 100
As France Goes, 73
Asia, 5, 6, 7
astronomy, 170
Aswan Dam, xiv, 197, 219
atomic weapons. See arms race; nuclear
    weapons
Austria, 29
automation, 181

Baghdad Pact, 219
Batista, Fulgencio, 132 n.
Battle, Laurie C., 15 n.
Battle Act, 15, 17-18, 82, 92, 93
Belgian Congo, 125 n.
Belgium, 23
Ben Gurion, David, 119 n.
Benson, Ezra Taft, 189, 190, 191
Berlin, 212-214; see also Germany
Betancourt, Romulo, 133 n.
Bilbo, Theodore, ix
Bill of Rights, 162, 163
biology, 170
bipartisanship, 210-211
birth control, 148 n., 224-226
Bismarck, 173
Blaine, James G., ix
Bolívar, Simón, 132

Bolivia, x
Bourguiba, Habib, 65, 71, 73-74, 78, 79
Bowles, Chester, 143, 148 n.
Brazil, 139
Bryant, William Cullen, 188
budget, U.S., x, xi, xii, 40, 154-155
Bulganin, Nikolai, 167
Bunche, Ralph, 175 n.
Burke, Edmund, 54
Burma, 167

Calais, 33, 38
Cambodia, 61, 64 n.
Cambridge Modern History, 33
Canada, 23, 151, 152, 153
Capehart, Homer, 33 n., 105
captive nations, 14-18
Carroll, John, 27
Castro, Fidel, 132-133
Ceylon, 197
Chamberlain, Joseph, ix
chemistry, 170
Chiang Kai-shek, 102, 103-104
Chile, 139, 221
China, 37, 48-49, 141-144, 183, 222
Churchill, Winston, ix, 8 n., 10, 13-14,
    45, 193, 216
civil liberties, xiii, 161-166
Clark, Joseph S., Jr., xiii, 165, 178
Cleveland, Grover, ix
Cobden, Richard, 157
Communism
  in India, 147
  and Indochina, 57-61
  and Israel, 121
  and Middle East, 107, 110-111, 219
  in Poland, 86-87, 90-91, 92
  and U.S., 26-27, 163-164
  and Vietnam, 61, 63, 64
Constitution, 161-162, 179
Cooper, John Sherman, 142, 148 n.,
    220-221
Cuba, x, 132, 139, 141
Curtis, George William, 189
Czechoslovakia, 23, 85

Damascus, 72
Declaration of Independence, 174, 199
Decline and Fall of the Roman Empire,
    45
defense strength, U.S., 34-36, 38-40

229